What Can a Modern Jew Believe?

For Dr. Alan S. Rokoff, שלום רב ראלן סנגוף המלמד

בברכת רב ומיבצול ומאת

לב׳ד

What Can a Modern Jew Believe?

GILBERT S. ROSENTHAL

Gilbert S. Rosenthal

Wipf & Stock
PUBLISHERS
Eugene, Oregon

WHAT CAN A MODERN JEW BELIEVE?

ISBN 10: 1-59752-868-4
ISBN 13: 978-1-59752-868-9

Manufactured in the U.S.A.

For my grandchildren

Sabrina Beth Stacks
Isabelle Adina Stacks
Benjamin Aaron Shure
Alison Hannah Shure

"Grandchildren are truly like children."
Yevamot 62b

Contents

Contents

Preface

IT IS my pleasure to extend my thanks to those who assisted me in bringing this book to fruition. The staff of the Hebrew College Library, Newton, Massachusetts, was notably helpful and courteous. Librarians Harvey Sukenic and Mimi Mazor were constant sources of aid whenever I needed to locate important books. My sister-in-law, Susan Teller, of Moshav Neve Ilan, Israel, read an earlier version of the manuscript and offered some keen insights from an Israeli educator's perspective. I thank my son-in-law, Nelson Stacks, for resolving some thorny technical problems in producing the manuscript. I am also grateful to the staff of my publisher, Wipf and Stock, for advice and guidance throughout the birthing process of producing this book.

The lion's share of accolades and appreciation belongs to my dear friend, Elissa L. Schiff, who edited the entire manuscript with an unfailingly critical eye and an impeccable feeling for language and grammar, as well as an abundant reservoir of Jewish knowledge. I can never thank her enough for the many hours, days, and weeks she invested in this project as a gift of true friendship.

Several chapters appeared in different forms in *Midstream, Judaism, Conservative Judaism*, and *The Journal of Religion*. I am grateful that their editors afforded me the opportunity to express my views freely and reproduce some of those essays in this volume.

The Bible translation I utilized is generally that of the Jewish Publication Society, although where I felt its version to be inadequate, I used my own. All translations of rabbinic sources as well as Hebrew material are mine. I deliberately avoided footnotes or endnotes in order to facilitate matters for the reader and help the reader follow the arguments without distractions. All abbreviations of sources follow the guidelines of *The Society of Biblical Literature Handbook of Style*.

These chapters reflect the evolution of my thinking from my days as a young and callow rabbi, to a mature veteran of five decades of service to God, Torah, and the Jewish people. In a sense, they are a summing up of what I have learned over the past 50 years. Happily, I was blessed along the way with a life's partner and a true love, my wife, Ann. She read the entire manuscript (as she has read all of my writings) and shared her reactions and criticisms. But more importantly, she shared our life experiences as we grew together from young newlyweds to mature grandparents. As Rabbi Akiva said of his beloved wife, Rachel, "All that is mine belongs to her." So it has been with us—and for that uniquely special blessing, I am profoundly and eternally grateful.

Gilbert S. Rosenthal
Needham, Massachusetts
December 2006—Kislev 5767

Introduction

THE STORY is told of the famous Reform rabbi, Zionist leader, and social activist, Rabbi Stephen S. Wise that he had contracted with a well-known publisher to write his autobiography. Wise was so preoccupied with his many activities that he had failed to produce a manuscript. One evening, he ran into his publisher, whom he had studiously avoided, at a banquet. The publisher greeted him and boldly inquired, "Dr. Wise, have you made any progress with your autobiography?" "As a matter of fact I have," replied Wise. "The former title was, *My Twenty Years of Battling for a Principle*. I've changed the title to, *My Thirty Years of Battling for a Principle*." I can identify with Rabbi Wise's struggle: A rabbi wrestles with numerous problems in the course of his or her rabbinical service. And high on the list is the constant internal battle with theological issues—issues that never seem to disappear and often become more vexing and challenging as the years flit by. I have been wrestling with theological concerns for close to a half-century; I presume I shall continue to do so as long as God grants me life and intelligence. The final resolution of inner doubts and questions, challenges and dilemmas still eludes me—and probably always will.

I should begin with a disclaimer and point out that I am not a theologian. I am a rabbi and historian of ideas; I have always been fascinated by the development, changes, and metamorphosis of different concepts and notions. But that does not preclude my right to investigate and speculate about theological notions and draw my own conclusions. After all, no one holds a monopoly on Jewish thought, and no license is required to dabble in theology, which means, literally, "the knowledge of God." Catholic theologians require a *mandatum* or license from the local bishop to teach theology at a Catholic university; happily that rule does not apply to Jews. Moreover, as Maimonides wrote, "The gates of investigation are never shut." And he also exhorted us, "Accept the truth from whoever offers it." I have tried to sift and select my sources from the Bible, Talmud, Midrash, and medieval and modern expositors, commentators, and interpreters. I hope that none of my more learned readers will conclude that I have manipulated the sources to support my stance. I have endeavored to select and interpret fairly, if a bit personally and idiosyncratically, without violating the true meaning of the texts, searching for, what Dr. Max Kadushin dubbed, "emphatic trends," or what in music is described as "leitmotifs," major, recurring themes. I have listed some of the more important sources with the hope that the reader will go and check them and learn more. At the same time, I have deliberately not included copious footnotes that are valuable for the scholar but put off the average, intelligent reader for whom this volume is intended.

This book reflects my own changing thinking and evolving understanding of what Judaism is all about. It is also the result of the many questions and challenges, doubts and uncertainties expressed to me over the past five decades or so by hundreds—perhaps even thousands—of men, women, and children who wanted to learn more about what Judaism stands for and what it means to be a believing Jew. "Much have I learned from my teachers, more still from my colleagues, but most of all from my students," suggested the sages (*Ta'an.* 7a). Bright, sharp, literate, challenging students are a welcome asset for any teacher or rabbi. They prod us to evaluate and reevaluate our stances and to reassess our positions. Undoubtedly, my own thinking has undergone change and has evolved from my student days when I thought I had all the answers. How wrong life proved me to be!

But humans ought to grow and develop intellectually and morally, even as they do physically. Heraclitus remarked that you cannot enter the same stream twice: The stream has changed and moved on, even as you have changed. The combination of experience, reflection, maturation, and deeper learning, as well as triumphs and tragedies, joys and sorrows must inevitably shape and reshape our views hundreds of time in the course of our lives. That is as it should be because, as Plato noted, in the name of Socrates, the unexamined life is not worth living, and we either evolve constantly or we stagnate. Professor Mordecai M. Kaplan taught senior homiletics at the Jewish Theological Seminary for many years, prior to becoming professor of the philosophies of religion. Once, he rehearsed a student who was to deliver his senior sermon in the Seminary synagogue on the following *Shabbat*. Dr. Kaplan praised the sermon fulsomely. The student delivered the sermon, and in class a few days later, Kaplan criticized it sharply. "I don't understand," complained the confused student. "A few days ago in the rehearsal you praised my sermon without reservation." "Yes" replied Kaplan, "that is true, but I have grown since then."

I am a teleologist: I believe that there is a *telos*—a goal or purpose to all creation. I like the statement attributed to Rav, one of the architects of the Babylonian Talmud, who declared: "Everything that God created in this world is for a purpose and nothing has been created in vain" (*Shabb.* 77b). Nothing is more teleological than our people—the Jewish people, *Am Yisrael.* Deuteronomy 7:6–7 stated this principle boldly: "For you are a people consecrated to the Lord your God: of all the peoples on earth the Lord your God chose you to be His treasured people. It is not because you are the most numerous of peoples that the Lord set His heart on you and chose you—indeed, you are the smallest of peoples." We were not chosen to be great in numbers or mighty in military prowess; other nations and religions fill that role. No, God selected us for a higher purpose, a loftier goal: to be a kingdom of priests and a holy nation. And our people must never lose sight of that goal.

If we are to serve as a holy nation, we must live passionately as Jews, or we will not live. Dr. Abraham Joshua Heschel wrote, "One who thinks that one can live as a Jew in a lackadaisical manner has never tasted Judaism." I believe that is the truth. But I do not subscribe to the view that it doesn't matter what a Jew believes or doesn't believe as long as he or she performs the *mitzvot.* This position, espoused by most of the Orthodox world and I presume, subscribed to by many in the ranks of the other streams of Judaism, is a distortion of Judaism. Such an attitude is, suggested Heschel, "religious behaviorism," and that is not what Judaism is all about. I remind my readers that Jeremiah insisted that God wants us to understand and know Him (Jer 9:22–23). We *do* possess a theology; we *do* cherish specific principles and ideals, concepts and notions. It is not enough merely to "do Judaism"; it is essential, in my view, that we "believe in Judaism." After all, we introduced the most radically new ideas into the pagan world, namely: monotheism, the dignity of all humans, social justice for all levels of society, and messianic redemption—just to name a few. Ideas live and vivify; they shape human thinking and behavior; they affect society and nations, and ultimately the world of men and women. "Nothing is as powerful as an idea whose time has come," wrote Victor Hugo. There is a purpose to all of these ideas, and it is incumbent upon all humans to uncover and mine that purpose, to enrich and be enriched in the process.

It is quite true that one of the main differences between Judaism and Christianity, and, to a lesser degree, Islam, is that we Jews do not profess a saving creed, a statement of faith such as the Christian Nicene creed, the acceptance of which guarantees salvation. The closest formulation of a creed is the recitation of the *Shema* from Deuteronomy 6:4 proclaiming God's unity. But that is merely an affirmation of our belief in one God; it is not in itself salvific; it does not assure us of "salvation."

Actually, Jews are not really that preoccupied with saving their souls. As Michael Wyschogrod puts it, "Judaism is not a salvational religion." We really don't go about wondering if we will be "saved" from the fires of Hell or whether or not our behavior or beliefs merit salvation for our souls. In all my long career, I never met a Jew of any religious orientation who indicated that the reason for observing a particular mitzvah was to gain entry into Heaven. And I rarely encountered even the most fervidly Orthodox rabbi who suggested that one's heterodox beliefs and practices merited an afterlife in Hell. Believing Jews accept the principle that, "All Jews have a portion in the age to come" (*Abot*, prologue to chapter one).

I am also not a literalist. I do not necessarily cherish *mitzvot* because they are the literal word of God, which is the "fundamentalist" perspective. If I were an Orthodox Jew, this would suffice for me: God has commanded this or that mitzvah and there is no further discussion because I do as the *Metzaveh* (Divine Commander) has commanded. I admire the zeal of my Orthodox brothers and sisters for whom this approach is both spiritually compelling and psychologically fulfilling. But I cannot accept this conception of Judaism, nor, evidently, can most of world Jewry. For me, the idea of living a full Jewish life stems partly from my passion to assure *the creative survival of the Jewish people*—that yet has much to offer towards the enrichment of humanity. I keep *mitzvot* as *if* God has commanded them; I pray *as if* God hears my prayers (though I have deep misgivings about the notion of an Omnipotent Creator of the universe taking note of puny me and my equally insignificant prayers); I live Jewishly *as if* my very soul depended on it; I study Torah *as if* the preservation of Jewish learning hinged on my intellectual investment.

I also believe that the Divine Force in this universe withdrew after the creation (*tzimtzum*, contraction, is the mystical term of the Kabbalah), allowing humans to fill the void and shape the world according to their wishes. God has thereby *empowered human beings*; He has given us the choice of good and evil, of life and death, to do with this planet as we choose. The essence of our humanity is free choice and the ability to shape our destinies as well as the destiny of society and the world. This is the very core of our humanity; without free choice we are little more than puppets of the Divine and thereby not accountable for our behavior. But I do believe in the accountability of humanity, which makes a belief in an omnipotent God who micromanages our daily lives a logical absurdity.

Above all, I believe in the need for the *creative survival of the Jewish people*. I stress, as Dr. Mordecai M. Kaplan stressed, the *creative* survival of our people. It is not enough just to survive: Animals and plants and bacteria survive, but their survival is not necessarily creative and might even prove harmful. I want our people to survive to be creative, to add to the wisdom of thinking humans; to augment the blessings of science and industry, medicine and the arts, and the intellectual and esthetic components. But if we are to accomplish those goals and fulfill our destiny as a teleological people, we need to do our best, summon our innermost resources, and live creative and rich Jewish lives. We are a small people; we number perhaps13 million in the world. Salo W. Baron estimated that there should have been at least 100 million Jews in the world, had it not been for persecution, pogroms, massacres, forced conversion, and expulsions. Sergio della Pergola calculates that had the *Shoah* (Holocaust) not annihilated six million Jews, we should number 32 million today by natural growth. So our numbers are shrinking; we have fewer and fewer Jews on whom we may count to live up to the standards laid down for us in the Torah and by the Divine charge. And that worries me most profoundly.

Consequently, we need all the help we can get; we must count on each and every Jew. Very early in the days of the State of Israel, Prime Minister David Ben-Gurion needed an ambassador to Romania—preferably someone who spoke the language—so he summoned to his office the famous painter, Reuven Rubin, who hailed from Romania and was fluent in the language. He informed Rubin that he was to be the next Israeli ambassador to his old country. Rubin hesitated: "But Mr. Prime Minister, what do I know about being an ambassador?" Ben-Gurion replied, "What do I know about being a prime minister? But there are very few of us, so each of us must do his duty to the best of one's ability." In truth, there are very few Jews in this world; consequently, each Jewish man and woman must do his or her duty to the best of his or her ability so that we may yet flourish and enrich humanity. One way to start is by clarifying how each of us conceives of Judaism and its great principles. And that is the purpose of my book: to prod people of intelligence who care about being Jewish and view their Jewish identity as more than merely an ethnic or national designation, to think, ponder, and engage fertile ideas in order to cross-pollinate them, and bear lovely flowers and sweet fruits.

Points to Ponder:
Introduction

1. How do you understand Maimonides' mandate, "The gates of investigation are never shut?" Are there no limits? And how are we to evaluate what is really true or not in our ongoing search for truth?

2. Granted that we all grow and change, are there no constants in life? Is everything subject to change or reinterpretation? Are there no abiding truths or principles that endure forever?

3. How do you react to the tale of Rabbi Mordecai Kaplan's critique of the student sermon as an illustration of how he constantly grew and evolved?

4. Do you agree with the author's thesis that there is a teleology in life and that there is a purpose, not always known to us, to everything?

5. Does Judaism emphasize creed or deed? Are both intrinsic to Judaism?

6. Do you think much about "salvation" of your soul, or do you view this as irrelevant to your life as a Jew and a human being?

7. The author is deeply concerned about the *creative survival* of the Jewish people. Does this resonate with you? And what comprises *creative survival*?

8. The author cites statistics that reveal we are a shrinking number of Jews in the world. Are numbers important? Could we accomplish more and feel safer with a larger Jewish population? Or is quality rather than quantity the more important of the two?

9. How have your own beliefs changed over the years?

10. Draw up a list of essentials for your own personal credo.

Abbreviations

Hebrew Bible

Gen	Genesis
Exod	Exodus
Lev	Leviticus
Num	Numbers
Deut	Deuteronomy
Josh	Joshua
1–2 Sam	1–2 Samuel
1–2 Kgs	1–2 Kings
Neh	Nehemiah
Ps/Pss	Psalm/Psalms
Prov	Proverbs
Qoh	Qohelet (Ecclesiastes)
Isa	Isaiah
Jer	Jeremiah
Ezek	Ezekiel
Hos	Hosea
Mic	Micah
Zeph	Zephaniah
Zech	Zechariah
Dan	Daniel

New Testament

Matt	Matthew
Gal	Galatians
1–2 Thess	1–2 Thessalonians

Talmud

All Talmudic references in the text are to the Babylonian Talmud (*b.*) except where the Talmud of Eretz Yisrael is indicated (*y.*).

m.	Mishnah
b.	Babylonian Talmud

y.	Talmud of Eretz Yisrael (*Yerushalmi*)
t.	*Tosefta*
Abod. Zar.	*Avodah Zarah*
Abot	*Avot (Pirkei Avot)*
B. Batra	*Bava Batra*
B. Metzia	*Bava Metzia*
B. Qam.	*Bava Kama*
Ber.	*Berakhot*
Erub.	*Eruvin*
Ed.	*Eduyot*
Git.	*Gittin*
Hag.	*Hagigah*
Hul.	*Hullin*
Ketub.	*Ketubbot*
Mak.	*Makkot*
Meg.	*Megillah*
Menah.	*Menahot*
Ned.	*Nedarim*
Pesah.	*Pesahim*
Qidd.	*Qiddushin*
Sanh.	*Sanhedrin*
Shabb.	*Shabbat*
Ta'an.	*Ta'anit*
Tem.	*Temurah*
Yebam.	*Yevamot*

Midrash

Abot R. Nat.	*Avot of Rabbi Nathan*
Mek.	*Mekhilta*
Midr. Pss.	*Midrash Psalms*
Gen. Rab.	*Genesis Rabbah*
Ex. Rab.	*Exodus Rabbah*
Lev. Rabbah	*Leviticus Rabbah*
Num. Rab.	*Numbers Rabbah*
Deut. Rab.	*Deuteronomy Rabbah*
S. Eli. Rab.	*Seder Eliyahu Rabbah*
Sifre Num.	*Sifrei Numbers*
Sifre Deut.	*Sifrei Deuteronomy*
Tanh.	*Tanhuma*

1

Why Religion?

RELIGION IS certainly prominently in the news these days. Scarcely a day passes without a front-page story in the newspapers or a prominent radio or television item dealing with some aspect of religion in our society. Regrettably, it is viewed as an increasingly ugly phenomenon. The swing to fundamentalism—or as I prefer to call it, *fanaticism*—is evident among all faith groups. There is a perceptible decline of religious tolerance worldwide as one faith group or another seems to want to dominate and even exterminate competing groups.

Just reflect on the chaos in Iraq and the carnage among Shiites, Sunnis, and Kurds. These bands of fellow countrymen are waging vicious battles against one another based on ancient enmities that go back over 1000 years. If this is the way they behave toward fellow Muslims, we can well imagine what they would do to Israeli Jews if they had the chance! Then there is the Wahhabi version of Islam disseminated by the Saudis—a version of Islam that is so fanatical and benighted, that it views other faith groups as infidels. These are the lessons spread far and wide with Saudi oil money, lessons that bore such tragic fruits on September 11, 2001 and on other bloody occasions. It seems as if Islam is waging a *jihad* against the West, or as they prefer to call it, against "the Crusaders and the Jews" (that is a bizarre linkage if ever I heard one!). Al Qaeda murderers, suicide bombers, and Muslim terrorists are bloodying the landscape with their senseless and mindless deeds. The seeds of their fanatical calls for war against the infidels have been transported beyond the Middle East to cities in the West. Not enough people cared terribly when Israeli buses and pizza parlors and markets were blown up; now the plague has struck Spain and England, Chechnya and Egypt. Every time the cry, "*Allahu Akhbar*—God is great!" resounds, every time we hear another mass murderer of women and children extolled as a "martyr," we should be incensed. A martyr is one who lays down his or her own life for a sacred cause, not a person who slaughters innocents in the name of God. One eminent moderate Muslim put it this way: "Not every Muslim is a terrorist, but these days it seems as if every terrorist is a Muslim." And we wait in vain for the leading Muslim scholars and imams to condemn such actions and issue *fatwas* (decrees) denouncing such behavior whether against Christians or Jews or Hindus or any other faith as a violation of the Koran and Islamic law and religion. Some in America have issued such condemnations; few have followed suit in Arab lands. It is shameful that Islam, which once served as the beacon of intellectual enlightenment, science, the arts, and philosophy and religious tolerance while Christian Europe wallowed in the Dark Ages, has sunk so low. It hurts to think that whereas we Jews fared better under the Crescent than under the Cross through the centuries, Islam is now the hotbed of anti-Jewish agitation and murderous behavior.

I certainly do not wish to give the impression that only Islam has "bloody borders" (to use the phrase of Samuel Huntington in his important volume, *The Clash of Civilizations and the Remaking of the World Order*). Christianity's borders are deeply stained as well. I need not tell my readers what crimes were perpetrated against Jews for centuries under Christianity, whether in its Catholic or Protestant forms. The Crusades, the Inquisition, the brutal wars of religion that wracked Europe—all add up to a bloody and black page in the history of religious intolerance. And for a more recent example, I remind my readers of what the Christians did to the Muslims in the Balkans only a few years ago. Nor can we ever forget that the *Shoah*, the Holocaust, was perpetrated in the heart of Christian Europe, with the churches standing virtually impotent or indifferent on the sidelines. Pascal said it well: "Men never do evil so completely and cheerfully as when they do it from religious convictions." No religion is untainted: not ancient Judaism, not Hinduism, not Buddhism—they all have authored their black pages of history. Professor J. Harold Ellens has recently edited a four-volume set, *The Destructive Power of Religion* (2004), and it makes for chillingly disturbing reading. Ellens argues that the conflicts we endure in society stem from the ancient Jewish-Christian-Muslim metaphor of a cosmic conflict between good and evil that feeds our aggressive drives and psychologically divides humanity into us versus them, those on the side of God and those with evil and the demonic.

Undoubtedly, the worst perversion of religion has been wars in the name of God. In the name of God we must conquer the New World! In the name of God we must battle the Saracens! In the name of God we must wipe out the Protestant heretics! And so it went down the ages. Marching into the trenches of World War I, the German soldiers wore on their uniforms the motto, "*Gott Mit Uns*—God is With Us." Once, they wrote it in bold letters on a placard and held it up for the British soldiers in the opposing trenches to read. The British knew no German and the next day they hoisted their slogan on a huge placard, "WE'VE GOT MITTENS, TOO." Perhaps Abraham Lincoln said it best in his remarkable Second Inaugural Address when he observed that both warring sides of the Union read the same Bible and prayed to the same God, each invoking God's aid against the other, but "the Almighty has His own purposes." "It may seem strange," he stated, "that any men would dare to ask God's assistance in wringing their bread from the sweat of the other men's faces; but let us judge not that we be not judged."

In truth, there is much to criticize in organized religions. The American philosopher, Morris R. Cohen, attacked what he called, "The Dark Side of Religion." He accused religion of historic opposition to science. He insisted that religion has fostered superstition, the belief in demonic possession, ghosts, angels, ancestral spirits, and other nonsense. Religion has fostered witchcraft and magic; it has opposed critical thought while emphasizing fear. It has engaged in endless cruelty and heresy hunting and sectarian battles that have taken untold lives. This cruelty, or "duty of hatred," stems from the belief in religious absolutes, he claims. Additionally, the gods are jealous of human happiness and engender in us a deep terror via a notion of sin. We are fearful of the torments of Hell because of organized religions. Religion has opposed the fine arts and birth control, and introduced censorship. Cohen concluded, "There may be more wisdom and courage as well as more faith in honest doubt than in most of the creeds."

Sigmund Freud was not as biting or harsh in his criticism of religion, but he did indicate that in his mind, religion is an illusion; he suggested that dogmas are not the residue of experience or reflection but "they are illusions, fulfillments of the oldest, strongest and most insistent wishes of mankind . . ." Illusions are not the same as error, he noted; they are derived from men's wishes, they are "wish fulfillment." "Where questions of religion are concerned, people are guilty of every possible kind of insincerity and intellectual misdemeanor."

Yet another source of criticism of religion stems from scientific circles. We are told that science and religion are incompatible; that science is based on fact, whereas religion is based on fiction; that science is the result of rational inquiry whereas religion is steeped in the irrational. Steven Weinberg, Nobel laureate in physics, put it bluntly: "I think one of the great historical contributions of science is to weaken the hold of religion." A word on the relationship between science and religion is in order. Let us recall that science consists of theories—some of which can never be proved totally. Moreover, scientific theories that are accepted today may be discarded tomorrow. A case in point is the Big Bang theory of the creation of the universe. Until 1961, the accepted theory of how this world came into being was that creation was continuous and there was no starting point. But then the Big Bang theory of creation was accepted to the horror of astronomers such as Fred Hoyle and others who fought the new theory bitterly. The Big Bang (which is actually closer to the Jewish notion that creation took place at a determined point in history) won out. Cosmologist James Peebles of Princeton University writes, "We don't talk about absolute truths, we seek approximations that pass tests." And he adds, "Theories are never complete. There is lots of room for improvement, which we call opportunities for research." Nobel laureate in physics Max Planck reminded us, "Science cannot solve the ultimate mystery of nature. And that is because, in the last analysis, we ourselves are part of nature and therefore part of the mystery we are trying to solve." And there are many unsolved mysteries in nature. One of the most vexing is the fact that the universe is expanding at an ever-increasing speed in violation of the laws of physics and no one knows why. So even scientists ought to be humble enough to admit that there is an element of mystery in creation and in nature; that they, too, must occasionally take the "leap of faith" Kierkegaard recommended to religious believers.

I have never been troubled by a so-called conflict between religion and science because they are two, separate realms. Harvard's late paleontologist, Stephen Jay Gould, suggested that religion and science are two non-overlapping magisteria, that is, they are two separate realms of authoritative teachings and may never meet but should be judged on their own merits. I agree that they are separate realms: The one seeks facts and asks the question, "How?" The other seeks purposes and goals and asks the question, "Why?" The one builds its structure on *experiments*. The other fashions its system on *experience*. Maimonides believed in *creatio ex nihilo*—that the world was created out of nothing, contrary to Plato's view that the world was fashioned out of primordial matter. But Maimonides was sufficiently rational to note that if science could prove to him the world were indeed created out of primordial matter, he would interpret the Torah to fit the accepted scientific view. In a word, the religious person is not required to discard logic and reason. As Professor Abraham Joshua Heschel noted, the very first of the thirteen requests we make of God in our daily *Amidah* prayer is the request that God grant us knowledge and intelligence. Without that uniquely human talent, what are we after all? I believe in evolution as the most plausible theory of how we humans got to where we are. But I believe that behind it all is the Creative Force we call, "God, " and it is incumbent upon people of religion to search for the "why" we are put on earth.

I think the greatest danger to religion and humanity these days (as I suppose it always was) is *fanaticism.* Winston Churchill defined a fanatic as "someone who can't change his mind and won't change the subject." Just look at what religious fanatics have wrought! A Hindu religious fanatic murdered Ghandi. A Jewish religious fanatic killed Rabin. What could have driven them to such heinous acts? "God told me to do it," they respond. I challenge: "God told you to violate the most basic of all His commandments, 'You shall not kill'? Maybe it was the Devil who told you to do this?" In a brilliant and poignant essay on Reinhold Niebuhr, Arthur M. Schlesinger Jr. summarizes Niebuhr's theology in these words: "There is no greater presumption than to read the mind of the Almighty, and no more dangerous individual than the one who has convinced himself that he is executing the Almighty's will." When one believes that he or she owns the keys to the kingdom; that he or she possesses the exclusive truth; that this faith guarantees salvation and none other—watch out! Beware the person who insists he wants to save your soul: he's apt to take your body in the process. Let me state bluntly that I believe a religion that condones racism, forced conversion, pogroms, heresy hunts, and massacres in the name of God is a false religion and a travesty. It is to be condemned and shunned like the plague that it is.

I see many dangers both to and from religion in America, these days. We are, unquestionably a religious people. Over ninety percent of Americans believe in God. Americans put their European cousins to shame when it comes to supporting churches and attending services weekly. But there has been an ominous swing to the right in religion in this country. The evangelicals and fundamentalists have gained ascendancy; the mainstream churches are in serious decline. President George W. Bush has set a new tone; as a "born-again Christian," he has articulated a position that troubles many. His faith-based initiatives have involved religious bodies in areas hitherto reserved for the government. Church and state issues are crowding the news. The Supreme Court has ruled that a judge may not display the Ten Commandments in an Alabama courtroom, so the stone monument has been removed. Frankly, I welcome the removal: I should much prefer that the Ten Commandments be installed in our hearts and lives where they might change the nature of society. The teaching of evolution has been banned in a number of states whose school science courses now include something called, "creationism," or, "intelligent design." I cannot believe that over 80 years after the famous Scopes Trial of 1925, when Americans were made to look so foolish because they allowed fundamentalists to expel evolution from Tennessee classrooms, we are still debating this issue. The U.S. Air Force Academy recently has been the scene of a controversy because the Superintendent and several Christian chaplains have been promoting a program of Christian proselytizing and fundamentalism. The conflict exploded after the chaplain who blew the whistle on this was transferred, leading to the creation of a special commission. The commission's report recommended that such activities are inappropriate on government grounds using public funding and must stop.

I am concerned about breaches in the wall of separation between church and state that our Founding Fathers wisely erected. Let us remember that the first Amendment to the Constitution provides, "Congress shall make no law respecting an establishment of religion or prohibiting the free exercise thereof." But the states supported established churches as late as 1833 in Massachusetts. And let us remember that no Jews could hold public office in Maryland until 1826, 1868 in North Carolina and in New Hampshire until 1878 because they were required to take a Christian oath on a Christian Bible. Do we want to go back to that situation? I should hope not. I am not arguing for the banishment of religion entirely from the public square. I do want *religious values* to shape our morality in government and society. But there is too much at stake to allow partisan religion to intrude increasingly in the public domain and make minority faith groups feel uncomfortable or unwelcome. Let us teach evolution and also indicate that there are those who reject it and adopt another viewpoint. Let us allow private prayer silently said before the beginning of the day in school but not inject public prayer that inevitably must become sectarian. Let us teach *about* comparative religions but not teach religion as such in public schools. We have enough divisive factors at play in today's world; we do no need yet additional ones.

Another development in the American brand of religion that troubles me is the growth of superstitions of the crudest types that have proliferated these days. Kabbalah centers have sprouted all over the country. A cluster of non-Jewish movie stars is currently taking Kabbalah classes. A more unlikely group of students of Kabbalah is hard to imagine. These are people who aren't even Jewish and who can't even read a word of Hebrew. And yet, they have the chutzpah to presume to enter into the most esoteric and difficult of all Jewish studies and to venture where only the most scholarly and learned sages have ventured previously! Many have taken to wearing red *bendles*—red bands around their wrists or ankles to protect them from evil forces. It amazes me that intelligent and educated people in the twenty-first century would actually believe that a red band on the body would ward off evil.

I turn to the religious situation in Israel. The nation of Israel, originally founded by secular Socialists who were generally antithetical to religion, has undergone remarkable religious transformations in its short history. The religious population has expanded so that that segment is exerting greater influence than previously. The Gaza disengagement highlighted the religious chasm most graphically. The religious right defiantly maintained that, "God willed us this land." The ultra-nationalist-religious elements insist that it has a Divine mandate to the Greater Land of Israel from the Mediterranean to the Euphrates. Their forcible removal from Gaza and several other settlements prompted a series of articles in the Israeli press wondering whether this is the end of "religious Zionism"—of a Zionism that preached it is a mitzvah to go out and settle all over the territories of what once was Eretz Yisrael. Land, in their judgment, is more important than lives or the path to peace, it would seem.

To make things worse, a number of prominent rabbis, as well as some American Evangelical leaders, blamed the disastrous tsunami in Southeast Asia that took over 200,000 lives on Prime Minister Sharon and his disengagement policy. As if this were not enough, some claimed the ruinous Katrina hurricane and flood that devastated New Orleans and Mississippi were Divine punishment of President Bush for supporting the disengagement. Others pointed to Prime Minister Sharon's devastating stroke as further evidence of Divine displeasure with Israel's policies. Apart from these outrageously cruel and callous words, there were some bloody deeds accompanying the disengagement, and they came from the Israeli side, not the Arabs. Two Israeli religious fanatics murdered eight Arabs and justified their actions as being religiously sanctioned. Apparently, for them, the commandment against murder does not apply to Arabs.

The Arab side is more despicable. Arabs seek justification in Islam for killing Jews. They proclaim it is Allah's will to not just drive out settlers but all Jews. They justify the most heinous acts of terrorism and murder in the name of the Koran. Hamas proclaims for all to hear, "God willing, we'll drive out all the Jews," again besmirching the name of God. One mass-murderer who slaughtered twenty-three Israelis, including six children and a mother of thirteen, leaving over 100 wounded, was a teacher and imam of his local Hebron mosque who wanted to be a "martyr!"

And what is the upshot of all of these data? Religion gets a serious black eye and is degraded. People view it as the *problem*, not the *solution*.

Its real goals and purposes are overlooked. As Jonathan Swift wrote, "We have just enough religion to make us hate one another but not enough to love one another." The result is *hillul ha-Shem*, the name of God is profaned, abused, degraded and cursed, and people tend to conclude, "If this is religion, I want no part of it."

A more balanced presentation of the role of religion in society is needed, however. It was monotheistic religion, after all, that did introduce the concept of human dignity. It ended human sacrifices, which is evidently the point of the remarkable story of the *akedah*, the binding of Isaac (Gen 22). It curbed pagan licentiousness and introduced a notion of ethics and morals to society. It stopped infanticide. It developed medical missions and brought schools to the worst and often most inhospitable places (although often it did so at the cost of local cultures in places such as the New World and Africa). It built hospitals and schools and colleges and great universities all over the world (including, let us recall, our own vaunted Ivy League colleges). It fostered great art and architecture and music that have enriched our culture beyond calculation. Ultimately, it led the fight against slavery and the campaign for civil rights, a striking illustration of how religion can affect public policy and legislation for good. Its legacy for good is enormous, and I shudder to contemplate how our world would have developed without the monotheistic religions. Truly, religion is the best possible armor but the worst possible cloak.

Consequently, we need to refocus on "Why Religion?" and what are the functions and goals and values religion seeks to foster and further? The word, "religion," is from the Latin meaning, "to bind together." That's an important clue: Religion is designed to bind people together via a system of beliefs and practices predicated on a belief in a deity. Religion is to serve as an amalgam, an adhesive power, a centripetal force that creates a community, a people, a religious body. Curiously, there is no word in classical Hebrew for religion. The modern term, *dat*, really meant "religious law" and is derived from the Persian. Some suggest *emunah*, "faithfulness," is a better term; others think *yirat shamayim*, "fear of Heaven," is more appropriate. And others prefer that we use the term, "Torah," which really means, religious teaching or instruction. No matter: we may not have developed a precise word for religion, but we surely understood its implications in our lives. We are and always have been the people of religion par excellence. But the first function of religion for us as for all other humans, I suppose, is to unite a group of people in a common system of beliefs and practices. For Jews, that is one of the main purposes of the *mitzvot* system.

Second, religion is a source of ultimate values and the guarantor of morals. It sets bounds and limits: this is prohibited, this is permitted; this you shall do, this you may not do! It sets parameters of proper and decent human behavior. Abraham commanded his children and their descendents, "They shall keep the way of the Lord and do righteousness and justice" (Gen 18:19). Dostoevsky wrote that, "If there is no God, then everything is permitted." In accepting the idea of a transcendent force in life, we restrict the animal urges and primitive drives that destroy human civilization.

Third, religion seeks the moral use of knowledge. It is not enough just to know; facts without values can be dangerous. The Nazi doctors who experimented on human beings in concentration camps had facts and were presumably pretty smart people. But they had no values; their knowledge was put to the most perverse and inhumane purposes. So I think Gould is not totally correct in suggesting that science and religion must *never* overlap: when they fail to overlap, human values are trashed or sacrificed to some false "gods." They must exist as two separate realms, and the Bible is not a textbook of paleontology or astronomy or geology just as the writings of Einstein or Gould or Stephen Hawking are not religious tracts. People who read the Bible as a science text degrade religion and demean science. Those who detect a clash between the two disciplines are establishing a false dichotomy. The point is: they should supplement each other when needed. Einstein put it well when he famously wrote, "Science without religion is lame. Religion without science is blind."

Religion seeks, fourth, to guide and humanize interpersonal relations. Judaism has developed an entire body of *mitzvot bein adam le-haveiro*, commandments regulating relations between one human and another. That relationship is built on three pillars: justice, truth, and peace (*Abot* 1:18). The prophets tirelessly sought to improve human relationships. Amos denounced those who crushed the head of the poor into the dust (2:7). Micah suggested that the three qualities we need to cultivate are, "doing justice, loving mercy and walking humbly and chastely before God" (6:8). Isaiah insisted we emphasize less the cult of sacrifices and free the prisoners, deal bread to the hungry, clothe the naked, and house the homeless (58:5–8). So important is the mitzvah of *tzedakah*, charity, that the rabbis of the Talmud suspended the normal prohibition of talking business on *Shabbat* and allowed such discussions of charitable campaigns to be conducted in the synagogue on *Shabbat* and even to go to the Roman theatres and circuses for that transcendent purpose (*Ketub.* 5a; *Shabb.* 150a). That is why it was such a mitzvah to try to help those millions of people in Southeast Asia who were ruined by the tsunami of 2004. And that is why we are horrified over the tragedy of the Katrina hurricane and flood in New Orleans in 2005 where old people in hospitals and nursing homes were literally abandoned to their fate, to drown or die of heatstroke. I am certain my readers shudder at the thought of abandoning old parents or grandparents. Is this the Christian way? Surely not: I certainly hope it is not the Jewish way. We have an obligation to our fellow beings because that is what religion is all about.

Fifth, religion must be a goad to activism. It must challenge and confront us to do something to battle evil and injustice. "Seek peace and pursue it," urged the psalmist (34:13). The sages interpret this verse to mean that we must actively seek peace at home and pursue it abroad (*Lev. Rab.* 9:9, p. 188). Judaism is not a passive faith; it is an active, dynamic religion that demands human involvement in solving society's problems and curing its ills. In his celebrated essay, "My Religion," Leo Tolstoy argued that his religion was summed up in the teaching of Jesus, "Resist not evil." If someone smites you on the cheek, turn the other one. If an evil person takes you to court for your tunic, give him your cloak. But do not resist evil (Matt 5:39 ff.). Judaism never subscribed to this view for two reasons. First, we learned that if one turns the other cheek to a bully, one gets smacked a second time—and even killed. Second, the only way to triumph over evil and injustice, tyranny and brutality in society is by actively battling it. The lesson of appeasement we learned in the 1930s when England and France sold out Czechoslovakia was that they achieved neither peace nor honor in their time, but they reaped the harvest of war and dishonor. Had the churches of Europe rallied together with the political parties against the Nazis when they had both the power and the following, we might have avoided the Second World War and the unspeakable horrors of the *Shoah*. But Europe's supine and craven reactions to the fascist and Nazi thugs remain an eternal blot on the record of Christianity—a blot that will not be expunged, I suspect.

Sixth, religion assures its followers, "salvation." Christianity preaches that those who believe and follow its tenets are assured that their souls are "saved." We Jews don't really talk very much about saving souls. We concentrate more on the *yeshua* or *geulah* of our society and people. But Judaism certainly discusses at length how to receive a *helek le-olam haba*—a portion in the age or world to come. Judaism teaches that "all Jews have a portion in the next life" except for egregious sinners (*m. Sanh.* 10:1; Prologue to *Abot*). Judaism also teaches that "the righteous of all nations have a portion in the next life," which Maimonides explains, includes all people who embrace the seven Noahide Laws, the basic minimum for civilized living. He also rules that we may never force people to accept Judaism because that is not the way to bring people under God's canopy, although we may compel savages to accept the basic Noahide rules.

And how does one achieve a portion in the afterlife? All kinds of answers are given. We must honor our fellow humans and never shame them—especially publicly. We must respect the human dignity of all creatures. We must deal honestly with others in business and professions. We must study Torah and cherish learning, participate in synagogue prayers and support communal activities. A remarkable statement of how to merit entrance to *olam ha-ba* is found in this Midrash (*Midr. Pss.* 118, p. 486):

> "Open for me the gates of righteousness." In the next life, the angels will ask a person, "What was your work on earth?" If he replies, "I fed the hungry," they will respond, "This is the gate of the Lord, those who fed the hungry may enter." "I gave water to the thirsty," and they will respond, "Those who gave water to the thirsty may enter." "I clothed the naked," and they will respond, "Those who clothed the naked may enter." Likewise for those who raise orphans, and those who do charity, and those who perform acts of loving kindness.

In short, the application of worship and learning to human relations, moral behavior, and good interpersonal relations make us *worthy* of "salvation" and guarantee us a portion in the age to come.

Consequently, as I view it, religion sets out the following goals:

- It strives to create a sacred community bound by transcendently holy norms
- It instills in us an uneasy conscience
- It seeks to make us better human beings
- It struggles to create a more humane society
- It comforts the afflicted and afflicts the comfortable

And we would do well to recall the words of Abraham Joshua Heschel: "Religion is a means, not an end. It becomes idolatrous when regarded as an end in itself."

There is yet one more extremely important function of religion in our lives. Religion must instill in us *courage and hope* so that so that we may face the gravest possible challenges unbroken and unbowed. In moments of testing when our faith is sorely challenged, we must *use* our faith, not *lose* it. Jeremiah said it: "For there is hope for your future" (31:15–17). Job said it: "Though He slay me, yet will I trust in Him" (13:15). The psalmist said it: "The Lord is my light and my salvation, whom shall I fear?" (27:1). Isaiah said it: "But they who trust in the Lord shall renew their strength" (40:31). This is Israel's messianic hope, one of our greatest gifts to humanity. This is our belief that weeping may linger for the night, but at the dawn there are shouts of joy; that today may be bleak and hopeless, but when the era of the messiah arrives, there will be light. Jews have always taken this teaching most seriously. I have no doubt that is one of the main reasons why we are still here. We have under the gravest of circumstances found comfort and courage, strength and solace in this ideal of the messianic salvation. As Maimonides phrased it in his famous Thirteen Principles of Faith, *Ani maamin be-emunah sheleimah, be-viat ha-mashiah*—"I believe with perfect faith in the coming of the messiah; and though he may tarry, still I do believe and will wait daily for his coming!"

Points to Ponder:
Why Religion?

1. Do you think that religion is currently receiving bad press? Is it justified?

2. What is the difference in your view between religion and fanaticism?

3. Do you agree that all religions have been tainted by some degree of violence in their history?

4. Science and religion seem to be more at loggerheads these days than in recent decades. Why is that so? Do you conceive of the two as in conflict? Are religion and reason incompatible? Or is the issue of science versus religion merely a red herring?

5. Do you agree that religions have brought great blessings to the world?

6. The author states that a religion that condones violence, forced conversion, and racism is a false religion. Do you agree? Are there circumstances in which religious coercion is justified?

7. We hear much these days about the conflict between evolution and religion. Do you perceive a conflict between the two?

8. Does America really require a separation between church and state or have we gone too far in banishing religion and God from the public square, as some aver?

9. Does the spread of superstition worry you and what should be our stand in confronting such beliefs and practices?

10. Should there be a separation of synagogue and state in Israel or is it essential for the State of Israel that the religious factor play a role in Israeli life?

11. How do you react to the notion that God struck down Prime Minister Sharon because of his disengagement from Gaza? Does your concept of a Deity ascribe to God the floods in the southern United States as punishment of sinners?

12. The author offers several definitions of religion, each describing its particular role. How would you define religion? And what do you see as the role of religion in your life and society?

13. The author states that religion seeks to spread the moral use of knowledge; that facts without values can be dangerous. Do you accept this thesis? Have your life experiences confirmed this to be true?

14. How do you react to Abraham Joshua Heschel's statement that religion is a means, not an end; that it becomes idolatrous when viewed as an end?

2

What Can a Modern Jew Believe?

For almost 50 years I have been wrestling with a momentous problem: What must a Jew believe? What can a modern Jew believe? Must a Jew believe anything? There are those who insist, "It really doesn't matter what one *believes;* what matters is what one *does.* We must perform the *mitzvot* irrespective of what we do or do not believe." Indeed, this seems to be the position of halakhically oriented Jews who observe Jewish law and pay little heed to the philosophy or theology behind that life-style. Professor Menahem Kellner in his book, *Must a Jew Believe Anything?*, has argued that a Jew need not believe anything because we do not possess a formal creed. At the same time, he rightly rejects the attempts of the new fundamentalists in Judaism who seek to make a halakhic issue out of beliefs, converting them into a litmus test of piety. Technically he is right: one may believe in nothing and still be a Jew as long as the person has not renounced the faith. But Solomon Schechter wisely observed that, "We forget that a life without guiding principles and thoughts is a life not worth living." And Abraham Joshua Heschel derided this non-thinking, mitzvah-oriented living as "religious behaviorism."

To be sure, Judaism is not a dogmatic faith. Still, as Max Kadushin noted, it does possess a few authentic dogmas such as belief in the Exodus from Egypt and that God revealed the Torah to Israel. But these few dogmas are remarkably undogmatic and flexible, allowing for a wide and variegated range of interpretations. The details of the Exodus were mooted by the sages while the issue of precisely how much of the Torah was revealed to Moses and Israel at Sinai was similarly disputed, as we shall see in the chapters on revelation and halakhah.

There have been various attempts to reduce Judaism to a few guiding principles and basic beliefs. Already in the Bible, we encounter such endeavors. For example, the book of Deuteronomy (10:12) posed the question, "What does the Lord your God ask of you?" And the answer is that we must revere and love Him, live by His commandments and walk in

His paths. The Prophet Micah formulated the challenge somewhat differently in what is indubitably one of the great distillations of religious teachings, when he demanded (6:8): "What does the Lord require of you? Only that you do justice, love mercy and walk humbly and chastely with your God."

The sages also wrestled with the issue. For example, there is an attempt in the Talmud (*Mak.* 24a) to reduce the 613 commandments to one basic precept. After a long series of opinions, the final view is the verse from the Prophet Habakkuk (2:4), "And the righteous shall live by his faith." Another attempt was made by the Babylonian *Amora*, Rava, who mused: "When we come to the next life for judgment, God will demand of us: 'Did you conduct your business affairs honestly? Did you set aside time for Torah study? Did you propagate the species? Did you hope for salvation? Did you engage in the dialectics of wisdom? Did you cultivate your intellect?'" (*Shabb.* 31a). I suppose everyone is familiar with the famous scene of the prospective convert challenging Hillel to convert him while standing on one foot (an exercise dubbed by Professor Louis Ginzberg, "acrobatic Judaism"). Hillel responded, "That which is hateful to you, do not do to your fellow human. That is the essence of the Torah; the rest is commentary. Now go out and study the rest!" (*Ab. R. Nat.*, A & B, 15 & 16, pp. 29b ff.; *Shabb.* 31a).

Obviously, these are aggadic or midrashic sources, which means they are in the realm of homiletics and theological fancy. Are there any halakhic or legal prescriptions of what a Jew ought to believe? The most importantly authoritative statement of this type is found in the Talmud in *Sanhedrin* 74a. We read of a momentous debate, held clandestinely in the attic of Nitza in Lod, at the time of the Hadrianic persecutions when the practice of Judaism was all but outlawed. The sages voted that there are three sins that may never be committed even at the cost of one's life: idolatry, sexual immorality (adultery and incest), and murder. If a person is commanded by the ruler on pain of death to commit any of these three, that person must submit to martyrdom. To put things positively, the three basic and inviolate principles of Judaism are: the belief in one God, sexual purity, and the absolute sanctity of human life.

Since the *Siddur*, the Jewish prayer book, is actually a crystallization of Jewish dogmas and beliefs, it is important to search the prayers for guidance on what a Jew must believe. The prayer book contains two essential dogmatic statements extracted from the Bible. I refer to the *Shema* (Deut 6:4) and the Ten Commandments (Exod 20:2–13 & Deut 5:6–17). The *Shema* is still recited several times daily; the Ten Commandments are no longer read publicly at daily services (for reasons that are not very clear), although they are found in most traditional prayer books. As Professor Moshe Weinfeld has demonstrated in his recent Hebrew volume on the subject, these two passages formed the core of Judaism's creed and were proclaimed daily, at the conclusion of which the entire congregation would affirm, "True and certain are these words."

The medieval Jewish philosophers, doubtlessly responding to the Christian-Muslim challenges to convert to the dominant faith, endeavored to formulate a basic creed for Jewry. Maimonides' Thirteen Principles (*ikkarim*) are the most celebrated formulation. The great sage of Fustat indicated that every Jew must believe in an eternal, omnipotent, omniscient God who revealed the Torah to Israel, whose last and greatest prophet was Moses, and who will ultimately send the messiah and resurrect the dead. But the ink was scarcely dry on Maimonides' text before critics began to carp and demur. The distinguished Spanish theologians, Hasdai Crescas (died c. 1412) and Joseph Albo (died c. 1444), rejected the Maimonidean formulation and reduced the thirteen to three: belief in God, revelation of Torah, and reward and punishment. The great Italian-Jewish scholar, Samuel David Luzzatto (1800–1865), denounced Maimonides for having been "seduced by Greek philosophy" and for "inventing his Thirteen Principles."

Naturally, what we believe as Jews derives from how we read the Bible as well as how we extrapolate those data through the eyes of the sages of the Talmud and Midrash who filtered biblical law and lore for us. The literalists maintain that every word, every tale is true; to challenge any one of them is heresy. Well, as Ira and George Gershwin pungently reminded us, "It ain't necessarily so." For example, how are we to interpret the tales of the creation at the beginning of the book of Genesis? Are we to understand the six days of Creation and the stories of Adam and Eve as literally true? I think not: after all, the Bible is not a textbook of history or astronomy or biology or paleontology. The Genesis tales consist of ancient sagas skillfully woven into our sacred scriptures, containing some profound moral lessons. First, they instruct us that there is an intelligent force behind creation. Second, the creation of the world came about in evolutionary stages culminating in the apex of creation: humankind. Third, there is a common ancestry for all humans; hence, we are all members of the same human family, so that none is superior to any other—no race, no religion, no national or ethnic group. Finally, we must affirm by word and deed the supreme worth of the individual and the transcendent value of human life, for we are all created "in the Divine image." These are, to my thinking, four of the essential teachings of the Creation saga.

Similarly, in approaching the Exodus tale, we must ask ourselves: "Do we really believe the story precisely and literally as recorded in the book of Exodus? The Ten Plagues, the struggle between Moses and Pharaoh, the precipitous exit in one night of 600,000 males above age 20 (which means a population of 2–3 million instantaneously departed Egypt), the miracle at the Sea of Reeds, the defeat of the Egyptian army—did it all happen as stated in the Torah?" I cannot be a literalist when approaching such seemingly implausible situations. But that does not mean I dismiss such stories as oldwives' tales or ludicrous flights of fancy. I think we must seek out the kernel of historical truth. And that kernel of truth implies: We wandered from Mesopotamia to Canaan and then to Egypt. Our fate changed for the worse, when, along with other Semitic people, we were subjugated and enslaved by the ruling Egyptian monarchs. But we never surrendered our dream to return to the land of milk and honey. Those dreams were revived and our people were galvanized by a man named Moses who led us out of slavery to freedom. From that experience, seared in our collective memories forever, we learned to abhor the bitter curse of slavery, to champion the sweet blessing of freedom, and to savor the indescribable joy of independence in our own land. These are the core values we should derive from the Exodus saga.

Reading the Bible literally is dangerous. It leads to excesses, fanaticism, and loss of faith if "proofs" are advanced that seem to refute its teachings and premises. Consequently, we must read the Bible for its values. And we must study the sages for their insights into texts as they derived values and norms from those texts. This is the approach, I believe, that can make the ancient texts speak to us moderns and offer us a credo for our tempestuous times.

Having reflected on the issue for so many years, I have concluded that there are five basic principles which, I am convinced, every faithful Jew must espouse. First, we must believe that there is one God. The concept is flexible and the tent of Jewish theology is broad enough to include the rationalist and the mystic; those who accept the notion of an omnipotent Deity and those who believe in a limited Deity; those who conceive of God as a supernatural force and those who view God as a natural process in humans and the cosmos. But the belief that there is an intelligent force at work in the universe and that the world is not just random chaos is fundamental.

Second, Jews must believe that God demands of all of us moral and ethical behavior; that the Ten Commandments are the basic legal code not just for Jews but ultimately for all humanity; that morals are not dependent on quixotic choice or subjective whims of conscience but are grounded in the infinite, a force beyond situational or individual dictates.

Third, we must believe that despite temporary setbacks and frequent frustrations, just behavior is ultimately rewarded and unjust behavior is ultimately punished. Whether it takes place in this world or in the next we cannot always say with assurance. But we must maintain confidence that there is a *din ve-heshbon*, a moral reckoning.

Fourth, every Jew ought to believe that *Am Yisrael*, the Jewish people, is God's elected people. We were chosen not because we are better than or superior to any other nation or faith group. Rather, God elected us via a covenant (*brit*) to teach His Torah to humanity and to emphasize ceaselessly that the essence of any religious faith consists of decent and moral behavior to all of God's creatures. We are a teleological people with the mission of teaching the world justice and righteousness, love and compassion, truth and peace, and the supreme worth of human life and dignity of all humankind created in God's image. Our mission is nothing less than *tikkun ha-olam*, mending the world and improving society so that God's kingship is established on earth. Rabbi Isaac Luria emphasized that we are God's partners in this sacred endeavor; that every action we take has cosmic significance; that by dint of human effort we can repair the cracks in the cosmos and restore the world to pristine perfection.

Finally, a Jew must preserve hope for a better future, as Jeremiah insisted in writing in the worst and bleakest days of Judean history, "for there is hope for your future" (31:16). This is the messianic faith of the Jew; it has sustained us in the blackest and bleakest moments in our long march across the pages of history. We must believe, despite all evidence to the contrary, that tomorrow can be better than today; it must be better.

But what if a Jew can't believe in a Deity who ordains certain behavior? How can such a person still live a Jewish life? Or is it an impossibility? Let me state candidly that I think it is futile to seek proof of the existence of God. All kinds of attempts to do so have been made by Jewish thinkers since the days of Philo of Alexandria and before him by Socrates and Plato and Aristotle; but I view these efforts as fruitless. For those who believe, no proof is necessary. For those who do not believe, no proof will suffice. In matters of belief, there are two basic approaches. The first is that of the person who says, "I fully believe, therefore I do. I believe firmly in a *Metzaveh*, a Commander; therefore, I observe, the *mitzvot*, the commandments." This is a fundamentalist approach to Judaism and if one can accept this premise, all flows smoothly. Fortunate is the person whose faith is so firm.

Regrettably, most modern Jews eschew this attitude and argue, "I cannot fully believe that God ordains this or that, yet I want to lead a Jewish life. What rationale is there for me? How can I do one without the other?" I remind such doubters that this was the situation of Israel as they stood at the foot of Mount Sinai. They had barely left Egyptian slavery and were about to be challenged to accept the Torah. Their faith was tenuous at best; after all, they were but a semi-idolatrous rabble, more pagan than monotheistic. And yet, when summoned at Sinai to accept His Torah they shouted, "We will do and we will hear!" (Exod 24:7). The sages, ever sensitive to the nuances of language, noted the peculiar order of the verbs: the proper order should have been, "We will hear and we will do!" They describe the Children of Israel as "a rash and precipitous people that placed its mouths before its ears" (*Shabb.* 88a). Martin Buber understands the peculiar order in the text to mean, "We will do in order to understand." Emanuel Levinas cites the Midrash that accepting before understanding is like an apple tree whose fruits precede its blossoms. "The experience," he suggests, "comes before the understanding."

Hence, I urge those Jews who cannot yet believe: Lead Jewish lives. Do the Jewish thing. Be part of *Am Yisrael* and the community and synagogue life. Immerse yourselves in Jewish learning and serious study. Experience *Shabbat* and *Yom Tov*. Commit yourselves to moral and righteous living. I am convinced that the rest will follow; the deep, abiding faith we all crave will ultimately engulf us in a warming embrace.

Frederick the Great once asked his court chaplain for proof of the existence of God. "The Jews, your highness; the Jews are proof of the existence of God." I consider this to be a strikingly potent insight. After all, we are still here despite the best efforts of so many civilizations, religions and nations to do us in—efforts that continue right now with unabated fury. No other ancient nation is represented on earth; great and mighty empires have long disappeared, turned to dust and detritus. But we are still here and have made enormous contributions to human civilization far beyond our meager numbers. So it is up to each of us to live up to our mission to be, in Isaiah's words, "a covenanted people, a light for the nations" (42:6) so that we might bring light and hope to a sorry world and help repair our fractured planet via *tikkun*. Can we not all agree at least on this one basic principle? Can we not put aside doubts and partisanship and pettiness and affirm at minimum this one, irreducible principle of faith? If we all agree that the Jewish people lives and must live and that we must do everything in our power, adopt every strategy and employ every means to insure its creative survival, then, indeed, we will live.

And this, I am convinced, is one principle in which all modern Jews can believe.

Points to Ponder:
What Can a Modern Jew Believe?

1. How do you react to those who insist that it doesn't matter what we believe; what counts is what we do?

2. What is the difference between a "dogmatic faith" and one that contains some dogmas?

3. Do you agree with Hillel that the essence of Judaism is love of fellow human?

4. Why do you think the recitation of the *Shema* and Ten Commandments was so important?

5. The author suggests that we must not read the Bible literally, but rather seek in it values. How do you react to this approach?

6. The author suggests that there are five basic principles we must all adopt if Judaism is to flourish. Do you agree with his selection?

7. Do you agree with Emanuel Levinas that the "experience comes before the understanding"? Is this a valid approach to heightening Jewish loyalties?

8. If a Jew cannot believe that God ordained patterns of living, how can he or she still retain Jewish observances?

9. What do you think of the suggestion that the existence of the Jewish people is proof of God's existence?

10. If you were asked to draw up a list of basic Jewish beliefs you accept, what would you include?

3

What Can We Believe about God?

I F I were to ask the average reader of these pages, "What is the central teaching or focal point of Judaism?" what would he or she say? My guess is, the reader would respond, "God is the central teaching and focal point of Judaism." And if I were to pursue my questioning and inquire, "What is there that is so special about the concept of God in Judaism?" my guess is the answer would be, "Monotheism—the belief in one God." And that person would be correct: Our unique contribution to religion and the world has been the notion of one God. No other ancient civilization even approached this remarkably revolutionary idea. Not the Assyrians or the Egyptians; not the Babylonians or the Persians; not the Greeks or the Romans—only the Jews fashioned a remarkably new concept that there is one God in this universe and none other.

This is a difficult chapter to write because in speaking of God, we are speaking of the ineffable, as Abraham Joshua Heschel has said. We are trying to talk about that which is not to be talked about, cannot be described, "sees but is not seen." How can mere mortals conceive, describe, portray in human words, and talk about the Deity? How can we finite mortals speak of the infinite? When Moses naively asked God for permission to see His face, he was told that, ". . . no man can see Me and live" (Exod 33: 18 ff.). The best Moses could do was to capture a sense of the infinite–much as one may perceive only the fleeting tail of a comet but never the comet itself. The medieval mystical *Shir Ha-Kavod* (Hymn of Glory) sung in many synagogues on Sabbaths and festivals, expresses the experience this way: "I have not seen You, yet I sing Your praise, I have not known You, yet I imagine Your ways . . . they have imagined You but not Your essence, they have fathomed You by Your works."

Yet we cannot quantify our experiential encounter with the Deity; nor can we measure our love or quantify our affections. And mountains of material have been written on this subject over the millennia: Because we can't measure it in a test tube or on a scale doesn't mean that love of

God or faith is an illusion or fiction. Sigmund Freud did describe God and religion as an "illusion," in his volume, *The Future of an Illusion*. Well, if so, it is a most universal and enduring one. Even the very name of God is a puzzle and a variety of terms for the Deity appear in the Bible: *El, Elohim, Ehyeh, Yah, YHVH, Shaddai*—all of these and more are divine names in the Bible. And the sages expanded the lexicon of divine names far beyond the biblical number as they sought to portray God's various attributes: The All Powerful, The Omnipresent, The Holy One, blessed be He, The Merciful, The One Who Spoke and the World Came into Being, Creator of the Universe, King of the Universe—and others. Finally, I think it is fruitless to try to prove the existence of God mathematically or philosophically as so many have endeavored throughout the ages. Such an exercise is one of futility. Only the actual experience of God can convince one beyond the shadow of doubt that, indeed, there is a living God of this universe.

At the outset, I should stress that the concept of a Deity in Judaism was one that developed over a considerable period of time. Additionally, I must emphasize that there have been and currently are many different and varied concepts of God. To argue that there is only one legitimate concept of God in Judaism, as some theological zealots have been doing these days, is to fly in the face of facts and ignore the body of evidence in the tradition itself. Moreover, our concept of God has evolved over the ages. Primitive Hebrews held to a primitive notion of God who demands some outrageous actions such as the murder of individuals or even whole peoples. But as our conception of the Deity matured, we came to realize that God insists on just and moral behavior; that He does not seek the death of the sinner but prefers that he repent and live, as Ezekiel phrased it.

Abraham is described in the Bible as the first monotheist (Gen 12) and there is a plethora of rabbinic legends expatiating on this theme. The best known, perhaps, and one which Hebrew school alumni will surely recall, is the one that tells us that Abraham's father, Terah, was an idol manufacturer. One day in his absence, Abraham, smashed all the idols and placed a stick in the hand of the biggest one. When his father came home he shouted at the lad, "Who has done this awful thing?" The young Abraham replied, "That big idol with the stick in his hand." Terah reacted derisively, "How can an idol of wood possibly do such a thing?" Abraham retorted, "If you agree that a statue of wood or stone could not act against other idols, how can you possibly worship such idols as a god?" Whether or not Abraham was indeed the first monotheist as we understand the meaning of the term is moot. Perhaps he was one of those who, in groping for a unified concept of the world, prepared the way for a more sophisticated and mature idea of monotheism—an idea that was to be more fully developed by Moses.

The Book of Exodus seems to suggest (Exod 6) that a new concept of the Deity was born with Moses beginning with his encounter at the burning bush. The Torah states that God explained to Moses that He had indeed revealed His divinity to the Patriarchs, Abraham, Isaac and Jacob. However, God did not reveal His full name (that is, His redemptive power) to the Patriarchs. Moses would be the first recipient of that extraordinary and revolutionary name and the concept accompanying it. The new name was YHVH, an obscure name whose pronunciation is still an enigma (the term, "Jehovah," used mostly by Christians is incorrect). The name evidently means, "He who causes to be"—i.e., God, the Creator of all. This name is so sacred to Jews that only the High Priest pronounced its letters fully when he entered the Holy of Holies of the Temple in Jerusalem on Yom Kippur, the Day of Atonement, and pious Jews until this day use a substitute for that sacred name. Thus, the revolutionary new concept introduced by Moses was that God is the creator of everything and the source of all life.

But it would be an error to assume that everyone experienced the Divine presence in a similar fashion. The sages stressed this point in a variety of their homilies and interpretations. For example, they inform us that at the Sea of Reeds, God manifested Himself as a warrior who defeated the Egyptian armies. At Sinai, God revealed Himself as the lawmaker and Divine partner in a sacred contract or covenant (*brit*). In fact, the sages underscore the multifaceted and diverse experiences of God's presence in history. "At the Sea of Reeds, God revealed Himself as a mighty warrior but afterwards He was like an old man full of gentleness and compassion" (*Mek. Shirata*, 2:30 ff.). "What a maid servant saw of God at that great moment at the Sea, Ezekiel and Isaiah and the other prophets never saw" (*Mek. Shirata*, 2:24–25). The prophets themselves had a very varied notion of God: "Moses saw God through a clearer lens, so to speak, than did any of the other prophets" (*Lev. Rab.* 1:14, pp. 31–32); "Isaiah saw God as would an urbane city slicker; Ezekiel viewed God through the eyes of a country lad" (*Hag.* 13b). Each generation, then, each person, each spiritual leader, and each prophet or sage views the Deity somewhat differently from the others. The rabbis tell us that Abraham viewed God as a mountain; Isaac experienced the Deity in a field; Jacob envisioned God in the home (*Pesah.* 88a). To put it differently, Abraham's God was a transcendent Deity; Isaac's was viewed in nature; Jacob thought of God in a more intimate, domestic setting as the force for family and human love.

As the sages suggested, "God revealed Himself, each according his or her individual capacity" (*Tanh. Yitro* 17, pp. 40a–b). To speak of only one, legitimate concept of God is quite untrue to the tradition of Judaism.

What can we say about the Jewish concept of God? First of all, the Bible tells us that God is the creative and transcendent force in the universe; that there was an intelligent spirit behind it all; that it was not merely an accident. "In the beginning God created heaven and earth" (Gen 1:1). He was already there at the very beginning of recorded time. Only the scoundrel (*naval*) denies this reality and reflects to himself, "there is no God" (Ps 14:1). Isaiah quotes God as indicating, "I am the Lord who creates light and darkness, who makes peace and evil. I am the Lord who does all of these things" (45:7). The Midrash (*Exod. Rab.* 5:14) imagines this exchange among Pharaoh and Moses and Aaron: "Pharaoh asked Moses and Aaron, 'Who is your God that I should listen to His voice?' They replied, 'The universe is filled with the might and power of our God. He existed before the world was created and He will continue to exist when the world comes to an end. He formed you and infused in you the breath of life . . . He makes the rain and dew descend and grass grow. He also forms the embryo into the mother's womb and enables it to emerge as a living creature.'" Additionally, Judaism believes that creation is not a one-time event; creation is ongoing. As the *Siddur* reminds us in the Morning Prayer, "God, in His goodness, renews each day the Act of Creation."

As we humans contemplate the cosmos, the movement of the stars and planets, the superlative design of the universe, we are moved inevitably to proclaim, "How great are Your deeds, Lord!" (Pss 33, 95–99, 103, 104; Job 40). "The heavens declare the glory of God and the firmament shows His handiwork," sang the psalmist (19:2). "Lift up your eyes and see who created these," urged Isaiah (40:26). In the unique design of the world, the biblical writers detected the Divine Force. The sages of the Midrash (*Gen. Rab.* 39:1, p. 365) depict Abraham chancing upon a palace, one day. He noticed that as there were many rooms and the lights were lit in the palace, he reasoned that there must have been an architect of the palace: It had not just sprung up out of nothing. Likewise, he reasoned, there must be an architect for the universe. Maimonides put it this way: "When a person contemplates how wondrous and great are God's deeds and creations, he will perceive in them His boundless and immeasurable wisdom. At once, that person will be moved to love, praise and exalt God's great name and yearn with a deep longing to know Him" (*Mishneh Torah, Yesodei Ha-Torah*, 2:1–2).

Equally startling and challenging is the miracle of birth and the mystery of the human body—still among of the great enigmas of life. After all these millennia, we should imagine that we know all there is to know about the human being. Yet, the ancient puzzle articulated by the psalmist, "What is a human being after all?" remains. Incredibly, there are still organs in our bodies that defy medical understanding and confound the physicians. And I know physicians and surgeons who are still humbled by the experience of human birth, even after witnessing thousands of such events. The recent discovery of the human genome impels us further to proclaim, "How marvelous are your deeds, O Lord!"

Monotheism is the other great imperative of Judaism and its doctrine of God. God is one and unique—the only Creator of the universe and the only source of its moral order. The *Shema* prayer that a Jew recites several times daily and is taken from Deuteronomy 6:4 ff. phrases this belief unequivocally: "Hear O Israel, the Lord is our God, the Lord alone" (or, "the Lord is one"). A Jew says this on rising in the morning, proclaims this at morning and evening services, recites it on the bed before retiring for the night, and exclaims this at the last moment of life before dying. No prayer is as important, grabs the soul, stirs the emotions, bespeaks the essence of the Jewish faith for which so many have lived and died as—the *Shema*. The Ten Commandments reiterate the central position monotheism occupies for the Jew: "I am the Lord your God. You shall have no other gods besides Me" (Exod 20:1 ff.; Deut 5:6 ff.). The great hope for the future of humanity is that the Lord shall be one and His name one" (Zech 14:9). The sages share this eschatological vision in their comment, "Today God is one but is called by many different names. In the future, His name will be one also" (*Pesah.* 50a).

Judaism also insists that God is pure spirit, not to be represented by any human or animal or celestial form. This was a clear reaction to the grossness of paganism that concretized the deities in the form of humans, animals, insects, or celestial bodies. There was, to be sure, a school of mystics in rabbinic times that depicted God's bodily features and dimensions. But they are hardly representative of the mainstream of Jewish theology. Maimonides wrote that any representation of God in bodily images is idolatry. Rabbi Abraham ben Daud of Posquières did criticize him harshly for this stating that "greater men than you believed otherwise." However, most scholars do not think that Rabbi ben Daud was necessarily espousing the cause of those who conceived of God in bodily form; rather, he was defending the right of those mystics to their concept of God, in keeping with the elastic theology so typical of Judaism. Nevertheless, the normative view of God is that He cannot be represented in any physical form. Maimonides' position is phrased in the popular *Yigdal* hymn that is sung at Sabbath and other services: "He has neither bodily attribute nor body; nothing can be compared to His sanctity." Consequently, the earlier depictions of biblical scenes in Jewish art portraying human figures from the Biblical tales were gradually phased out into nonobjective portraits or depictions as the iconoclastic view of the Deity gained supremacy.

In view of this data about Judaism's refusal to depict God in physical or human ways, how can we interpret terms in the Bible and Talmud and Midrash that speak of the "hand" of God or the "finger" of God? What are we to make of portrayals of the Deity as wearing *tefillin* and praying and studying Torah? The Talmud explains that the Bible uses familiar, human terms to impress upon us the meaning of Godhood and to make concrete and understandable that which is so recondite and abstract. Maimonides dealt with this challenge at length in his *Guide of the Perplexed* and he disposes of the challenge by telling us these are mere metaphors. Other philosophers explain that we cannot speak the divine language; hence, we must use human terms (inadequate and crude though they are) to describe God and God's impact on our lives and the world.

Another striking understanding of God is that God is devoid of sex or sexuality. As Yehezkel Kaufmann noted, this is no accident: Judaism broke completely with paganism that was replete with gods who were sexual objects, who procreated, who fornicated, who murdered and who exhibited the panoply of human behavior. Hence, in the Bible, God is neither born nor married nor the parent of others. The names for God are not really masculine but neutral (there is no neuter gender in Hebrew). And there is no name for goddess in classical Hebrew, no doubt a reflection of the Biblical writers' revulsion with female deity pagan fertility cults such as the worship of Ashtoret (Ishtar).

Judaism speaks of a God as both omnipotent and omniscient—who can do anything and knows everything. "Nothing is too difficult for God" (Jer 32:17). God is the all-powerful creator of everything on earth and in the heavens; God is a Deity who can bring about miracles—whether the splitting of the Sea of Reeds or the victory of the few ill-armed Israelites over their powerful and well-equipped enemies. God creates the rain and the wind and life itself and is frequently referred to as *Ha-Gevurah* or *Ha-Gibbor*—the all-powerful One. In the daily *Amidah* prayer, we reiterate the phrase, "The God, the Great, the Mighty and the Awesome One . . ." Paradoxically, this is a Deity who has chosen to limit His powers, yielding much to humans so that they are not mere automatons or puppets or hapless and inert victims of fate. Rabbi Akiva's famous paradox phrases it well: "All is foreseen, yet free will is given to humanity" (*Abot* 3:15). Another sage states that, "a human being must reflect that there is a seeing eye and a listening ear and all his deeds are recorded in a divine book" (*Abot* 3:19). God knows all—even our innermost thoughts, as Jeremiah tells us (17:10), and the psalmist reiterates several times (33:14). In the liturgy we affirm, "You know the secrets of the universe." Even the halakhah reflects this theological bent as this legal ruling indicates: "Why does a robber compensate the victim fourfold while the thief pays fivefold damages? The robber knows that there is a God and he steals openly. The thief, however, does so clandestinely as if he can fool God and collect future assets" (*B. Qam.* 79b). Once, Rabbis Israel Salanter, the great master of *Musar*, ethical teachings, was traveling by wagon from one town to another when he passed a field of ripe wheat in which the harvested grain was bundled, awaiting the harvesters. The teamster stopped the wagon, looked around to be certain that no one was present, jumped off and scooped up a number of bundles of wheat, and started to mount the wagon. "Stop!" cried out Rabbi Salanter, "someone is watching." The terrified teamster dropped the wheat, jumped back in the wagon, whipped the horses and sped off at top speed. After some time, he turned breathlessly to Rabbi Salanter and asked, "Who was watching? I saw no one." "He was watching," replied the Rabbi, pointing to heaven.

Judaism's God is omnipresent and everywhere, for God is the ruler over heaven and earth and sea. He is Creator of heaven and earth (Gen 14:19) and Master of all realms (Ps 139:7–10). His realm is not limited by geography. Indeed, the heavens are His throne and the earth is His footstool; how can humans possibly encompass His majesty in a temple or house of worship? (Isa 66:1ff.). As Yehudah Halevi phrased it so beautifully, "Lord where shall I find You and where shall I not find You?" God is the Deity in every facet of nature—in heavens and earth, in sea and mountains. Unlike pagan religions that circumscribed the areas of sovereignty of their many gods, Israel's God is limitless; His divinity permeates all reality. "His glory fills the world," reflected Isaiah and the psalmist (Isa 6:3; Ps 148:13). "God is everywhere like the rays of the sun. As the soul fills the body, so God fills the world" (*Sanh.* 39a). The rabbis query, "Why did God reveal Himself in a bush in the wilderness? God chose an area that is un-owned property so that His word belongs to all humanity" (*Mek. Bahodesh*, 2:236). God is often referred to in rabbinic parlance as *Ha-Makom*, the All-Present, and in every *berakhah* we find the formula praising God, "*Melekh ha-olam*, Sovereign of the universe." Biblical stories are designed to stress this idea of a universal God whose realm encompasses all reality. When Hagar flees with her son Ishmael from Sarah's wrath to the wilderness, God is there to intervene and save them from death. When Moses wanders in the wilderness of Midian, a land not at all associated with Eretz Yisrael or any other holy place, God appears to him in a burning bush to stress that His sanctity is not limited to one land or one continent or tribe. When Jonah naively seeks to escape from God and his mission to preach repentance to the people of Nineveh and flees on a boat from Jaffa to Tarshish calculating that God's power does not extend to the sea, he is taught a painful lesson: He is cast overboard by the distraught sailors, swallowed up by a great fish who, after Jonah confesses his sin and praises God, vomits him up on dry land. The Hasidim stress the universality of God. "Rebbe, I'll give you a dollar if you can show me where God dwells," a Hasid once challenged his master. "And I'll give you two dollars if you can show me where God doesn't dwell," replied the Rebbe.

And yet, the same Judaism that speaks of a transcendent God who creates all reality also preaches the notion of a God who is in intimate connection with humanity. The psalmist put it succinctly: "God is near to all who call upon Him, who call upon Him in truth" (Ps 145:18). When we stand before God in prayer, we address Him in the second person: "*Barukh ata Adonai*—praised are You, Lord . . ." Indeed, all blessings begin with this same, intimate formula–a formula that bespeaks a certain familiarity with the Deity. Max Kadushin described this relationship as "normal mysticism." We are told that, "God hears even a whispered prayer; can you imagine a God nearer to us humans than this one?" (*y. Ber.* 9:1, 13a). The sages developed the notion of the *Shekhinah,* God's sacred presence (note: it is a female noun and is often considered to encompass the "female" aspects of the Deity) that inhabits the human world and is in close proximity to us—when we merit it. The mystical school in Judaism especially enriched and developed by the kabbalists of the Zohar circle and later in the version of Rabbi Isaac Luria (1534–1572), expanded the notion of the *Shekhinah.* The kabbalists preached a concept of a remote, transcendent God whom they dubbed, *Ein Sof,* the Infinite One. But God is in contact with earthly creatures via a series of ten emanations (*sefirot*). The *Shekhinah* is often identified with Israel with whom God comes in intimate contact via the emanation, *Tiferet* (beauty), a contact made more intimate and vivid as Israel observes *mitzvot* such as Torah study or Sabbath observance. Additionally, the Lurianic School stressed that each of us is endowed with a *nitzotz,* a divine spark. It is up to us humans to reunite the divine sparks with the Source of all through our sacred deeds. The Hasidim further developed this notion of God's proximity or imminence, often referring to God by the familiar, diminutive Yiddish term, *Tattenu*, Our Father. "Where does God dwell?" queried the Kotzker Rebbe. And he answered his own question, "God dwells wherever humans let Him dwell."

The Jewish concept of God is inextricably bound up with moral behavior. Let us remember that when God revealed Himself to Moses it was in connection with the battle to free the Hebrew slaves. And when God revealed His Torah at Mount Sinai, He proclaimed, "I am the Lord your God who brought you out of the land of Egypt." God is the Liberator who expects freedom for all creatures and who disdains slavery and oppression. God is holy and expects of all Israel to lead holy lives: "You shall be holy for I am holy" (Lev 19:2). Isaiah spoke of "God who is sanctified by righteousness" (5:16). Indeed, one of the more frequent rabbinic terms for God is, *Ha-kadosh barukh Hu*, the Holy One, blessed be He." God demands that we lead holy lives in emulation of Him and His attributes (*imitatio Dei*): Just as God is merciful and tender, so must humans be merciful and tender. God insists on moral behavior, reminding us that sacrifices and prayers, no matter how extravagant, are hypocrisy if social injustice prevails. "Shall you steal, murder, commit adultery and come to My house and proclaim, 'We are saved!'" (Jer 7:9). "Let not the wise man glory in his wisdom nor the powerful man in his power, nor the rich person in his wealth, but let him glory in this: He shall know Me for these are the qualities I want" (Jer 9:22 ff.). God insists on moral behavior: "It has been told to you, O man, what is good and what the Lord your God requires of you: to love mercy, do justice and walk humbly and chastely with your God" (Mic 6:8). When justice is done in society, in the courts, in the market places, it is as if God's *Shekhinah* is present (*Sanh.* 7a). When injustice and oppression reign, God, so to speak, conceals or hides His presence (Isa 45:15; 57:17). Truth, justice, righteousness, compassion, love, and peace are manifestations of Divinity in the world. We are commanded to emulate these attributes of the Divine—not God's qualities of retribution against the sinners or punishment of the wicked.

"But how can we speak of a God of justice when we read of the bloody horrors associated with the conquest of Canaan described in the Book of Joshua?" This painful question has been addressed to me on more than one occasion. My reply consists of several elements. First, the description in the Book of Joshua is a stylized Bronze Age tale of conquest that is not incontrovertibly historic. The fact is that the so-called "ethnic cleansing" of the aboriginal peoples of Canaan was hardly total; the sages of the Mishnah indicated that there were still descendants of the original native tribes in their time. Second, what occurred was not so much physical destruction of the local peoples as much as absorption of those groups into the Jewish people religiously and ethnically. Finally, and most importantly, we must remember that the Children of Israel were semi-barbarians who had only recently been freed from slavery in Egypt, who still were tempted to worship a golden calf, and whose concept of God was scarcely a mature and fully developed one. They did not yet grasp the meaning of a God who demanded righteousness and justice, truth and peace. They were a people in the process of fathoming God, a God who is constant and unchanging and demands moral actions from His children. But if God never changes, our concept of a Deity is constantly evolving from the immature one of the ancient Hebrews, to the fully developed Deity worshipped by the Jewish people in rabbinic times. It has taken many centuries for Israel to truly grasp God's charge to Abraham that he shall command his descendants "to keep the way of the Lord by doing righteousness and justice" (Gen 18:19).

Judaism also teaches that God is the Master of history, that historical events are not merely random happenings or chance. There is a cycle in human events: humans sin, God punishes, humans repent and are forgiven and reconciled with God. All human events such as the Exodus from Egypt or the destruction of the Temples in Jerusalem, first by the Babylonians, then at the hands of the Romans, are reflections of the will of God. Isaiah viewed the Assyrian attackers as God's agent in punishing wicked Israel; Second Isaiah considered Cyrus of Persia, God's anointed redeemer of Israel from the Babylonian exile. And some Talmudic sages described Titus and the conquering Romans as God's emissaries who were sent to devastate Judea as punishment for the people's corruption.

Since the Holocaust, this view of a God of history has been subjected to withering criticism. Did God will the death of six million of His chosen people? Did God deliberately have the Nazis murder over a million Jewish children? Was Hitler the agent of God's vengeful punishment of Jews for the sins of modernity, as some Hasidim would have it? Critics of this theology call it an abomination and a desecration of the notion of God who is *El rahum ve-hanun*, a compassionate and forgiving Deity. Of all the theological concepts of God in Jewish thought, the one that posits a God of history has been the one most severely criticized and even rejected by many. As Albert Einstein averred, "God does not play dice with the universe." There are natural laws in this universe that are not breached by anyone—including God. How could a good and compassionate Deity have looked on and not intervened while six million of His chosen ones were slaughtered in the most bestial manner? Does God not have better things to do than punish mortals? How could He not have intruded and stayed the hands of the murderers? Theologians such as Richard Rubenstein have totally rejected the notion of God of history. Since Auschwitz, some even speak of the "death of God." Yehudah Amichai, the late, great Israeli poet mused that after Auschwitz there is a new theology because, "the Jews who perished in the *Shoah* now resemble their God who has neither image of a body nor a body."

The concepts of God in Judaism have undergone numerous permutations, in antiquity, then in the Middle Ages, and again in modern times, especially since the Holocaust. Yehudah Halevi's ideas about God were fashioned by Plato's thoughts, as were Solomon ibn Gabirol's writings. Maimonides was heavily indebted to Aristotle and he refers to God in his writings as "the Active Intellect"—a very Aristotelian notion. Hasdai Crescas was indebted to the Greek rationalists. Rabbi Moses de Leon, editor of the Zohar, was greatly influenced by mystics from other religious traditions. Bahia ibn Pakuda owed much to the Sufi Muslim mystics. And Rabbi Isaac Luria obviously utilized some rather startlingly pagan myths in weaving his rich tapestry of mysticism that conquered much of the Jewish world in the sixteenth and seventeenth centuries.

In modern times, we have witnessed the impact of the Enlightenment and rationalism on Jewish thought. Moses Mendelssohn, one of the fathers of the Jewish Enlightenment in Western Europe, reflected those trends in his understanding of God. Mordecai M. Kaplan, the great iconoclastic religious naturalist-humanist, wrote of God as the power or process that makes for human salvation, and he rejected totally the notion of a personal, supernatural Deity. Martin Buber, heavily influenced by Existentialism, fused that school of thought with Hasidic ideas and spoke of God as experienced in all meetings or human encounters. Abraham Joshua Heschel, also under the sway of Existentialism and deeply indebted to his Hasidic background, talked about God as the "ineffable" and as the feeling of "radical amazement" we experience in contemplating the world. More recently, different notions of what God should mean to us have been propagated with varying degrees of success. Clearly, as I have tried to emphasize several times, there is no one, single, "orthodox" concept of God in Judaism. There are certain parameters; there are particular limits beyond which one may not go and still be considered a Jew—but that is it. The theological tent of Judaism is broad and wide and deep enough to accommodate starry-eyed mystics side-by-side with cool rationalists; kabbalists together with Reconstructionists. And that is one of the glories of Judaism, I think.

The modern age has certainly challenged the belief in God—and religion in general—as never before. Science has taught us the notion of a mechanistic universe subject to inexorable and inviolate laws of nature. The general approach of scientists has been to deny the notion of a personal Deity who intervenes in human affairs, shaping world events and even suspending the laws of nature. Darwin's theory of evolution challenged the Genesis version of creation and undermined the faith of many in the Bible and in God the Creator. Marxism insisted that religion is the opiate of the people and derided the concept of God. Freud maintained that religion is merely an illusion and that God is just a projection of the ideal father figure. And Bertrand Russell suggested, "Man creates God, all-powerful and all-good, the mystic unity of what is and should be."

Despite the assault of modern science on the idea of God, there are scientists who have moved tentatively to the notion of an Intelligent Force behind the creation of the universe. More than a few of the leading astronomers and cosmologists are receptive to the notion of a Creator, these days. Albert Einstein wrote that he arrived at a belief in a Deity as he gazed in "rapturous amazement at the harmony of the natural law, which reveals an intelligence of such superiority that, compared with it, all the systematic thinking and acting of human beings is an utterly insignificant reflection." Harvard astronomer Owen Gingerich indicated in an interview that he does not believe in an "Intelligent Force" but in an "intelligent force" because the world is not just crazy randomness. Frankly, I do not understand the difference between an "Intelligent Force" and an "intelligent force." The point is: this extraordinary and unique world of ours, this awesome cosmos, this verdant, fruitful planet Earth replete with its varied life forms, is not just chance, the result of a Big Bang, the random meandering of human development from ameba to homo sapiens. Moreover, I fail to see why a religious person finds the Darwinian theory of evolution incompatible with religious beliefs. The Book of Genesis clearly is on the side of the notion of development in stages, notwithstanding its mythological view of the beginnings of Adam and Eve. Rav Kook propounded the belief that the evolution of life from lower to higher life forms is evidence of God, the Creator. And I think every time astronomers discover a "new" planet or star or solar system, they are affirming the Jewish liturgical belief that "God, in His goodness, renews each day the act of creation of the universe." Curiously, the Midrash records the view that God destroyed various worlds before creating this one (*Gen. Rab.* 9:2, p. 68).

But this understanding of purposeful creation and the teleological evolution of life forms and species is not the whole story. Dostoevsky argued that if there is no God, anything is permitted. And that is certainly evident in the tragedy of the twentieth century—a century marked by two world wars and the Holocaust, mostly perpetrated in Christian Europe. But the reader might rejoin, "What of all the blood spilled in the name of religion? After all, just look at the modern-day jihadists and how they murder in the name of Allah!" The only answer I can suggest is: These are the most abominable perversions of religion that teaches love of neighbor and justice for all peoples. With all of its failings and shortcomings, religion instills in us a conscience that troubles us and gives us no rest in the face of evil and cruelty. Without that conscience, that deeply ingrained sense of right and wrong, then indeed, everything abhorrent is permitted.

I think that we might accept the notion of a *self-limiting God—a Deity who has deliberately stepped back, contracted and removed Himself from human affairs and history in order to leave room for us humans to choose freely good or evil, life or death.* In other words, we might find satisfaction in the thought of a limited Deity who is restricted by the laws He Himself established in our world. When Abraham argued with God over the fate of Sodom and Gomorrah, insisting that God could not destroy the entire city if there were at least ten righteous people there, he appealed to the idea that the Judge of all the earth must do righteously; that even He is bound by the laws of *tzedek u-mishpat*, righteousness and justice that He established (Gen 18:23 ff.). Similarly, Moses appealed to God after the Golden Calf episode not to destroy the entire people for the sins of a few, for that would violate His laws of justice and furnish ammunition for the pagan challenges to Judaism (Exod 32:9–14). And the daughters of Zelophehad won their appeal to inherit their father's estate in the absence of brothers, because justice was on their side and amazingly God conceded the point, stating, "The plea of the daughters of Zelophehad is just" (Num 27:1–7). These are but a few examples of the fact that God in the Bible does indeed concede points to us humans and is, so to speak, self-limited in His power and knowledge. Interestingly, God's concessions are invariably on the side of compassion and justice—never injustice or cruelty. God cannot act unjustly for to do so would violate His own inviolate standards.

The Midrash expands on this bold nation of God conceding to humans, thereby limiting His power. For example, in the case of Abraham's appeal for justice at Sodom and Gomorrah, the sages have God state to Abraham, "If you think I have acted improperly, teach Me and I will act accordingly" (*Tanh. Vayera* 10, p. 91). In evaluating Moses' insistence that

35

God spare the innocent after the Golden Calf matter, the sages celebrate Moses' victory over God who, "unlike a king of flesh and blood, passes a law and is first to keep it, not violate it" (*y. Rosh Hash.* 1:3, 57b). Reflecting on the successful suit of Zelophehad's daughters, the rabbis observe, "Fortunate is the person to whom the Holy One, blessed be He, concedes in a debate." At the very end of the famous legend of the purity of a certain type of oven, a text we shall discuss in our chapter on halakhah, Elijah is asked what was the Holy One's reaction to the rabbis' victory over His own ruling. He replied: "God laughed joyfully, proclaiming, 'My children have defeated Me!'" (*B. Metzia* 59a). In other words, God wants us humans to triumph over Him in such matters because He has chosen to limit His powers in order to enhance ours.

The concept of a self-limiting God is unusual but not rare in Jewish thought. The mystics of the Kabbalah wrote of *tzimtzum*, of God contracting into Himself after the act of Creation, so as to allow room for humans and animals. Maimonides argued that God is not the source of evil—we are; and God allowed us free will to choose the path of life. Abraham ibn Daud proposed that God, of His own free will, yielded His foreknowledge of our actions so that we might freely choose. Gersonides agreed that God knows the future generally but not specific human actions in particular situations; otherwise there could not be free will. And Joseph Albo, a firm advocate of divine omnipotence and omniscience, agreed that God can not do a physical or logical impossibility. In short, there are sufficient precedents and opinions to validate the belief in a self-limiting Deity. I believe such a concept of God serves two main purposes: 1) It affirms the idea of free will so that each of us is responsible for his or her deeds; 2) It helps resolve the gnawing problem of who created evil. As free creatures endowed with the ability to choose, we are the source of most evils in this world, because, "Everything is in the hands of Heaven except the fear of Heaven" (*Ber.* 33b). I believe that the modern Jew can more readily accept this notion of God than the more popular one of an all-powerful, all-knowing Deity.

Additionally, I think that modern Jews can accept the twofold belief that God is the creative force in the universe as well as the moral force in this world of humans. Kant wrote of his perception of God in the starry sky above and in the moral order down on earth. This is precisely what the psalmist sang about in a variety of contexts. "In righteousness I see Your face" (Ps 17:15). The sages interpret this to mean that whenever a person gives even a small coin to a poor person, that individual perceives God's sacred presence. In other words, when we humans do acts of justice and charity, kindness and compassion, we perceive divinity in our lives and society. Additionally, the Psalm suggests that justice and righteousness are evidence of God in our lives and world. I interpret this to mean the greater the forces of justice and righteousness in society, the greater the evidence of a God in the world.

Second, the psalmist stresses that God is perceived in the order of the cosmos: "The heavens declare the glory of God, and the firmament show His handiwork" (19:1). Psalm 146 combines the two concepts of what God should mean to us:

> God Who made heaven and earth, the sea and all that is in them; Who preserves truth forever. Who performs justice for the oppressed; Who gives bread to the hungry; the Lord frees the prisoners. The Lord opens the eyes of the blind; the Lord raises up those who are bowed down; the Lord loves the righteous. The Lord protects the strangers and strengthens the fatherless and the widow . . ." (146:6–9)

Can I prove absolutely and irrefutably the existence of God? I think not: But as I have stated before, for those who believe, no proof is necessary; for those who do not believe, no proof will suffice. I believe that God is manifest in this world in the power of creativity, in the cosmos, and in the unique mystery of the human being. And God is present in the power of righteousness in society. We humans are constantly challenged to make God's sacred presence manifest by our actions. When we do justice and righteousness, when we display compassion and love, when we fight for freedom and peace—God is present. As Jews, when we perform sacred deeds—*mitzvot*—God is manifest. Our Torah study, our prayers, our performance of *mitzvot* between humans and God and between human and other human strengthen God's *Shekhinah*. In a remarkably bold image, the Talmud teaches that God is weakened when we neglect these *mitzvot* but strengthened when we perform them (*Ta'an.* 7b). In an equally startling homily, the sages taught: "When you are My witnesses, I am God. When you are not My witnesses, I am not God. When you are united and of one counsel below, My name is glorified and praised on high" (*Sifre Deut. Ha-Berakhah* 346, p. 144a). The sages, in another striking homily, depict God as proclaiming to Israel, His beloved, that He has given them His beloved law as if to say, "By virtue of Israel's adherence to law (*din*), I am exalted and sanctified" (*Deut. Rab.* 5:7 on Isa 5:16, 56:1 & 61:8). The mystics build on these foundations and teach that our actions on earth and our performance of *mitzvot* have a cosmic impact and affect the Deity.

We aspire as Jews and as human beings not to become God, but to become God-like by emulating Him in the performance of sacred deeds. We sanctify God's name through the performance of those deeds *(kiddush ha-Shem)* for we are partners with God in fashioning a new and better society, a more beautiful and perfect world. This reduces somewhat God's absolute power while enhancing human forces. But that makes God no less God, the object of our worship, guarantor of our moral values, and ultimate reason for our hope in a better future for humanity and the world.

Points to Ponder:
What Can We Believe about God?

1. Do you think that God is the central teaching of Judaism?

2. Do you think it is fruitless to try to prove the existence of God?

3. The author insists that there are many legitimate conceptions of God within the parameters of Judaism. What are the implications of this notion of the Deity?

4. The Midrash makes it clear that each of us experiences God differently and this shapes our concept of God. Have you come to this conclusion in your own life?

5. Of the several proofs for the existence of God, which appeal to you the most?

6. How do you interpret the Kotzker Rebbe's insight that God dwells wherever we humans let Him dwell?

7. Does the idea of emulating or imitating God's ways appeal to you?

8. The Holocaust seems to have destroyed the idea of a God of history? Do you agree?

9. Has the Holocaust shaken your acceptance of the concepts of an omnipotent and omniscient Deity?

10. How do you understand Einstein's aphorism that God doesn't play dice with the universe?

11. How has modern science challenged the traditional ideas about God? Has this challenge been significant in your life?

12. Do you agree with Dostoevsky that, if there is no God, everything is permitted?

13. The author suggests we might find a belief in a self-limiting God more acceptable. Do you agree with his suggestion?

14. The author bases his belief in God on the evidence of a creative force in the universe and the power of righteousness in society. Do you accept these criteria?

15. For those who believe, no proof is necessary; for those who do not believe, no proof will suffice. Do you agree with this thesis?

16. How do you react to the mystical concept that our actions strengthen or weaken the Deity?

4

Can We Believe in Revelation?

SINAI WAS an event of unparalleled significance. For the Jewish people, it was the supreme moment when God revealed the Torah to Moses and the Children of Israel. For Christians and Muslims, it was an unsurpassed moment unequalled until the resurrection of Jesus and the revelations to Muhammad. Traditionally, Jews have always believed that God literally spoke to Moses and Israel (Exod 19:20; 20:1; Deut 4:1 ff.). Jews reaffirm this notion daily when we lift the Torah scroll and proclaim, "And this is the Torah which Moses placed before the children of Israel by the word of the Lord, through Moses." Whenever a Jew is called to the Torah for an *aliyah*, the honoree recites the *berakhah* announcing, "Praised are You, Lord, our God . . . , who chose us from all the peoples and gave us His Torah, praised are You, Lord, who gives the Torah."

The Mishnah of *Sanhedrin* (10:1; 90a), in one of the very few dogmatic statements of belief in rabbinic literature, indicates that the person who denies that the Torah is from heaven (i.e., is of Divine origin) loses his or her portion in the afterlife. And the Mishnah *Abot* (1:1) opens with a clear and almost unequivocal statement: "Moses received Torah at Mount Sinai and passed it on to Joshua, who passed it on to the elders, who passed it on to the prophets, who passed it on to the men of the Great Assembly." The usual rabbinic interpretation of this passage is that Moses received both the written and oral Torahs from God. But there is more to say about this intriguing passage as we shall shortly see. Maimonides lists this dogma as number eight in his Thirteen Principles of Faith.

Orthodox Judaism has made the belief in *Torah min ha-shamayim*, the Torah was revealed from heaven by God, the central pillar of its approach to Judaism. Rabbi Samson Raphael Hirsch, the great neo-Orthodox leader of German Jewry in the nineteenth century, stated bluntly that this is the foundation of all of Judaism: that the entire written and oral Torahs were given at Sinai. Rabbi Joseph Hertz, late Chief Rabbi of British Jewry and editor of the popular Hertz *Humash*, wrote that Judaism stands or falls on this principle that God revealed the entire Torah to Israel at Sinai. This teaching defines an Orthodox Jew these days, and separates Orthodoxy from liberal Judaism irrevocably.

For most modern Conservative and Reform Jews, I think, this principle poses a grave challenge to faith and the hardest notion to accept. Did God really speak to Moses and the Children of Israel? Is every word of the Torah divinely inspired? Is every law of the Torah, therefore, binding on us forever? Is there not an error in any of the Torah? Is it all really perfect for all times? If a person can accept the fundamentalist position, then all else flows easily. But if not, does not the entire structure collapse like a *sukkah* in a hurricane?

The challenges to the concept of revelation for modern Jews are several, and they are formidable. The scientific challenge questions the biblical views about creation as well as the miracles described in the Bible such as the splitting of the Sea of Reeds at Moses' behest and the sun standing still at Joshua's command. Scientific learning contradicts the notion of creation in six days and nights; it also challenges the belief that human beings came into this world at one time and completely developed. Moreover, science dismisses the miracles of the Bible as contrary to the laws of the universe and of logic.

Biblical criticism has propounded the documentary theory, a theory that virtually every critical Bible scholar accepts in various degrees. This theory posits the view that the Bible is not the work of one hand or one person but that at least four different sources comprise the Five Books of Moses, and that numerous writers and editors fashioned the other works of the canon. The critical school notes the development of language, laws, and ethical insights—an evolution that encompassed at least a thousand years. Untold numbers of human hands edited, emended, and stitched together the great epic we refer to as the *TaNaKh*—the Hebrew Bible. Archaeological discoveries of ancient Semitic civilizations have demonstrated beyond a shadow of doubt, that the Hebrew civilization was influenced by and owes much to the ancient cultures that surrounded it—the Canaanite, the Phoenician, the Assyrian-Babylonian, the Egyptian, and the later invaders, including the Greeks and Romans.

Then, too, many moderns are filled with moral qualms and even revulsion at the questionable moral and ethical blemishes of the Bible. Capital punishment is an accepted form of punishment for some 37 crimes in the Pentateuch, ranging from murder to homosexual behavior to cursing parents. The annihilation of the seven aboriginal peoples of Canaan at God's insistence is deeply troubling. The scene describing how the Prophet Samuel hacks to death King Agag of Amalek (1 Sam 15) never fails to evoke questions and even revulsion by worshipers and students of the text alike. Was this truly God's wish? Has God commanded such heinous acts? Let me phrase the dilemma this way: If the Bible is the complete and inerrant word of the Lord, how can it contain unjust and even horrendous rules and countenance unseemly actions? If our moral qualms and misgivings are justified, how can we consider the *entire* Bible to be the word of God?

Of course, the notion of God "speaking" to humans is startling. Modern men and women wonder if this is possible, and they question why there are no such Divine interventions or prophetic revelations these days—troubled days during which Divine intrusion in history is so sorely needed.

These are substantial issues and mighty challenges that cannot just be dismissed cavalierly.

The fact is, *matan Torah*, literally, "the giving of the Torah," is one of the genuine rabbinic dogmas. The medieval sages and philosophers refer to it as, *"maamad har Sinai,"* and they list it as one of the indispensable Jewish beliefs. Still, it is a remarkably flexible dogma. For example, we do not know to this day where Mount Sinai is. The so-called Mount Sinai where the monastery of Santa Katerina is located is at best an early Christian site of no historical or religious significance. I should think such an important historic site that changed the direction not only of Israel but of the Western world would have been noted, along with Jerusalem. But its location remains a mystery. Moreover, the date of the revelation of the Ten Commandments to Moses is in dispute with some sages insisting it took place on the sixth of Nissan while others held it was the seventh of Nissan. Some sages insisted the Torah was handed down to Moses on the eve of the Sabbath while others maintained that the Torah was given on the Sabbath.

What language did God speak in revealing the Torah? And how much of the revelation did Israel actually hear? Rabbi Jose ben Hanina said that God spoke in Hebrew alone. Others logically argued that God spoke the only language the Jews understood—Egyptian. Other sages insisted He spoke in four tongues: Hebrew, Latin, Arabic, and Aramaic (*Sifre Deut. Ha-Berakhah*, 343, p.142b). But yet another view maintained that God spoke in the 70 languages of the world so that every human being could grasp the message and decide whether or not to accept the commandments (*Shabb.* 88b and parallels). Some sages tell us that God gave the Torah to Moses and his descendants alone and that Moses generously shared it with all Israel. Some argued Israel heard only the first two commandments; others insisted that Israel heard all the commandments in one celestial voice. Yet another opinion stated that the entire world heard the commandments of God.

The sages debated the physical form of the Torah. The Torah is rather clear that the Ten Commandments, at least, were inscribed on two stone tablets. But there were some rabbis who insisted the Torah was given "scroll after scroll" (*megillot, megillot*) while others argued that it was given in one complete scroll simultaneously (*Git.* 60a). And there are numerous fanciful references to the Torah being handed down in fire.

More significantly, what was the mood of the people at the time? Were they willing to bind themselves to the covenant? Or were they compelled by the Deity to accept the laws and teachings? Several sages fancifully noted that God suspended the mountain over their heads like a great bowl and compelled the people to accept the Torah on penalty of death: "If you accept this Torah, well and good; if not, I will drop the mountain and there shall be your burial place" (*Shabb.* 88a and parallels). But the very opposite opinion is put forth by many sages who spin a charming legend that God went around peddling the Torah and offering it to a variety of nations, all of whom refused it, until Israel finally eagerly accepted the Torah of its own free choice (*Mek. Bahodesh*, 2: 234 f. and parallels).

Perhaps more important than anything else is the issue of how much of Torah was revealed at Sinai and how much was subsequently filled in. Here, too, the dogma proves to be typically *undogmatic* and remarkably flexible. A fair number of sages insisted that the Patriarchs and Matriarchs observed some if not many of the laws of the Torah long before Sinai. Several insisted that Abraham observed not only the main laws such as circumcision (which the book of Genesis indicates was a Divine command to Abraham and his children) but even the minutiae of the Sabbath laws (*Lev. Rab.* 2:9, p.50; *Yoma* 28b and parallels). Some argued that God dictated the entire Five Books to Moses, including the description of his death. Others, however, insisted that Joshua authored the last verses of the Pentateuch describing Moses' death and burial (*B. Bat.* 15a).

Rabbi Akiva and his school of thought advanced a "maximalist view," maintaining that everything was given at Sinai, including the entire written Torah, the oral Torah, and all of the prophecies of the prophets of Israel as well as rabbinic debates in the academies and even future questions that future scholars will raise in the rabbinical academies and *yeshivot* (*Ber.* 5a and parallels). This rather remarkable view, which Abraham Joshua Heschel dubbed, "a theological exaggeration," would seem to squelch any attempt to enhance growth or development in Jewish law. On the other side of the theological spectrum, Rabbi Yishmael articulated a "minimalist view." He insisted that neither the entire written nor the oral Torah was revealed to Moses at Sinai: "Could Moses have learned the entire Torah in forty days and nights? Is it not said that 'it is longer than the earth and broader than the sea?' (Job 11:9). Moses had but forty days and nights on the mountain. Hence, we must conclude that God merely taught him the general principles (*klalim*)" (*Exod. Rab.* 41:6; *Sotah* 37b and parallels). Moses and other sages and prophets filled in the details as the subsequent generations unfolded. When the sages described laws of the Sabbath and holidays, as well as other legal matters, as "lacking scriptural bases" and compared them to "mountains suspended by hairs," they were espousing the minimalist view of Rabbi Yishmael and his school of law and theology (*m. Hag.* 1:8).

Was Sinai a one-time event or was it part of a process of revelation that has continued? Do humans play a role in the revelation process? Or are we merely passive recipients of the Divine will? A number of sages argued that there are post-Sinaitic revelations of Torah. For example, the prophets, such as Jeremiah and Ezekiel occasionally instituted new laws. Rabbi Aha stated, "Things not revealed to Moses were later revealed to Rabbi Akiva and his colleagues." This is evidently the point of the fascinating tale of Moses' visit to the academy of Rabbi Akiva where he understood not a single thing in the legal debates that unfolded before him. Finally, one sage declared, "It is a halakhah given to Moses at Sinai," at which point Moses' mind was set at ease and he felt comforted and gratified (*Menah.* 29b). Every new insight in the law is "like a revelation from God," suggested the rabbis. The moment at Sinai is relived whenever a father teaches his son Torah or when one studies it himself. The sages derived their authority to introduce laws or legislate from the Sinaitic process that began so long ago and continues down through the ages. Thus, they inaugurated calendar dates for the festivals on the basis of the statement that "it is a law for Israel, a judgment for the God of Jacob" (Ps 81:5). In other words, the sages act in lieu of the Lord in setting the calendar. The delightful debate over the permissibility of a certain type of stove ends with the ringing affirmation, "The Torah is not in heaven any longer" but has been handed over to human hands to be decided by majority vote. I shall discuss these intriguing selections in a later chapter; for now, it suffices to cite them briefly as stark examples of how the *event* of Sinai was transformed into the *process* of Sinai and how humans are, in a sense, *partners* with God in shaping laws and morals.

The medieval sages never doubted that Sinai took place. Yehudah Halevi argued simply that 600,000 adult males plus women and children stood at the foot of Mount Sinai and heard God's charge to the people. What more convincing historical evidence is there than that? Maimonides lists the belief in the Torah having been revealed by God to Moses and Israel as one of the basic *ikkarim* (principles). He insists (in what is evidently a refutation of both the Christian and Muslim claims to superseding revelations) that no further revelation of Torah took place, and he sides with Rabbi Akiva that both the written Torah and oral Torah were revealed at Sinai. Rabbi Joseph Albo agreed that Sinai was a fact, but he adopts Rabbi Yishmael's position that only general rules were laid down. Some medieval scholars (such as Rashi) were believed to have written their great commentaries and interpretations "under the influence of *ruah hakodesh*, the Holy Spirit." And mystics such as Abraham Abulafia, Isaac Luria, Haim Vital, and Joseph Karo held similar views about themselves and their writings.

When we come to modern times, we encounter a multiplicity of interpretations of the meaning of revelation. The Orthodox, as we have noted, cling fervently to the literal notion that the Torah was revealed at Sinai, although they sometimes equivocate as to how much was actually given and how much was revealed in subsequent ages by prophets and scholars.

The Reform movement has rejected the literal notion of revelation, affirming that the ethical and moral laws derive from Sinai but denying that the ritual rules such as *kashrut* and *Shabbat* are divinely revealed legislation. Many Reform thinkers, such as Rabbi Leo Baeck, maintain that revelation is ongoing and continuous and must not be reduced to a single event in human history.

The Conservative movement has accepted the notion of continuous revelation, understanding Sinai in a *nonliteral* way, envisioning a series of ongoing encounters with God in a process or series of revelations. Additionally, Abraham Joshua Heschel suggested that we must interpret Sinai to imply a "minimum of revelation and a maximum of interpretation." In other words, the essence is from God; the understanding is from humans.

Practically alone among modern Jewish thinkers, Rabbi Mordecai M. Kaplan denied the belief in Divine revelation of the Torah, viewing it instead as a pious myth. He reversed the classical formulation of Jewish faith, arguing, "God did not reveal the Torah to Israel; the Torah reveals God to Israel." Consequently, he reduced the *mitzvot* from Divine fiats to "customs and folkways." In short, Torah is stripped of divinity and reduced to the creation of the human mind and the will of the people, and the *mitzvot* are regarded as anthropological and sociological phenomena.

Franz Rosenzweig and Martin Buber wrote of an ongoing encounter with the Divine, of which Sinai was but one moment, albeit the defining moment. But this non-fundamentalist position led Buber to non-observance of the *mitzvot* whereas Rosenzweig gradually and inexorably was impelled to greater observance of the *mitzvot*.

How then can we moderns view revelation? And does it hold significance for those of us who can no longer accept the idea that God literally spoke to Moses and dictated the Torah to him at Sinai? I, for one, cannot reduce the Bible to just another ancient text containing sagas and myths and legends of an ancient civilization. Not can I accept the notion of a Jewish legal system reduced to sociological norms and idiosyncrasies. Jews throughout the ages did not lay down their lives to protect "folkways and customs." And while I do not read my Bible literally, I do seek within it values that resonate even after the passage of millennia.

First, we should bear in mind that although revelation is a Jewish dogma, it is, like all the other dogmas in our faith, a very elastic and flexible one. I tried to demonstrate earlier that even within the rabbinic understanding of the notion, there is wide latitude. The place, the date, the spirit, the form, the language, and most significantly, the content of the Torah revelation—all these critical issues were mooted by sages over the ages.

Second, revelation is not a one-time *event*: it is a *process*. Note that the Mishnah states, "Moses received Torah at Mount Sinai." The usual Hebrew syntax should have called for the accusative case: "Moses received *the* Torah (*et ha-Torah*)" at Sinai. But that is not the way the text reads. Consequently, I suggest the implication is that Moses received the *essential* or *nuclear* Torah at Sinai beginning the long process of interpretation and re-interpretation that still occupies us to this day. It is important to recall that the Bible itself indicates that the editing of the text occupied many minds over several centuries. The first recorded editing is noted in the days of King Hezekiah (eighth century B.C.E.); the next in the time of King Josiah (seventh century B.C.E.); then the texts were sifted and submitted to a major editing in the days of Ezra (fifth century B.C.E.), whose contribution to the process of creating Torah was so great that the rabbis compared him to Moses. Finally, the Talmud indicates that at the great conclave of Yavneh, around 90 C.E., the sages voted on which books belong in the canon and which do not. If books such as Ezekiel, Ecclesiastes, and Song of Songs were truly God's literal word, how could sages possibly have opposed their admission into the canon, as many did? But they were ultimately included by majority vote, while books such as Ben Sirah and Jubilees were excluded.

Third, I also believe that the seeds of Torah were planted by many hands over the millennia, beginning before Moses' days, continuing down through a period of 1,000 years or so, blossoming into a foliating tree with its leaves and flowers and fruits that still flourish and live after all these centuries. The original seeds may not seem to bear any physical resemblance to the foliating tree, but they are intimately related biologically and genetically. We ought to understand revelation, therefore, as an on-going process—a process that, in a sense, continues daily. The sages interpret the verse from Deuteronomy 11:32, "I give you this day these commandments," to mean, "They should be as precious to you today *as if* you received them today at Mount Sinai. They should be as familiar to your mouths *as if* you just heard them today" (*Sifre Deut. R'eah*, 58, p. 87a). This remarkable insight is dramatically highlighted when a Jew takes an honor to the Torah and recites the traditional blessings, the conclusion of which reads: "Praised be You, God, Who gives the Torah." Note the present tense of the verb, "Who *gives*"—not "Who *gave*." The process of fathoming and interpreting God's will and commands is on-going and never-ending.

Fourth, revelation is accorded to specially gifted people; not everyone is so privileged. There are different types of revelation in very different realms. The great musician or artist who produces a unique masterwork has been gifted by God. The scientist who conceives of the inconceivable and the physician who discovers a breakthrough in treating illness are equally the recipients of revelation. And the prophets were very special, very uniquely gifted vehicles for the dissemination of God's religious and moral teachings. Precious few humans in history have been so privileged; few have been worthy of God's gifts and summons. Now we can understand that a cultured nobleman from Jerusalem such as Isaiah or a highly educated priest named Jeremiah could have uttered such remarkable thoughts in such exalted language and poetic style thousands of years ago. But how shall we explain that a country lad who tended sycamore trees and herded goats, named Amos, could have formulated such remarkable teachings in such a literary style way back in the eighth century B.C.E. unless God had implanted the words and thoughts in his soul? I view this phenomenon as the revelation of God's word, for no other explanation can, in my judgment, adequately interpret this phenomenon of prophecy.

That is why we accord these creative geniuses of the spirit all the honors we can muster.

Fifth, revelation was and is perceived by people differently. That suggests that no single understanding of God's revelation is necessarily invalid. Rabbi Levi taught that God's voice is heard by each one of us individually and differently: the young person according to his capacity, the elders according to theirs, and the little ones according to theirs (*Exod. Rab.* 29:1). The Kotzker Rebbe interpreted the first of the Ten Commandments as follows: "Why does the text state, 'I am the Lord your (singular) God'? This teaches us that each perceives God in his or her own way. Revelation depends on the capacity of each person." This explains why some persons heard God's command and applied it in a heinous way, while others heard the same command and applied it benignly; why some understand the injunction, "You shall not murder," to exclude the killing of "heretics," while others interpret the command to mean, one may never shed blood except in self-defense. There are many different interpretations of God's commands. The sages put it this way: "Just as a hammer splinters rock into many slivers, so is a biblical verse capable of many interpretations" (*Sanh.* 34a). Elsewhere they suggest that there are seventy facets to Torah. "Why are the words of the Torah to be compared to figs? Just as figs, at different stages in their development, have different tastes (*taam*), so the words of Torah, as long as a person reflects on them, he or she finds new reasons and interpretations (*taam*)" (*Eruv.* 54b). Maimonides suggested that the stories in the Bible serve a double function: Either they seek to verify one of the fundamental beliefs of the faith or they seek to regulate human actions so as to remove injustice and violence between human beings. And he adds: "In reading the Bible, you must reckon with the fact that there is often a hidden level not immediately apparent to the eye. If you fail to perceive the inner truth, the failure is apt to be yours—not the Bible's" (*Guide of the Perplexed*, 3:50).

However, there must be a limit to the extent of an individual's perception of the Divine will. The individual understanding of each injunction must be filtered through the lens of moral standards. A just God may never commit an injustice. This is the point to that remarkable scene in Genesis 18 where Abraham argues with God in a vain attempt to save the lives of the wicked residents of Sodom and Gomorrah. "Shall not the judge of all the earth do justice? How can You sweep away the righteous with the sinners?" And God is compelled to concede to Abraham that if there are righteous people in those iniquitous cities, He will spare them. If God is bound by His moral laws and incapable of committing an evil act, how much more so are we humans expected to uphold His standards of justice and righteousness. A person who believes that God commands criminal behavior has egregiously misread and distorted the Divine will.

Finally, there is a continuous dialogue between God and Israel—a dialogue that sets as its goal the clarification of ideas, concepts, laws, norms, and injunctions first set down for us at Sinai. That is evidently the intent of this suggestive Midrash (*Sifre Deut. Berakhah* 355, p. 148a):

> Israel says, "O Jeshurun, there is none like God." And the Holy Spirit proclaims, "God is Jeshurun's deity." Israel says, "Who is like You among the gods, Lord?" And the Holy Spirit proclaims, "How fortunate are you, Israel, who is like you?" Israel says, "Hear O Israel, the Lord is our God, the Lord is One." And the Holy Spirit proclaims, "And who is like your people Israel?"

This dialogue has been actively evolving since the time of Abraham. It was heightened at Sinai in Moses' day. It carried over into the era of the prophets. It flourished in the rabbinic era. And it has continued through the centuries down to our day. The perpetual dialogue between God and His people proceeds to unravel the Divine will in law, ethics, morals, and ideas. God seeks us out as He endeavors to renew the act of creation. He needs humans, notes the Midrash, even as a king needs guests to inhabit his palace and enjoy the food and drink and other blessings. For what joy can a king experience with no one to share his blessings? Loneliness is not just a human affliction; without a blessed humanity, God is alone in a vast cosmos. And we humans need Divine guidance as we grope and lurch, unsteady travelers in search of the Divine goal for humankind.

Points to Ponder:
Can We Believe in Revelation?

1. Orthodox Judaism insists that Judaism stands or falls on the belief that God revealed the Torah on Sinai to Moses. What is your reaction to this notion?

2. How can one believe in the Divine origin of the Torah in the light of biblical criticism?

3. If the Bible is the complete and inerrant word of God, how can we account for some of the horrifying rules and bloody deeds commanded by the Deity?

4. Do you believe that God literally spoke to Moses at Sinai?

5. The concept of *matan Torah* is remarkably flexible, suggests the author. How is this so? And what are the implications of this view?

6. Why did many rabbis stress the notion that God offered the Torah to all the nations of the world?

7. Heschel attacked the concept that the entire Torah was revealed at Sinai, arguing for a "minimum of revelation and a maximum of interpretation." What are the implications of his approach?

8. Why is it important to stress that Sinai was not just an *event* but part of a *process*?

9. Kaplan denied revelation at Sinai and reduced the *mitzvot* to "customs and folkways." Do you believe this is a sufficient rationale for Jewish observance?

10. How is it that some people interpret Torah in a heinous way while others interpret benignly?

11. The sages compare the words of Torah to figs. Why is this metaphor so striking?

12. The author suggests that each individual's perception of Torah must be filtered through the lens of moral standards. Do you agree with this approach?

13. How do you interpret the idea that Israel and God are in perpetual dialogue?

5

What Is a Human Being?

For two-and-a-half years a momentous debate raged in the academies of ancient Israel in the first century B.C.E. The subject of the debate was a rather unusual one: Would it have been better had humans never been created or not? The illustrious school of Hillel declared that it was a good thing for humans to have been created. The competing school of Shammai disagreed and asserted that it would have been better had humans not been created. Finally, after exhaustive debates, the academies voted and the majority declared that Shammai was right: Humanity never should have been created. But now that we are here, let humans scrutinize their deeds and live the best possible lives (Eruv. 13b). Typically, the law is according to Hillel and not Shammai, except in a number of cases. But in this extraordinary case, Shammai's view is the accepted one. This remarkable debate and its unexpected outcome give us an insight into the Jewish view of the nature and capabilities of humanity. And it is a realistically sobering perspective, indeed. Humans, as we have seen, are capable of colossal evil and diabolical deeds: We now have the capability of destroying civilization as we know it. At the same time, humans are capable of correcting their failings and foibles and of building a better world.

The controversy launched by the schools of Hillel and Shammai so many centuries ago continues unabated until today. Some of the greatest, most thoughtful, most sensitive people from Maimonides to Martin Buber have debated the issue passionately. Anne Frank wrote in her famous diary, "In spite of everything, I still believe that people are really good at heart." (One can only wonder if she would have written so optimistically in Bergen-Belsen where she tragically met her death some months later.) Abraham Joshua Heschel suggested that God has a vision and expectation of humans and it is our task to receive it: "That's why man is a messenger for God—the messenger." William Faulkner, upon receiving the Nobel Prize for Literature, declared, "I believe that man will not merely endure. He will prevail. He is immortal, not because he alone among creatures has an inexhaustible voice but because he has a soul, a spirit capable of compassion and sacrifice and endurance."

On the other side of the ledger, Sigmund Freud wrote, in a letter to Oskar Pfister, "I have found little that its 'good' about human beings on the whole. In my experience most of them are trash, no matter whether they publicly subscribe to this or that ethical doctrine or to none at all . . . If we are to talk of ethics, I subscribe to a higher ideal from which most of the human beings I have come across depart most lamentably." In a recent novel by the great Israeli novelist and Holocaust survivor Aharon Appelfeld, it is said of one of the main characters (undoubtedly Appelfeld himself), "He does not believe either in God or in man. Not in God—because he cannot see Him. And not in men—because he does see them and he knows that they are prone to sin."

What comprises the essence of a human depends on the reference frame one adopts. Biochemists, for example, have one view of humanity. Many years ago I remember seeing a chemical chart of the components that make up the human body. The average man at that time was about five feet, ten inches tall and weighed 150 pounds. His body contained enough fat to make seven bars of soap, enough iron to fashion a medium sized nail, enough sugar to fill a sugar bowl, enough lime to whitewash a chicken coup, enough phosphorus for 2,200 match heads, enough magnesium for a dose of milk of magnesia, and sufficient potassium and sulfur to explode a toy cannon. In those days, a human's ingredients were worth some 98 cents!

Biologists speak of humans as the end product of a long chain of evolution: We have evolved from simple cells to the ameba to primate animals to anthropoid apes to Neanderthals to humans, all different branches from the same root. And we are still evolving. There is nothing in the Darwinian theory of evolution to challenge religious teachings, as we have already noted. The Bible is not, after all, a textbook of biology or cosmology or paleontology and its recounting of the Creation in the space of one week as well as its mythic description of Adam and Eve are hardly historical facts. The Bible is the national history of the Jewish people on a religious foundation, as Arnold Ehrlich observed. It is a textbook of theology and morals; it describes the search of one people for God and how that people covenanted itself to God through the medium of commandments and faith. Modern biology has discovered that we humans are comprised of genes, the basic unit of all human development. The recent discovery and mapping of the human genome in June of 2000, inform us that each human cell contains a nucleus with 23 pairs of chromosomes, one from each parent. Each chromosome is made up of a long chain of DNA (an acid) wrapped around proteins. A molecule with intertwined strands shaped like a double helix makes up DNA. Each of us contains 3 billion chemical letters holding about 30,000 genes. Upon discovering the intricate encoding governing our genetic material, scientists were amazed and surprised to note that we humans are really almost the same biochemically; that differences in our genomes are slight. Moreover, our human genomes are not terribly different from those of lower animals such as mice and fruit flies. What does this all mean? Dr. Francis S. Collins, director of the Human Genome Project, stated: "We have caught the first glimpses of our instruction book previously known only to God." Additionally, as geneticist, Dr. Luigi Cavalli-Sforza, has noted, we now realize our common ancestry springs from Africa and differences among humans are essentially quite superficial, such as skin color or texture of hair.

Modern psychologists view humans very differently than biologists. Since Freud, they have conceived of us as a bundle of competing drives— drives that are in constant tension, forever struggling for dominance. The drive for love (eros) contends with the death wish (thanatos). The battle among the ego, the id, and the superego (conscience) is viewed as a never-ending, dynamic struggle. Freud considered the sex drive as the most potent and pervasive force in civilization. Jung disagreed and posited the view that the fear of death is humanity's basic drive. Alfred Adler insisted that the feeling of inferiority lay at the foundation of all human character.

Lawyers adopt different criteria for evaluating human worth. In the wake of the September 11th tragedy that took 3,000 lives at the hands of terrorists in the year 2001, the United States Congress set up a special Victims Compensation Fund headed by an eminent attorney, Kenneth Feinberg. One of his most painfully daunting tasks was to evaluate in monetary terms the worth of each deceased individual. How can one possibly assess the fiduciary value of a victim who was murdered on that bloody day? And yet, every day juries make awards in accidents or wrongful death suits and they consider a variety of factors in assessing human worth.

But none of these disparate theories can really explain the great mystery of life, namely, the leap from animal to sentient human; from the profane to the Divine; from the irrational beast to the intelligent, reasoning human being. No scientist can truly describe how the predatory, hunting animal became the inventive, creative human capable of law and morals, of art and music, of literature and science. No scientific explanation can sufficiently sketch for us how the beast evolved into a creature that displays tender love and compassion. Only the person of faith, I think, can meet this challenge with any degree of assurance.

What does Judaism say to all of this? What is anthropology according to the Jewish faith? The early chapters of the Bible begin with a magnificent and optimistic description of the origin of humans. "And God said, 'Let us make humans in our image and in our likeness'" (Gen 1:26–27; 5:1; 9:6). And so humanity was created in the moral, ethical, and intellectual image of the Divine. God breathed into Adam the breath of life, a bit of divinity, a spark of God Himself. Only after creating Adam does God describe the process of creation and the world He has fashioned as "very good." Humanity is created *be-tzelem Elohim*, in the image of God. That is an extraordinary description and a uniquely challenging notion, indicating, as Yair Lorberbaum has demonstrated, that humans are an extension of God. Like the Creator, we humans can create even life itself. Like the Author of the moral imperative, humans can choose between the moral and immoral, the good and the bad. Like the Divine Intellect, humans may employ discernment and intelligence for building new worlds and, yes, for destroying old ones. "Precious is humanity," suggested Rabbi Akiva, "an extra degree of God's love was granted humans since they are created in God's image" (*Abot* 3:14). Paradoxically, humans are an amalgam of the Divine breath or spirit and the dust of the earth (Gen 2:7). As the sages put it, "The soul is from heaven, but the body is from earth" (*Sifre Deut.* 306, p. 132a). There are three partners that comprise every human being: God, father, and mother (*Qidd.* 30b). Perhaps this is the way the ancients understood the role of both nature and nurture in shaping a human character. The psalmist rapturously sang that "man is but a little lower than the angels, and with splendor and glory You have crowned him" (Ps 8:5–6). Actually, the medieval philosophers insisted that the righteous person stands on a higher plane than even the angels in heaven.

What is the most important teaching in the Bible concerning humans? Rabbi Akiva maintained, "Love your neighbor as yourself" (Lev 19:18). But Shimeon ben Azzai disagreed: The most important teaching of all is, "These are the generations of humanity" (Gen 5:1f.). Rabbi Akiva believed the goal of the Torah is to imbue love for fellow humans in us. But Ben Azzai insisted that once we acknowledge the common ancestry of all humanity, we must behave justly and lovingly toward each other (*Sifra Kedoshim* 4, p. 89b).

Since God created us all in His image, we are all brothers and sisters, children of God, descendants of Adam and Eve—part of one great *mishpahah*, family. Legend has it that Adam was created from the dust of the four corners of the earth, a multicolored dust, dust from various nations and continents. Furthermore, God created humanity out of one mold, stamped with the impression of Adam, the prototype of us all. And yet, not one person is exactly like another; diversity is both the will of God and a blessing (*Sanh.* 37a–38b). From this it follows that humans are a microcosm of the creation; that a human being is the equivalent of the entire world. Hence, if we cause grief to one single individual, it is as if we cause grief to the entire world (*Sefer Hasidim*, 44, p. 103). The Talmud is very insistent on this point: "He who destroys a single life [this is the original reading], it is as if he had destroyed an entire world; but he who saves a single life, it is as if he had saved an entire world" (*m. Sanh.* 4:5). Whoever sheds the blood of another human "diminishes the image of God in the world" (*Mek. Bahodesh* 2:262). Bloodshed is permitted only in self-defense and when no other option is available. Suicide is viewed as murder, except in very limited circumstances, for, as Maimonides argues, "the body of a human being does not belong to him or her but is the property of God, the Creator." Likewise, active euthanasia is tantamount to murder. We may not shorten the life of a dying person although we are not required to take superhuman or heroic measures to prolong suffering so that passively allowing the patient to die naturally would be valid. The greatest of all the *mitzvot* is, therefore, saving human life (*pikuah nefesh*). Nothing supersedes that—not even Yom Kippur. Thus, if someone is taken ill on Yom Kippur, even if there seems to be no immediate danger to life but only a possibility, we are not just allowed but required to seek medical help even if it means desecrating the sacredness of the day. "Nothing may stand in the way of saving human life" is the accepted principle in Jewish law and ethics (*Yoma* 82a ff.).

The Jewish notion of *kevod ha-beriyot*, human dignity, flows from all of these sources and concepts. It is a rich concept, full of suggestive ideas and nuances. "Who is honored? Whoever honors every human being" (*Abot* 4:1) because "another's honor must be as important to you as your own" (*Abot* 2:10). One must never disgrace another or shame another, especially in public. To do so is to forfeit one's share in the next life. There is an interesting division of opinion whether the penalty for insulting or injuring another person varies with the status of the victim. Rabbi Yose insisted all depends on the status of the victim: If he or she is important or distinguished, the penalty is higher. But Rabbi Akiva argued that "even the poorest persons are regarded as descendants of Abraham, Isaac and Jacob," and that status is equal in the realm of torts and insults (*m. B. Qama* 8:6). Judges and communal leaders must respect the human dignity of all (Maimonides, *Mishneh Torah, Sanh.* 24:9). We may violate positive and even negative commandments to safeguard human dignity. For example, an elderly person is not required to return a lost object he spots in the street because it might impair his dignity. Similarly, a priest, who is normally forbidden to come in contact with a dead body, may violate that prohibition in order to bury an unattended corpse and accord the dead appropriate dignity and honor. Even a criminal has dignity, so that the body of an executed criminal must not spend the night on a gallows or stake. "Why," asked Rabban Yohanan ben Zakkai, "must a cattle thief pay five-fold the value of the stolen cow but four-fold the value of a stolen sheep? The reason is the cow walked by itself but the thief had to carry the sheep on his shoulders thereby impairing his dignity" (*Mek. Nezikin* 3:99). In short, in the clash of a positive commandment to preserve human dignity versus any of the Torah commandments, the mitzvah of human dignity overrides the others (*Ber.* 19b–20a).

All of these sources bolster the view of the school of Hillel that views humans optimistically and insists that it was a good thing that God created humanity, despite all the failings and foibles.

But there is also the other side of humanity—the side that impressed the members of the school of Shammai who viewed humans through a pessimistic lens, maintaining that it would have been better had God not created the human race. Quite so: The Bible does not seek to gloss over the inclinations of humans to sin. "The inclinations of man's mind are evil from his youth" (Gen 6:5 & 8:21). "Who can say, 'I have cleansed my heart. I am purified of my sin?'" (Prov 20:9). "Indeed, I was born with iniquity; with sin my mother conceived me" (Ps 51:7). "There is not one good man on earth who does what is good and doesn't sin" (Qoh 7:20). "Can mortals be acquitted by God? Can man be cleared by his Maker?" (Job 4:17). "Most devious is the heart; it is perverse—who can fathom it?" (Jer 17:9). These are but a sampling of the numerous verses and tales in the Bible that underscore one theme: human beings are prone to sin. Reinhold Niebuhr observed, "The Bible has a higher view of the stature of man and a lower view of the virtue of man." And Yehezkel Kaufmann has suggested the Bible is the record of human rebellion against God and His law. All of this evidence hardly makes for a lofty image of humanity, I suggest. Just examine the record of human perversity and you will fathom Shammai's pessimism. And that record of human perversity appears from the very genesis of humankind.

It did not take Adam and Eve very long to succumb to sinful or rebellious urges. They violated the one mitzvah given them and were expelled from Eden: Paradise lost! Cain kills his brother Abel and becomes history's first murderer, a fratricide, no less! The generation of the great Flood is so perverse that God decides to wipe them all out and begin afresh with Noah and his family. But Noah and his sons are barely out of the ark that has saved them from the flood waters when they sink into despicable acts of sinfulness. Sodom and Gomorrah were the most perverse and depraved of cities; their names have become synonymous for sin and iniquity down through the ages, long after God destroyed them. These examples are culled just from the earliest chapters of Genesis, and things barely improve as humans mature: Indeed, they just get worse.

The sages of rabbinic Judaism tried to fathom the dark side of humanity. They created the theology of duality of all humans, suggesting that every person is endowed with two conflicting drives, the *yetzer tov* or good urge, as well as the *yetzer ha-ra*, the evil urge, often personified as Satan or the Angel of Death. These two drives are innate to humans, for God created them both from the very beginnings of human life on earth; they are in perpetual conflict within our souls until the day of death. The challenge to all of us is: Which of these two opposite inclinations will win out?

Several times in the Talmud and Midrash, the rabbis record a strange myth about the primeval humans in Eden. They tell us that the serpent, the source of sin in humanity, copulated with Eve and injected in her the filth or venom of sin (*Abod. Zar.* 22b and parallels). It was only the acceptance of the Torah at Mount Sinai that purged Jews of this pollution. This seems to suggest the notion of "original sin"—a notion that was to become a hallmark of Christianity that substituted faith in Jesus for the Torah as the salvific force that would expunge the original sin. But normative Judaism never really elevated this strange myth into a fundamental belief. Yes, men and women are prone to sin; but they are not inexorably destined to sin because the Torah enables their *yetzer tov* to overpower their *yetzer ha-ra*. Curiously, this mythic notion of the original sin that was shed by normative Judaism but became a cornerstone of Christian doctrine, reemerged in the mystical Judaism of the Kabbalah and became a fundamental teaching of the kabbalists and mystics.

Still, mainstream Judaism has not accepted the pagan distinction between body and soul, the dichotomy of dualism that maintains the view that the soul alone is godly, while the body is sinful by its very nature. To be sure, we extol the virtue of the soul as the very breath of God. We pray each morning, "God, the soul You have implanted in me is pure . . . You ultimately will take it back to You, its source." At the same time, we do not denigrate the body as profane or the source of sinfulness. We view the mind as the source of sin. A suggestive debate is recorded between a Magi and Rabbi Amemar in which the Magi claimed the top half of the human body is of Ahurmazda, the god of light and good, whereas the bottom half is of Ahriman, the god of darkness and evil. Rabbi Amemar rejected this argument, noting that if this were so, why would Ahurmazda allow the lower half, Ahriman, to excrete and pollute the land with waste products? (*Sanh.* 39a). I recall a discussion that took place in the class of Rabbi Abraham Joshua Heschel on the subject of a *gartel*, a waist sash worn by Hasidim to distinguish between the upper torso in which are contained the brain and heart of a human—the spiritual and intellectual elements of a person—and the lower torso, in which are contained the organs of excretion and sexuality. The Hasidim assert that we should wear a *gartel* at prayer to separate between the holy and the profane. Dr. Heschel, himself the offspring of a famous Hasidic dynasty, rejected this view reminding us that the most profane actions we humans perform emerge from the brain and the tongue.

Consequently, Judaism is life-affirming and not ascetic; it exhorts us to enjoy the gifts of life within the bounds of propriety and normal behavior, avoiding excess or gluttony. Qohelet urged us to enjoy life with the woman we love, to indulge in wine and good food, and wear attractive, white outfits. The rabbis considered the Nazirite, who took a vow to abstain from wine and intoxicants, as well as haircuts and shaves, to be a sinner, rather than a saint, and they discouraged excessive fasting (*Ned.* 10a). There were times when a mood of asceticism crept into Judaism, notably after the calamitous destruction of the Temple and Jerusalem by the Romans. There actually were sages who argued against savoring meat or wine at the time and who sought to curb marriages or marital festivities, insisting, "How can we enjoy these pleasures of life when the Temple lies in ashes?" But saner and soberer minds prevailed: Life must go on with some degree of normal behavior. Rav taught that in the future days, a human being will be challenged by God to give a reckoning for all the blessings in life a human could have experienced but failed to do so. The Talmud urged us to enjoy a lovely home, a lovely wife, and lovely utensils and furnishings. We are commanded to recite a blessing when we behold beautiful people, trees and plants.

And even though ascetics cropped up periodically in the Jewish community, they never advocated celibacy. In Mishnaic times, only Ben Azzai is recorded to have been a celibate, and he was forced to defend his action, embarrassingly admitting that his heart was in love with Torah, allowing no room for the love of a woman. Writing around the year 1200, Rabbi Judah

He-Hasid, the pious, reflected on the impact of the era of the Crusades and all the tragedy and destruction it had brought Jews and Europeans. Contrary to normative Jewish thought, he was convinced of the innate evil of humanity; he suggested that the power of the *yetzer ha-ra* was infinitely more potent than the power of the *yetzer tov*; and he advocated a life of asceticism and repentance, effectively despairing of humanity and of this world, hoping that he would be a martyr *al kiddush ha-Shem*, for the sanctification of God's name. More in keeping with normal Jewish doctrine, Maimonides suggested, both in his *Mishneh Torah* law code and in his philosophical masterwork, *Guide of the Perplexed*, that the golden mean is the best way to lead one's life and that we should avoid extremes in food and drink, moral behavior, and religious fervor.

The mystics of sixteenth- and seventeenth-century Safed did specify the times appropriate for sexual intercourse with their wives, but they never advocated celibacy. Marriage and children have always been viewed in Judaism as the goal and ultimate blessing for all men and women, and the family is the nuclear institution in Jewish life and always has been. Genesis stressed that, "It is not good for a human to be alone" so that God made a helpmate for Adam, namely, Eve. The twin goals of life would then be realized in marriage: companionship and propagation. Traditionally, Judaism does not recognize "alternate lifestyles" as legitimate, no matter what contemporary mores dictate, and I firmly believe most Jews view family life and marriage between man and woman as the norm.

The twentieth century, dubbed by Isaiah Berlin "the worst century in European history," has confirmed the pessimistic view of humanity as hopelessly in thrall to, what the kabbalists label, the *Sitra Ahra*—the dark side, the evil side, and the destructive side. Charles Dickens, observing the carnage of the Crimean War in 1854, wrote to a friend that he felt "something like despair to see how the old cannon-smoke and blood-mist obscure the wrongs and sufferings of the people at home." Things haven't changed much since then: Governments still distract their citizens from their domestic woes with bloody adventures abroad. Two world wars cost tens of millions of lives and ravaged whole continents. The *Shoah* (Holocaust) virtually destroyed a once flourishing European Jewry. Communism, fascism, Nazism, and other bestial "isms" originated in Christian Europe— the center of religion, culture, and creativity and the citadel of Western civilization. Frankly, I still cannot fathom how Germany, the land of Goethe and Beethoven, Schiller and Kant, could have spawned the murderous Nazi ideology that annihilated most of Europe's Jews and shattered much of Christian Europe. The psalmist had warned that humans are like beasts that perish (Ps 49:21). The sages took this to mean that when a person behaves like a beast, wild beasts will ultimately consume him. Wild beasts dressed in human clothes were, indeed, let loose upon the world in the Second World War. For many, God died in Auschwitz; for others, Christianity died there. And for still others, as Abraham Joshua Heschel articulated it, man—not God—died in Auschwitz. The psalmist concluded rashly that "all human beings are false" (Ps 116:11). Perhaps he was not so rash, after all: There is much to support that negative view of humankind. Humans are hopelessly addicted to violence and aggression, it appears; their bloody historical records bear that out. Humans are cruel and jealous, querulous and nasty, ungrateful and arrogant, egocentric and thoughtless. "Out of the crooked timber of humanity, nothing straight can be fashioned," observed Kant. "If you pick up a starving dog and make him prosperous, he will not bite you," wrote Mark Twain. "This is the principle difference between a dog and a man."

We had hoped that with the end of the bloody twentieth century and the unexpected collapse of the Soviet empire and conclusion of the Cold War, the world would finally enter a new millennium of justice, co-operation, and peace. But the new wars of terrorism that have spread their venom seem to have replaced the older, more traditional forms of warfare, disillusioning many of us and confirming the opinion of those who maintain a grim evaluation of the virtue and decency of human beings. Who could have anticipated the bestial ferocity of the attacks of September 11, 2001? Who could have predicted that the *jihad* of modern-day Islam would morph into such a monstrosity that displays neither pity nor humanity; evinces no respect for human life, and shows no compassion for those of different nationalities or religious denominations? We had naively thought that the *Shoah* had enlightened humanity as to the lethal results of anti-Semitism so that hopefully, that ancient scourge might be ended once and for all. We were wrong: The plague has resurfaced with a renewed virulence in Europe and in Muslim lands. The moral failings of the United Nations that relentlessly condemns Israel but itself stood by indolently as Hutus slaughtered 800,000 Tutsis in three months in Rwanda and has done little to alleviate the suffering of the residents of the Darfur region of Sudan have compounded the widespread mood of despair and disillusion-ment. These tragic developments seemingly confirm the pessimistic views of humanity held by Rabbi Yisrael Salanter, the great nineteenth-century moralist. Salanter wrote that humans must work at improving themselves by first tackling their external behavior so as to ultimately modify their internal instincts and moral traits, enabling God to help them conquer the innate evil urge, and change their characters for the good. Without such character changes, there is little hope for humans to prevail over the beasts, I think.

Reflecting on all that has transpired since the end of World War II when we anticipated the dawning of a new age of peace and international justice, I must confess my sense of despair. I truly believed that the United Nations would prevail in saving succeeding generations from the scourge of war; that nations would finally beat their swords into plowshares and their spears into pruning hooks. The Cold War dashed those hopes and shattered those dreams. Then, with the collapse of the Iron Curtain and the Soviet Union, I thought that maybe all would finally turn out for good and for blessing and democracy would triumph at last. Instead, the twenty-first century has brought forth a new scourge: the scourge of brutal, bestial, mindless terrorism, whose only goals seem to be murder and mayhem. William Butler Yeats, mulling over the carnage of the First World War, mused that, "the best lack all conviction while the worst are full of passionate intensity." These words still preserve their cogency and relevance, I believe.

In the wake of the Second World War, the Existentialist School of philosophy despaired altogether of humanity, convinced that humans are, indeed, innately depraved. Secular philosophers such as John Paul Sartre, and religious thinkers, including Reinhold Niebuhr, were certain that humans are hopelessly addicted to sin. As I review the bloody events of the twentieth century, I still am stunned by the Holocaust and appalled at the endless struggle of the State of Israel to survive overt and avowed enemies who are intent on destroying her. I feel disgusted by the ineptness of the United Nations and its flaccid and feckless members. I am horrified over Islamic fanaticism. Consequently, I am also tempted to accept the notion that humanity, on its own, is beyond redemption.

And yet, Judaism insists that all is not lost, that we are sentient, choosing individuals, and that we are free men and women with the capacity to choose good or evil, life or death. This notion of free will is a basic Jewish tenet. Already in the early chapters of Genesis, it is clear that God endowed us with the ability to choose. Adam and Eve did not have to eat the forbidden fruit and be expelled from Eden; they chose freely to do so. Cain did not have to murder Abel; God warned him that sin crouched at his doorstep but that he could prevail over it if he so opted. The people of the generation of the Flood were not fated to bring destruction on themselves; they freely went the way of perversity and wickedness. The Book of Deuteronomy places the choice before us all: "Behold, I give you this day the choice of good and evil . . . life and death. Now choose good and life" (Deut 11:26–28; 30:15–20). And the prophets of Israel presented a stark choice to their rebellious and fractious contemporaries: Either keep God's Torah, do good, and deal honestly and justly with each other, or you will be punished most severely. The people had the option—and they usually failed and paid a fearsome price for their transgressions, including two exiles from their land and the loss of their two Temples.

But always, the way of *teshuvah*, repentance, was kept open for them. All that they had to do was to select freely the proper path. We did not ever subscribe to the view summarized succinctly in the Yiddish word that all is *bashert*, preordained. This fatalistic position, typical of Buddhism, of much of Islam, and of Calvinist Christianity, is definitely not typical of Jewish thought or beliefs.

The Midrash describes the formation of the embryo informing us that before the process begins, the Holy One, blessed be He, decrees what its end will be. God decrees whether it will be male or female, weak or strong, poor or rich, short or tall, ugly or beautiful, fat or thin, despised or vulgar. God also ordains its history. But God does not decree whether he or she will be a *tzaddik* (righteous individual) or a *rasha* (wicked individual) because that decision is in the hands of each human being. The Talmud states several times clearly and unequivocally, "Everything is in the hands of Heaven except the fear of Heaven" (*Ber.* 33b and parallels). We are responsible for our deeds. In Jewish law, a person is considered as always forewarned; he or she cannot claim ignorance of the norms against murder or mayhem, torts or damages (*adam muad le-olam:* B. *Qama* 26a and parallels). We are and must always be liable for our actions and pay the price of our follies. In Elie Wiesel's words, "Not all are guilty, but all are responsible." Rabbi Akiva formulated the notion of free will versus determinism in his famous paradox: "Everything is seen (or foreseen); yet free will is given humanity. And everything depends on the majority of one's deeds" (*Abot* 3:15). I take this to mean that we are all creatures of both nature and nurture, of genes and free will, heredity as well as environment. If we were to accept the doctrine that all is predetermined by Divine grace and election, to use a Calvinist term, then no person can ever be held accountable for sins and crimes. But that would lead to an intolerable situation in society of no accountability: We might as well close down all the jails and free all the murderers and scoundrels. Judaism rejects this understanding of human psychology, as I interpret it. We are, to be sure, partly the creatures of our genetic makeup, certainly in a physical sense, and perhaps even in a temperamental or emotional sense. But not in a moral sense: We are moral masters of our fate; we set our own course and chart our journey on this earth. "God helps lead the person on the path that person chooses" suggests the Talmud. Maimonides ruled in his *Mishneh Torah (Teshuvah,* 5:1–2), and in several other sources, that free will is guaranteed to us all:

> A human being is master of his fate and free will is given to all of us. If a person chooses to do good and be a saint, the power is in his or her hands; if the person chooses to do evil and be a wicked person, the choice is his or hers . . . Do not delude yourself with the nonsense spread by fools that states that the Holy One, blessed be He, preordains from birth whether a person will be righteous or wicked. Every person can be as righteous as Moses or as wicked as King Jeroboam.

May humanity prevail? Will decency triumph? Will civilization survive? John Paul Sartre insisted that human-created evil is "absolute and irredeemable." William James mused: "Man, biologically considered, is the most formidable of all beasts of prey, and indeed the only one that preys systematically on his own species." Are they correct? Will we transform this beautiful, verdant, fertile planet into yet another desolate, moon-like celestial body, like so many billions that float around the cosmos, sterile, dead, devoid of life? I believe it is all up to us. Fundamentally, we must actively struggle against the evil within ourselves and in our society and fashion a better world. "All that is necessary for the forces of evil to triumph in the world is for enough good people to do nothing," exhorted Edmund Burke. We have seen the results of human indifference to intolerable evil whether in the *Shoah* or in Cambodia, in Rwanda and the Sudan, in Ethiopia and the Balkans. The world's leaders did not take Hitler's threats seriously; they dismissed them as the ranting of a lunatic, confidently assuaging the nations of Europe, as well as their Jewish populations, that this madness would pass, that sanity would prevail, and that it was all empty rhetoric. What a fearsome price we paid for that folly! This explains why Israel views very seriously the threats of Arab groups such as Hamas, or the leaders of Iran, when they threaten to wipe Israel off the map. Never again may we turn a blind eye and ignore evil in other parts of the world, for sooner or later it engulfs us, as well.

The sages suggested several ways in which we might battle and overcome the *yetzer ha-ra,* the satanic forces in humanity and society. First, we must stimulate and strengthen the *yetzer tov,* our good nature, to struggle against the evil side. Second, we must study Torah and absorb its teachings. Third, we should recite the *Shema* and accept God's kingship over us. Finally, we must reflect on the day of death and the judgment that we will all ultimately face (*Ber.* 5a; *Abot R. Na.* A, 16, pp. 62 ff.).

Additionally, we humans must shed our hubris, our over-weaning pride and arrogance, and cultivate a greater sense of humility. "The most important product of knowledge is ignorance," declared Dr. David J. Gross, Nobel laureate in physics. That seems to be the theme of the poignant prayer on the High Holidays that follows the *Musaf Kedushah*. The *hazzan* usually chants this section in a particularly melancholy and moving fashion: "Adam! Adam! His origin is dust and to dust he will return. He is like a fragile vessel, like the grass that withers, the flower that fades, the shadow that passes, the cloud that vanishes, the wind that blows, the dust that floats, the dream that flies away." We are technologically geniuses but moral pygmies. We have harnessed the atom, sent men and women into space, reached the moon, glimpsed the farthest stars and planets, engineered the genes, and operated on the human heart and brain and eye. But all this has infused in us a sense of arrogance and uncontrolled pride, the pride described by the Torah, in these words: "My own power and the might of my own hand have won this wealth for me" (Deut 8:17). In Barbara Tuchman's words, "The appetite for power is old and irresponsible in humankind and in its action almost always destructive." Regrettably, this newly found power has not been accompanied by a new sense of moral responsibility, of care for our planet and its natural resources, of respect for the dignity and freedom of all human beings. Quite the contrary: We are in greater peril than ever before because there is no balance of power between two superpowers. Weapons of mass destruction, now available to rogue nations and terrorists groups, threaten to incinerate our planet and obliterate its inhabitants.

The Midrash informs us that God deliberately created the mosquito before humans to deflate human arrogance so that if we become too pompous, the mosquito reminds us, "I preceded you in the order of creation!" We need recall that little legend as we survey the unchecked hubris that seems to have infected the inhabitants of our earth. The Hasidic master, Rabbi Simhah Bunam, put it this way: "A person should always carry two texts in his pockets. One should read, 'The world was created for me' (*M. Sanh.* 4:5), while the other should read, 'I am but dust and ashes'" (Gen 18:27). This, I think, is what we modern Jews might believe about humanity's nature, fate, and future. Perhaps ultimately, through radical moral reeducation along these lines, we will attain the capacity for good, for life, and for peace envisioned by our Creator when He set in motion the process of creation.

Points to Ponder:
What Is a Human Being?

1. What do you make of the debate between Hillel and Shammai over the creation of humans and the surprising fact that the law is according to Shammai?

2. How has the discovery of the human genome affected the Jewish understanding of humanity?

3. How do you understand the concept that humans are an extension of the Divine?

4. How do you interpret the statement that humans are the product of father, mother, and God?

5. Rabbi Akiva and Ben Azzai disagreed over the most important teaching of the Bible concerning humans. What is the practical difference between them?

6. "He who destroys a single life, it is as if he destroyed an entire world." What are the implications of this teaching? And what of the opposite: "He who saves a single life, it is as if he had saved an entire world"?

7. *Pikuah nefesh* is described by the author as "the greatest of all *mitzvot.*" Do you concur with his judgment?

8. The author notes that Judaism teaches that we are endowed with two urges: the *yetzer tov* (good urge) versus the *yetzer ha-ra* (evil urge). How does this fit in with our modern psychological understanding of human beings?

9. What are the ramifications of the myth of the serpent copulating with Eve?

10. The author writes that Judaism is life-affirming and not ascetic. Can you prove or disprove this thesis?

11. Rubenstein wrote that the God of history died at Auschwitz. Heschel wrote that man, not God, died in Auschwitz. Which view appeals to you?

12. Given our knowledge of genetics and psychology, can you accept Judaism's stress on free will? Do you agree that everything is in Heaven's hands except the fear of Heaven?

13. Do you concur that if unchecked, arrogance will destroy humanity and our civilization?

14. The author argues that we are technological giants but moral pygmies. Do you feel his evaluation is accurate?

15. We learned that Rabbi Simhah Bunim carried two Jewish texts in his pocket. What texts would you carry in yours?

6

Are Jews the Chosen People?

THE CENTRAL point of Jewish theology and the key to an understanding of the nature of Judaism, is the doctrine, "God chose Israel as His people." So argued Kaufman Kohler, the eminent Reform theologian in his classic work, *Jewish Theology*.

"The idea of race or national superiority exercises divisive influence, generating suspicion and hatred," countered Mordecai M. Kaplan, in one of his less vehement rebuttals.

What is the correct meaning of, "God chose Israel"? What does the concept of "chosen people" imply? Is it critical to Judaism and still valid and meaningful today? It is not featured in the catalogue of dogmas drawn up by Maimonides or Joseph Albo. Still, it has been terribly important and potent in the eyes of world Jewry throughout the ages.

The Bible is clear on the matter: God chose Israel to be His own beloved treasure and first-born son. The process began with Abraham, Isaac, and Jacob and continued throughout the centuries. In the words of Nehemiah (9:7):

> You are the Lord God who chose Abram, who brought him out of
> Ur of the Chaldeans and changed his name to Abraham. Finding
> his heart true to You, You made a covenant with him to give him
> the land of the Canaanites. . . .

God singled out Abraham because He was confident that Abraham would "instruct his children and his posterity to keep the ways of the Lord by doing what is just and right . . ." (Gen 18:19). In a sense, chosenness as mission was already born. Later in our history, God extended the choice of the Patriarchs and Matriarchs to include all of Israel. Standing at the foot of Mount Sinai, Israel was informed that God had selected them not because of their numbers—for they were a small and militarily impotent people—but because He loves them (Deut 7:6 ff.). He sees their unique potential to become a "treasure people," a "Kingdom of priests and a holy nation," a nation that would emulate God's sanctity by sanctifying their lives. The verb, *bahar*, sums up the unique relationship between God and Israel (Exod 19:5–6). It connotes "choose, love, delight in, test, refine, bring near, set aside, and sanctify." And it is applied not just to the people but also to Eretz Yisrael, Jerusalem, the Temple, the tribe of Levites and Aaronide priests, the prophets, and the house of David who would furnish kings to rule Israel.

The election of the Jewish people is not viewed in the Bible as a one-sided love affair. Quite the contrary: Israel was required to respond and reciprocate. It was only after the people proclaimed with one voice, "All the things that the Lord has commanded we will do" that they became truly His treasured people (Exod 24:3, 7; Josh 24:14 ff.).

Election was invariably linked to a mission and that included teaching monotheism, curbing human arrogance, ending violence, lust, greed, chauvinism, warfare, and ushering in a new society. In a word, election is merely a *means* to the final *end*; it is teleological. Alas, that mission frequently entails suffering and martyrdom as described so dramatically by Second Isaiah, whose poems on the "suffering servant of the Lord" are so poignantly prophetic (Isa 41:8 ff.; 42:6; 43:10; 49:8). He described God's servant in these harsh words: "I offered my back to the floggers, and my cheeks to those who tore out my hair. I did not try to hide my face from insult and spittle." And the psalmist picks up the theme: "You let them devour us like sheep. You disperse us among the nations. You sell Your people for no fortune. You set no high price for them. You make us the butt of our neighbors, the scorn and derision of those around us" (Ps 44:10 ff.).

To be sure, election tempts a people to arrogance. If God has singled out one nation as beloved, there is the natural tendency to feel superior, to assume one may do no wrong, to conclude if Israel is chosen, others are rejected. The prophet Amos confronted such hubris, and he injected the theme of *noblesse oblige* to counter it (3:2 and 9:7): "Concerning the whole family that I brought up from the land of Egypt. You alone have I singled out of all the families of the earth—that is why I call you to account for all your iniquities." Jeremiah, too, battled the overweening pride of Judeans who were convinced that as God's elect that could do as they wished with impunity, that no harm would ever befall them, their land or temple (Jer 7:1–12).

Is the election eternal and irrevocable regardless of Israel's behavior? There is some ambivalence in the Bible: some authors suggested ominously that Israel's sinful ways will lead to horrible consequences. But others insisted that no matter how sinful or perverse the people may be, Israel's election is forever. As Isaiah put it, "For a little while I forsake you, but with vast love will I bring you back" (54:7–10).

Rabbinic theology was built on the biblical foundations of chosen people and preserved and expanded on the ambivalent themes already propounded in the Bible. For example, the sages debated sharply whether God compelled Israel to accept the Torah and become the elect of God or whether Israel elected God. One famous legend describes God suspending Mt. Sinai over Israel, threatening them with instant destruction should they reject the Torah (*Shabb* 88a). Conversely, a popularly taught tale found in many sources in the Talmud and Midrash depicts God peddling the Torah among the various nations of antiquity only to be spurned because the demands were unreasonable. Israel alone accepted the challenge with a ringing affirmation, "We will do whatever we are commanded" (*Sifre Deut.* 343, p.142b and many parallels). It was Israel's willingness to accept the Torah that qualified it as God's own people. In the words of Rabbi Jose ben Simon: "Because you stood at Sinai and accepted My Torah, you were called 'Israel' as all the other nations are called by specific names. But once you accepted My Torah at Sinai, you were called 'My people'" (*Tanh. Vaera* 1:9a).

These legends recall the old saw, "How odd of God to choose the Jews; it's not so odd, the Jews chose God." Israel Zangwill put it aptly: "It's not so much a matter of *chosen* people as *choosing* people." There is a dialectic to it all; a process of reciprocity is at work.

A similar ambivalence crops up over whether chosenness is forever and irrevocable or contingent upon Israel's behavior. Rabbi Yehudah bar Ilai insisted that only if Israel conducts itself as children will they remain His children. But Rabbi Meir demurred, insisting, whether Israel behaves or not, "You are children of the Lord" (*Sifre Deut.* 96, p. 94a). Elsewhere, Rabbi Meir stressed that "even though you are full of blemishes, you are God's children."

There seems to be universal consent among the sages that election has a purpose; that it is not just a quirk of fate that we were chosen; it is teleological, as this famous rabbinic homily indicates (*Sifra Kedoshim* on Lev 19:2, p. 86b): "'You shall be holy for I, the Lord, am holy.' Said the sages, You must consider yourselves part of the king's retinue and emulate Him. Just as He is compassionate and merciful, so must you be." In a word, the elect of God must engage in *imitatio dei*, emulation of the deity. We do not become gods ourselves; we become God-like.

The election entails suffering, even as Deutero-Isaiah had predicted, observed the sages. But the suffering ennobles our people. And while God chose Israel, He has not rejected other nations. Some are chosen; all are loved. He has "attached His name to Israel in a special and unique way," but He is sovereign over and loves all people (*Sifre Deut.* 31, p. 73a).

As the new Christian church gained ascendancy, chosenness became a polemical issue and assumed an even greater role in Jewish ideology. In breaking with Judaism, some of the writers of the New Testament (especially Letter to the Hebrews, chapter eight) suggest that Judaism is obsolete, outmoded, and superseded by the new faith in Jesus. The Church Fathers expanded on this theme, and carried it to the extreme that God had rejected or forsaken His former chosen people. Justin Martyr, for example, pointed to the loss of the Temple in Jerusalem and crushing defeat at the hands of the Romans, loss of sovereignty, and ensuing dispersion as convincing proof of this new status. Although Paul, in his Letter to the Romans (chapters 9–11), specifically rejects this supersessionist or displacement interpretation of historical events and reemphasizes that God has not forsaken Israel for He does not revoke His gifts or renege on His promises, the view that Judaism is a failed religion, at worst, or a mere prelude to Christianity at best, prevailed. The New Israel has superseded the Old; God has replaced the Old Testament with the New; the chosen people is now the Church. The national election of Israel has been replaced by individual election to eternal life without regard to people, race or station. God has substituted the election of a faith community for the choice of a nation or people. A number of the polemic battles over this issue between rabbis and *minim*, "heretics, sectarians," reflect the increasingly sharp tensions between the two groups. "He has turned away and withdrawn from Israel," argued a new Christian. "Not at all," countered the sages, "His hand is forever stretched over them to protect them." Another *min* challenged Rabbi Hanina: "Now that your Temple is destroyed and you cannot cleanse yourselves from your uncleanness, you are defiled and God no longer dwells among you." The Rabbi replied, "It is written, 'He dwells among them in the midst of their uncleanness'" (Lev 16:16).

To meet these onslaughts, I believe the sages elevated the idea of chosenness to near dogma status and crystallized it into the normative Judaism of the liturgy. The prayer recited as one is called to the Torah for an *aliyah* (honor) says it succinctly: "Praised are You, Lord our God, King of the universe, who chose us from all the peoples and gave us His Torah. Praised are You, Lord, who gives the Torah." This theme appears frequently in the Sabbath and Festival *Kiddush*, the *Amidah*, in the blessings prior to the *Shema*, and elsewhere. But note: chosenness is never an end in itself;

always it is linked to spiritual vocation, study of Torah, *mitzvot* such as *Shabbat* and *Yom Tov*, and service to God and humanity.

Faced with the double challenge of not one but two daughter religions, Christianity and Islam, medieval Judaism needed to discover a *raison d'être*. Both faiths preached a theology of displacement and supersession of the mother faith; both denigrated Judaism, periodically expressing their contempt in violence and expulsions. Chosenness provided that needed *raison d'être*. Although most philosophers took the belief in the chosen people seriously, viewing it as an essential teaching of Judaism, none elevated it into a dogma of faith. Interestingly, neither Saadia Gaon nor Maimonides stressed the notion of chosen people. In fact, Saadia warned Israel not to be arrogant, for all nations are God's and election does not imply exclusion of others. Maimonides barely mentioned the concept in his *Guide of the Perplexed*. But Yehudah Halevi adopted a "racial" concept of Judaism and Jews, considering the gentiles inferior. Maimonides strongly rejected this racial interpretation of the chosen people. He wrote that "we believe in a prophet because of what he says, not because of his descent." He clearly spurned a "biological" approach to Judaism, as is evident in his famous letter to Ovadiah, the proselyte:

> I received your inquiry asking whether you, as a convert to Judaism, are entitled to say in your daily prayers, "Our God and God of our Ancestors." Indeed, you may say all of these blessings without changing the wording. You are just like any native-born Jew in this regard . . . for Abraham is your spiritual father, and our inheritance is yours as well, since there is no racial distinction in our faith.

The mystics of the Kabbalah reinterpreted chosenness in a remarkably bold fashion. The well-known aphorism of the Zohar, "The Holy One, blessed be He, the Torah and Israel are one," articulates the views (often erotically expressed) that Israel unites or cohabits with God via the media of Torah and virtuous behavior. Lurianic Kabbalah taught that all Israel forms a messianic entity charged with the mission of releasing the sparks of sin encased in the world via the process of *tikkun*, mending, or repairing society, and reuniting those sparks with the infinite Source of all.

The modern era and the Enlightenment subjected the notion of chosen people—along with other basic tenets—to searing criticism. Chosenness seemed to be outdated and embarrassing. Worse, it cast other nations in an invidious light. Moses Mendelssohn substituted the idea of "mission," the belief that God has mandated Israel to spread His sacred teachings of monotheism and morality far and wide. This position was eagerly endorsed by the newly emerging Reform movement and even the great neo-Orthodox Rabbi Samson Raphael Hirsch. Kaufmann Kohler, Herman Cohen, Leo Baeck, and Martin Buber stressed the teleological meaning of chosenness, in that Israel's election has a higher purpose. "The people of Israel has been charged to lead the way to righteousness and justice," is the way Buber phrased it. Baeck, a survivor of the Nazi Holocaust, reflected: "Every people can be chosen for a history, for a share in the history of humanity. Each is a question which God has asked, and each people must answer. But more history has been assigned to this people than to any other people . . . The word of the One God penetrated this people from its beginnings." Abraham Joshua Heschel regarded chosenness as a "spiritual act," for Israel is a "spiritual order" and in order to be a people, we have to be more than a people; we must be a "holy people." He insisted:

> We have not chosen God; He has chosen us. There is no concept of a chosen God but there is the idea of a chosen people. The idea of a chosen people does not suggest the preference of a people based upon a discrimination among a number of peoples. We do not say that we are superior people. The "chosen people" means a people approached and chosen by God . . . It signifies not a quality inherent in the people but a relationship between the people and God.

Only Mordecai M. Kaplan, the notable iconoclast, rejected the idea totally as "generating suspicion and hatred," and he expunged it from his prayer book much to the ire of the Orthodox world. In fact, some ultra-Orthodox fanatics actually burned his new prayer book, proof—if proof is required—that no one group has a monopoly on crazies and fanatics. In a remarkable outburst in class that I witnessed, he heatedly dubbed the doctrine "racism and Nazism," much to the horror and hostility of the students.

Today's Reform Jews preserve election as a mission to spread God's teachings and moral lessons to humanity. The Conservatives interpret it teleologically: We are a people dedicated to the service of God and covenanted to build a just and compassionate society throughout the world. The Orthodox seem to accept the notion of election, and with few exceptions, their theologians take it seriously, understanding election to mean that Israel is covenanted to live by the precepts of the Torah. Curiously, the new crop of Reconstructionists seem less troubled by the idea than their founder and are content to allow the option of either the traditional blessings or the Reconstructionist formulation. More recent theologians such as Eugene Borowitz, David Hartman, and Irving Greenberg have recast the doctrine into "Covenant theology." For example, Eugene Borowitz finds that the traditional view that God chose us from all people and gave us the Torah clashes too much with our sense of history. He prefers covenant theology because it expresses his belief "in an enhanced reciprocity between God and people."

Does the idea of the election of Israel still serve a function? Has it yet value and validity? I believe it is still a compelling vital component of Judaism.

First, chosenness recognizes the unique contribution of this tiny speck of a people that spawned two major faiths and brought the message of ethical monotheism to billions the world over. And we continue to enrich this planet disproportionately: We are less than one percent of the total population and contribute over twenty-five percent of the list of Nobel laureates.

Second, we draw inspiration from the notion of election and are urged on to spread God's word to an often cruel and indifferent world. As long as violence, bigotry, oppression, and wars afflict us, this world is unredeemed and the teleology of our election assumes greater importance. We are to engage in *tikkun ha-olam*, mending our fractured world and improving our society. The notion of the chosen people goads us to be loyal Jews, lead Jewish lives, champion righteousness and justice, love and peace, and be involved as God's partners, as a "kingdom of priests and a holy nation." We are a people created in the image of the Divine, partners in an ongoing dialogue as both the chosen and the choosing.

Third, the rebirth of the State of Israel has added a new dimension to the ancient summons. The State must not be just another political entity or Levantine state, and "normalcy" is the very antithesis of our chosenness. As I shall explain in my chapter, "Why Eretz Yisrael?", the State of Israel must be different and extraordinary, a laboratory of the highest Jewish and human values exemplifying the prophetic ideals by championing righteousness, social justice, as well as equal treatment for all faiths, ethnic, and economic groups. If it is to become a "nation like all other nations," as some demand; if it is to evolve into a "normal nation," as some would have it, it will forfeit its cachet. It must be a light for the nations and a banner for all peoples.

Finally, I believe that election offers us a transcendent *raison d'être* for remaining Jews in a gentile society even as it has inured us to withstand the pressures of paganism, Christianity and Islam. After all, "Why be a Jew?" still resonates and assumes ominous implications in a secular society. We certainly paid a steep price for our stubbornness in refusing to join the mainstream, and our bloodied footsteps have stained the terrain of many a land. The late, eminent Protestant theologian, Markus Barth, son of the greatest Protestant theologian of the twentieth century, Karl Barth, wrote in his volume, *Israel and the Church:* "Israel has been from the beginning of her existence and still is the symbol of the cost and value of being God's chosen people and His instrument among the nations of the world. For Israel proves it is worth the prize to suffer defamation and persecution for the sake of God who is one. So the Jews show what a high calling it is to be both God's servant and God's child." If we are not the elected Suffering Servant of the Lord, then why continue our perilous journey? But if we believe that we are still His elect with tasks still undone, with, in the words of Robert Frost, "promises to keep, and miles to go before I sleep," then we proceed on our march across history's pages fortified by the belief in the mystery and majesty of our role:

> You are one and Your name is one
> And who is like Your people, Israel,
> A unique nation on earth.
>
> (From the Sabbath afternoon prayer)

Points to Ponder:
Are Jews the Chosen People?

1. How is it possible for Kohler and Kaplan to take such opposite views on the election of Israel?

2. How do you understand chosenness as mission?

3. What is the meaning of, "a Kingdom of priests, a holy nation"? Does it appeal to you?

4. According to Second Isaiah, election entails suffering. Is that not a deterrent to being Jewish?

5. What are some of the dangers inherent in the belief in our chosenness?

6. Some prefer the term "choosing people" to "chosen people." What is your reaction to these two terms and which do you prefer?

7. How did the sages meet the Christians' challenge that they were the new chosen people of God?

8. Contrast Yehudah Halevi's view on election with Maimonides' position. How do they resonate in our day?

9. Is election as mission really that different from the original concept?

10. Does "Covenant theology" appeal to you more than election and if so, why?

11. Do you think election offers us a reason to remain Jews in a non-Jewish and often hostile world?

7

Halakhah: Divine or Human?

IS HALAKHAH, Jewish law, Divine or human? Or is it an amalgam of both elements? This is a fundamental question for understanding Judaism, which is, after all, a religion of *law*, not merely theology, of *action*, not just of faith. Law plays a crucially important role in Judaism that cannot be ignored without distorting the Jewish faith. To ignore halakhah is to misconstrue Judaism.

But what is the nature of halakhah? Interestingly, the sages seemed to believe that halakhah is a process, an unfolding of laws. Moreover, there is a parallel process of expounding the law that proceeds in heaven and on earth. God and His celestial *Beit Din* study, debate, interpret and vote on legal rulings simultaneously with the terrestrial courts and academies. An unusual *midrash* in the name of Rabbi Yehudah states that "not a single day goes by in which the Holy One, blessed be He, does not pass new halakhah in the celestial *Beit Din*, for it says in Job 37:2, 'Hearken well to His thundering voice, to the rumbling that comes from His mouth'" (*Gen. Rab.* 49:2, p.501). Doubtlessly, this is the inspiration for the statement of the eminent kabbalist, Rabbi Isaiah Horowitz (*Shelah*, died 1630) that "the Holy One, blessed be He, gave the Torah and gives it at every moment; the flowing fountain never ceases."

So we know that the sages viewed Torah as an evolving process with God Himself actively involved in its renewal. What place in the process do we humans occupy?

One school of thought, championed by Rabbi Akiva, insisted that *all* is in heaven; that everything was given at Sinai. Some partisans of this approach insist, in what Abraham Joshua Heschel dubbed "a theological exaggeration," that the entire corpus of the oral law including every future decision of the sages was revealed to Moses (*Ber.* 5a and parallels). Furthermore, Mar Samuel asserted that 3,000 *halakhot* given at Sinai were forgotten during the mourning for Moses and it is our task to try and discover those lost laws (*Tem.* 16a). Rabbi Eliezer ben Hyrcanus was the great exponent of this position. His legal rulings were either based on traditions from ancestors and previous scholars or else were conveyed to him from heaven via supernatural channels. The famous debate over the purity of a certain type of stove highlights the difference between Rabbi Eliezer and his colleagues. He ruled that an *Akhnai* stove is ritually pure while his colleagues demurred and declared it impure (*B. Metzia* 59b):

> "If the halakhah is according to my view let the carob tree prove it." And the carob tree was uprooted and moved 400 cubits. Said the sages, "We don't bring proof from a carob tree." If the halakhah is according to my view let this stream of water flow backwards." And the stream flowed backwards. Said the sages, "We don't bring proof from a stream of water." "If the halakhah is according to my views let the walls of the academy prove it." And the walls of the academy inclined as if to fall.
>
> . . . . .
>
> He persisted and said, "If the law is according to my view let Heaven prove it." Whereupon a *Bat Kol* (echo of a Divine voice) issued from heaven proclaiming, "Why do you challenge Rabbi Eliezer? The law always follows his views." Said Rabbi Joshua ben Hananiah, "It is not in heaven" (Deut 30:12). Said Rabbi Jeremiah, "The Torah has already been given at Sinai; hence, we pay no attention to a *Bat Kol* for You have written in Your Torah at Sinai, 'Follow the majority.'" (Exod 23:2)

Clearly, Rabbi Eliezer was relying on his learning and prestige plus a few miracles and Divine intervention against the majority of the sages. But as the great Polish commentator Rabbi Samuel Edels (*Maharsha*, died 1631) notes: "This shows that the power of the majority supercedes a *Bat Kol* because the Torah was not given to angels in heaven."

Another well-known tale on the issue of human versus Divine prerogatives in halakhah is found in the Talmud *Eruvin* 13b, again in the name of Mar Samuel:

> For three years Beit Shammai and Beit Hillel debated. Beit Shammai said, "The halakhah is according to us." Beit Hillel said, "The halakhah is according to us." A *Bat Kol* came went forth from heaven and proclaimed, "Both these and those are the words of the living God but the halakhah is according to Beit Hillel."

This famous tale, which, as Professor Avi Sagi notes, conceals more than it reveals, seems to reinforce that notion that whereas humans may debate halakhic rulings, the final arbiter is God in heaven. This approach denigrates the role of human beings: humans may neither create, nor change or reinterpret the law. At best they may only discover or recover the original, concealed *halakhot* via *pilpul* (debates, dialectic) and offer *hiddushim*, novel interpretations and insights.

The second school of thought, championed by Rabbi Yishmael, denied that *all* was given at Sinai. Indeed, only general principles were revealed to Moses; the rest was filled in by succeeding generations of scholars (*Hag.* 6a and parallels). Consequently, the role of humans in the halakhic process is affirmed and strengthened. After all, even in the Talmudic controversy about the stove cited above, we are informed that "the law is not in heaven" any longer, or, as Professor Menachem Fisch puts it, "it is beyond the reach of heaven." Several aggadic texts, some of which display legendary or mythic qualities buttress this view.

> Said Rabbi Yanai: "Were the Torah given cut-and-dried it would not have a leg to stand on." Said Moses: "Master of the universe, teach me the halakhah." God said to him, "Follow the majority. If the majority rules 'innocent,' he is innocent. If the majority rules 'guilty,' he is guilty. In this way the Torah may be interpreted 49 ways to rule impure and 49 ways to rule pure." (*y. Sanh.* 4:2, 22a).

Clearly God expects humans to debate all sides of issues in arriving at a conclusion by majority vote. Not only that, but we are told that God affirms and confirms decisions arrived at by human courts and ratifies them on high. So we read in the Talmud (*Mak.* 23b & *Meg.* 7a) on the verse in Esther 9:27, "the Jews undertook and irrevocably obligated themselves" to observe Purim, that "three laws passed by Israel were confirmed in the heavenly *Beit Din*." The three laws are the reading of the *Megillah* of Esther, greeting persons using God's name or a Divine epithet such as "shalom", and imposing tithes on the Levites to be given to the priests. In short, "they confirmed on high what was accepted below."

The same principle applies in setting the calendar: Heaven approves of human decisions on halakhic matters. The sages insisted that the Torah conferred on them the authority to proclaim which day is prohibited and which day is permitted, which labor is prohibited and which labor is permitted (*Hag.* 18a). And they went even further in strengthening rabbinic prerogatives:

> If the *Beit Din* ruled to move Rosh Hashanah to the next day, at once the Holy One, blessed be He, says to the angels, "Remove the *bimah* because My children have ruled to move Rosh Hashanah to the next day, as it says, 'For it is a law for Israel, a ruling of the God

of Jacob.' If it is not a law for Israel, so to speak, it is not a ruling for the God of Jacob. . . ." (*y. Rosh Hash.* 1:3, 57b).

In other words, God originated the core of the law but now it is up to us humans to continue the process of explication and interpretation. God merely confirms or assents to human actions.

This view of human involvement in the legal process is found in a quaint aggadah in *Gittin* 6b:

> The sages disagreed in the interpretation of the verse in Judges 19:2, "Once his concubine played the harlot." Rabbi Aviatar said that the husband found a fly in his food. Rabbi Jonathan said he found a pubic hair in his food. Rabbi Aviatar came across Elijah and asked him, "What is the Holy One, blessed be He, doing?" He replied, "He is discussing the question of the concubine in Gibea." "And what does He say?" Elijah responded, "My son Aviatar says such-and-such and my son Jonathan says such-and-such." Said Aviatar, "Can there possibly be uncertainty in the mind of the Holy One?" Elijah replied, "Both answers are the words of the living God."

In an even bolder legend, God and His *Beit Din* are depicted as turning to humans for help in deciding the law. This is the tale found in *Baba Metzia* 86a:

> They were debating in the heavenly academy the rule of a skin lesion. If the scab precedes the white hair it is unclean; if the white hair precedes the lesion it is clean (Lev 13:1–3). But what if we are unsure which came first? The Holy One, blessed be He, ruled "pure" but the members of the heavenly academy ruled "impure." They wondered, "Who will decide the issue? Only Rabbah bar Nahman who is a great expert in skin lesions and the laws of impurities." They sent the angel of death to summon him but as Rabbah was engrossed in Torah study, he could not kill him. The angel then caused a wind to blow so that the leaves rustled mightily. Rabbah thought that a cavalry troop was approaching. He stopped studying and exclaimed, "Better that I should die than fall into the hands of the government." And he died proclaiming, "Pure, pure" [thereby upholding God's opinion].

This aggadah is clear evidence that at least some sages believed that God Himself as well as His celestial academy turn to human beings for halakhic rulings and the authority of the sages supersedes even God's.

That halakhah is not stagnant or frozen and that we humans have a role to play in its growth and development is clearly the point of one famous text that comes down firmly on the side of human creativity in the halakhic process. I refer to the legend in *Menahot* 29b, a tale that reveals more than it conceals. Its purpose was clearly to indicate the methodology of Rabbi Akiva in expounding the written Torah by which every jot and tittle on the letters is built into great structures. Instead, we learn much about how we humans create and expand God's Torah. Rabbi Yehudah quotes the tale in the name of Rav:

> When Moses went on high he found the Holy One, blessed be He, sitting and tying crowns on the letters of the Torah. He asked God, "Who prevented You from writing whatever You wanted [Rashi: that You have to add additional crowns]? He replied to Moses: "There is a certain man named Akiva ben Joseph who, after many generations in the future, will interpret every single jot and tittle of the letters and build mounds of *halakhot*." Moses replied: "Master of the universe, show him to me." He said, "Turn back to the future." Upon doing so, Moses found himself in the academy of Rabbi Akiva so he sat at the end of the eighth row. He did not understand a single word of the discussion and he felt faint. They reached a certain matter in the discussion and one of the pupils challenged Rabbi Akiva, "Rabbi, how do you know this is the law?" Rabbi Akiva responded, "It is a halakhah given to Moses at Mount Sinai." And Moses' strength returned to him [Rashi: since Rabbi Akiva quoted him by name even though *he had not yet received this legal ruling of Torah*].

This unusual legend teaches some very profoundly crucial lessons. First, as Rashi observed, we see from the text that contrary to Rabbi Akiva's viewpoint, Moses had *not* received all of the Torah at Sinai. Second, we learn that the law develops and grows; it is not static or frozen. Third, each human being is free to explore and expand the Torah. Fourth, the Torah is clearly broader than the written text; its boundaries are set by *human* inquiry. Finally, human beings are God's partners in fashioning halakhah.

It is apparent from these sources I've marshaled, that the majority of the sages seem to have endorsed Rabbi Yishmael's understanding of the halakhah by which humans are invested with the authority to flesh out the basic Sinaitic principles. Indeed, it seems to be God's will—or challenge to us—that we humans continue the task He inaugurated. Let us remember the tale of the *Akhnai* stove, which I cited earlier and which ends with God laughingly proclaiming, "My children have defeated Me!" God *wanted* us to uncover and reveal, explain and elucidate, interpret and reinterpret, expand and amplify, improve and renew His essential Torah. An early medieval Midrash (*S. Eli. Rab.* 2, p. 172) offers an analogy of Torah and raw materials. It states that when God gave us the Torah it was like wheat and flax. Just as it is up to us humans to convert them into bread and cloth, so must we refine and enhance the basic teachings of Torah.

Am I reading too much into these texts? Have I distorted their true meaning? I think not and I have assembled some later commentaries to prove the point.

Rabbi Yom Tov ben Abraham Asbili (*Ritva*, Spain, thirteenth-fourteenth centuries) replied to a query about rabbinic authority from French rabbis by noting that God had shown Moses 49 different possibilities to permit or prohibit a matter but He indicated that "the prerogative will be handed over to the sages of Israel in every generation to rule according to their discretion." His younger colleague, Rabbi Nissim Gerondi (*Ran*, Spain, fourteenth century), considered it God's will that the wise men, not prophets of each generation reveal the halakhah. In one of his sermons, he noted that the Talmud had indicated that after the destruction of the Temple, prophecy was taken from the prophets and given to the sages (*B. Bat.* 12b). Consequently, "the power of deciding such matters has been transmitted to the scholars of the generations and their consensus is what God has commanded." Rabbi Joseph Albo (Spain, fifteenth century), the last of the great Spanish theologians, subscribed to the position of Rabbi Yishmael and argued that only "general principles were given orally to Moses at Sinai, briefly alluded to in the Torah, by means of which the wise men of every generation may work out the details as new issues develop."

Shifting to Poland, I cite the great legalist, Rabbi Solomon Luria (sixteenth century) who interpreted the phrase, "both these and those are the words of the living God" as follows:

> It is as if each sage received his ruling from God or from Moses even though no such thing was ever uttered by Moses . . . Therefore, the Torah transmitted the authority to the sages of each generation, each according to his intellect, to enhance and add to the teachings with the approbation of Heaven.

Rabbi Samuel Edels adopted a bolder view of the human role in shaping halakhah. He interpreted the verse from Isaiah 42:21, "that he may magnify and glorify [His] Torah" in a strikingly original way:

> You must not consider it wicked in God's sight for humans to add from their own intellect laws and prohibitions to those written in the Torah given by God . . . The Holy One, Blessed be He, wants

us to glorify and strengthen that which we increase so that it might be even more glorious and strong than the body of the Torah of the Holy One . . . And lest you argue, "Who appointed puny humans to make themselves partners of God who gave us the Torah and *mitzvot* by adding a new Torah and *mitzvot?*" To this God responds by citing the verse, as if to say, "Just the opposite! The Holy One wants this to happen. . . ."

I turn to a modern giant of Jewish learning, Rabbi Barukh Epstein (Russia, died 1942), who discusses this matter in several places in his renowned commentary on the Pentateuch, *Torah Temimah*. He notes the view of Rabbi Yehoshua ben Levi in the Talmud, who agrees with Rabbi Yishmael that "every future teaching of great scholars has already been given to Moses at Sinai" but he interprets it in quite a different way. He suggests that only the principles (*ikkarim*) of the laws were given; the ultimate decisions will be arrived at by students through their analytical powers and ability to fashion rules based on those principles. But his statement is not to suggest that the actual *pilpulim* were conveyed to Moses "as the narrow-minded have endeavored to prove in their interpretations of the Talmud, thereby undermining the effects of human striving and struggles in the Talmudic debates." Elsewhere, he proposes that the text, "by the hand of Moses" (Num 4:37) should be linked to the verse, "it is not in heaven" (Deut 30:12) indicating that "it is in human hands to resolve all doubts that accompany specific laws."

In short, it is the will of God that we humans abet the unfolding process of interpreting and elucidating the Torah begun at Sinai, for the Torah must be interpreted and reinterpreted in every generation, in every land, in the light of new and changing circumstances. Just as we are God's partners in completing the creation of the world (*Shabb.* 119b), so are we His partners in continuing the evolving understanding of Torah and halakhah, of teaching and law. As Rabbi Joseph B. Soloveitchik put it, we humans are God's partners and a reflection of God the Creator as we seek novel interpretations of the law for the "goal of the halakhah is uniting the creative force in man with the Creative Force of the universe." Professor David Weiss Halivni describes our role as "active partners in the creative process."

This understanding of halakhah as an ongoing process bestows on us both an honor and a challenge. It certainly is an honor to be viewed as a partner of the Divinity in shaping halakhah. But it is also a challenge to remain faithful to God's mandate to cultivate, invigorate, and reinterpret the halakhah.

Judaism without halakhah is no longer Judaism: it is an anarchical system of several loosely held beliefs. How can there be a Jewish religion if individual autonomy is the rule so that chaos reigns? As the eminent Reform rabbi and scholar, W. Gunther Plaut complained, ". . . our people lack a Jewish lifestyle . . . To defend the emptiness of their lives they shout, 'Freedom!' but they mean *hefkerut*, license to carry on with as little as possible, or at best, with what is convenient." Yet another renowned Reform leader and thinker, Rabbi Arnold J. Wolf, formulated the problem differently when he wrote, "Accordingly, the Reform movement will suggest or even instruct its adherents what political measures to support, while hardly requiring any ritual obedience, except for converts. . . . But there is no coherent standard for changing Jewish law except the spirit of the times, an epoch that its hardly worthy of emulation."

Conversely, Judaism with a frozen halakhah is an anachronism and irrelevant—a betrayal of the dynamism that has always shaped it, as the sources I have selected clearly indicate. Let us recall that the word "halakhah" means going, walking; it implies movement, process, activity—not stasis. Additionally, the noun is feminine (even as the word Torah is feminine), implying fecundity and growth. The very nature of halakhah is to grow and reproduce and multiply. "The law must be stable but it cannot stand still," wrote Roscoe Pound, the late Dean of Harvard Law School. And Professor Louis Ginzberg urged that "immutability must not be confounded with immobility." It is intolerable that the plight of the *agunah*, the woman unable to receive a *get* (Jewish divorce) because the husband is either missing or recalcitrant has not been properly addressed or resolved in the Orthodox community. It is even more galling knowing that the remedies exist within the parameters of halakhah. For example, there are five cases in the Babylonian Talmud of annulment of marriages—a procedure invoked on any number of occasions by the great adjudicator of the last century, Rabbi Moshe Feinstein. Yet, when Rabbi Emanuel Rackman and a handful of courageous colleagues invoke these remedies, they are pilloried and shunned for their heroic efforts.

Our faith is a tree of life; it has flourished and foliated in the past because we were bold and audacious in accepting the Divine mandate to serve as God's partners in creating new insights into Torah. When Jews were slaughtered by Greeks because they would not take up arms on the Sabbath, the sages reinterpreted the halakhah and conceived of the category of *pikuah nefesh*—saving a human life supersedes all the *mitzvot* including *Shabbat*. When the Torah's prohibition against any person "leaving his place" grew so onerous and strangling as to destroy the pleasure

88

of *Shabbat*, they eased the halakhah to allow movement as far as 2000 cubits outside the city limits. When economic pressures and the refusal to grant loans to the needy became unbearable, the rabbis circumvented the biblical prohibition against usury and conceived of a variety of legal loan instruments. That is how they kept halakhah alive; that is how they preserved Judaism as a living entity.

So the questions with which I began this chapter can now be answered: "Halakhah: Divine or Human?" The answer is: *both*. God, the source of Torah and halakhah entrusted to us mortals the sacred task of partnering with Him in exalting and glorifying Torah and *mitzvot*, in bringing all beneath the wings of the *Shekhinah*, the Divine Presence. Whether or not we are up to the challenge may well determine the future of Judaism.

Points to Ponder:
Halakhah: Divine or Human?

1. What are the implications of the view that halakhah is an evolving process?

2. The school of Rabbi Akiva maintained that every law and future interpretation of the law was given at Sinai. How can we reinterpret the laws if this is correct? If we adopt this stance, does not the law become a frozen and immobile element of Jewish life?

3. How do you understand the implications of, "Both these and those are the words of the living God"? And are there no limits to what constitutes the words of the living God?

4. The debate over the nature of certain skin lesions in which God's opinion requires human support seems to exalt the human role in legislation at the expense of Divine power. How do you react to that bold assertion?

5. The legend of Moses in Rabbi Akiva's academy seems to undermine totally the view that all was given at Sinai. How can you reconcile this opinion with belief in the Divine origin of Torah?

6. The great commentators conclude that God has given the authority of interpretation of Torah and halakhah to the wise men and scholars of each generation. But who is to determine who the wise men are? And what criteria are to be followed?

7. What are the implications of Rabbi Samuel Edel's view that God wants humans to be God's partners in adding to the body of Torah and *mitzvot*? And are there no limits or parameters?

8. The author suggests that it is both an honor and a challenge to be viewed as God's partners in shaping halakhah. How is this so? How do you view our role in the process?

9. Do you agree that Judaism without halakhah is an anarchical system of several loosely held beliefs? Can there be a Jewish religion without halakhah?

10. Reform Judaism insists on the principle of individual autonomy in deciding whether or not to abide by particular rituals. The author criticizes that approach as leading to anarchy and chaos. What do you think?

11. Orthodoxy argues that once we start manipulating halakhah, anything goes. Do you concur with this opinion?

12. Conservative Jews are committed to a system of halakhah but honor it more in the breach than the performance. What do you make of this?

13. "The law must be stable but it cannot stand still," wrote Justice Cardozo. How do you interpret his words?

8

Why Ritual?

JUDAISM IS a religion of law. All of our actions are regulated by a comprehensive system of *mitzvot*, commandments, that prescribes our behavior from the time we awaken in the morning until the moment we retire at night; from our birth throughout our life-cycle events until our death; from the fall festivals of Rosh Hashanah, Yom Kippur and Sukkot, to Passover and Shavuot in the spring and the summer season. *Mitzvot* control our every action both in personal life as well as in relationships to the outside world, in our family situations and in our business enterprises, in our personal actions as well as in our communal behavior. Furthermore, Judaism, as we have seen, teaches that these commandments derive from the Divine will—they are the commandments of God and part of the revelation of Torah, no matter how we understand that elusive concept. "Why is Israel called God's people?" wonder the sages. "Because of the Torah." Rabbi Shimon said: "Before you stood at Sinai and accepted My Torah, you were called 'Israel' just as the other nations are called by simple terms. But after you accepted the Torah at Sinai, you were called, 'My people.'" In another Midrashic passage, the sages state: "If it were not for my Torah that you accepted, I should not recognize you and I should not regard you more than any of the idolatrous nations of the world." Saadia Gaon summed it up succinctly: "Our people is a people solely by virtue of its Torah."

The Jew never regarded the laws of the Torah and Talmud as burdensome. Quite the contrary: It was always seen as a privilege to keep the Divine commandments. "Your statutes have been my song," proclaimed the psalmist (119:54). "The Torah is perfect and refreshing to the soul . . . the command of God is pure and it enlightens the eyes" (Ps 19:8–10). The sages stated emphatically: "The Holy One, blessed be He, wanted to bestow merit on Israel so He endowed them with Torah and a multiplicity of *mitzvot*" (*m. Mak.* 3:16). And the liturgy is equally clear in its gratitude for the commandments as this passage recited before the *Shema* indicates:

"With great love have You loved us, Lord our God . . . Imbue in us the will to understand, to discern, to hearken and to learn, to teach and to obey, to practice and to fulfill in love all the teachings of Your Torah. Deepen our insight into Your Torah and cause our hearts to cling to Your commandments . . ."

There are, theoretically, 613 *mitzvot*—365 negative and 248 positive—many of which are no longer relevant today, such as those connected with sacrifices, Temple worship, ritual purity, and agricultural regulations once observed in Eretz Yisrael. A Jew is expected to observe the relevant *mitzvot* with love and pleasure, *simhah shel mitzvah*, rather than with just fear and trembling (*Sotah* 31a) and without calculating the rewards awaiting the faithful (*Abot* 1:3). A Jew must invest his heart and soul in the service of God and fellow humans, cultivating inwardness, concentration, and intent (*kavvanah*), because "God desires the heart" (*Sanh.* 106b). The medieval ethicist and mystic, Bahya ibn Pakuda, wrote: "Know clearly that the duties of the limbs cannot be performed completely until the heart acquiesces and the soul agrees to do them and our inner impulses direct them." Whenever we perform a mitzvah—whether the eating of bread or the lighting of Sabbath candles or the study of Torah—we pronounce a *berakhah* and in the longer version, we recite a set formula, "Praised are You, Lord our God, King of the universe, who has sanctified us through Your commandments . . ." Moreover, we seek to beautify each mitzvah, to make it as esthetically appealing as possible, whether in the menorah for the Hanukkah candles or the *etrog* we choose to be use at Sukkot time (*hiddur mitzvah*, is the term for the esthetics and beautification of rituals). "This is my God and I will beautify Him" (Exod 15:2). Rabbi Yishmael wondered how it is possible for flesh and blood to beautify his Creator. He suggested that we beautify God through the performance of *mitzvot* and by making them as esthetically beautiful as possible. "I will obtain in His honor a beautiful *lulav* and *etrog* set and build a lovely *sukkah*. I will have made a splendid *tallit* and a fine set of *tefillin*" (*Mek. Shirata*, 2:25 and parallels).

When the apostle Paul defected from Judaism and created a new religion predicated on the belief in Jesus as the Messiah and Son of God, he faced the dilemma of what to do with the Torah and commandments. He was personally deeply ambivalent about following the *mitzvot* so that he could not quite bring himself to shed them entirely. The regimen of the commandments and his own inability to live up to them properly engendered in his soul a sense of guilt and frustration (Gal 3:12 ff.; 1 Thess 2:15–16). But in order to win over the pagan gentiles to the new faith, he knew that many *mitzvot* would have to be discarded, especially circumcision (often confused in the Greco-Roman world with mutilation and even castration) and *kashrut*, the onerous dietary laws. He believed that rabbinic Judaism of his time had overly stressed the letter of the law thereby killing its spirit. Consequently, he highlighted the spiritual over the external aspects of the Jewish religion. By doing so, Paul succeeded in enrolling many in the gentile world into the new Christian faith so that ultimately, by the fourth century C.E., the Roman Empire officially converted to Christianity under Constantine the Great.

In a similar attempt to highlight the spiritual and ethical essence of the Jewish faith nearly two millennia later, the Reform movement in Judaism that began in Europe in the early nineteenth century also deemphasized the importance of rituals such as Sabbath observance and dietary rules. Convinced of the need to "westernize" Jewish rituals and stem the defection of Jews from the ranks, the Reformers gradually diminished the role of the *mitzvot*, deleting *kashrut*, *Shabbat* restriction, festival norms, and rules of marriage and divorce. Rabbi Isaac Mayer Wise, architect of American Reform Judaism, sneeringly refereed to *kashrut* as "kitchen Judaism." Other Reform leaders described rituals such as *yarmulkes* (head coverings for worship) and *tallit* and *tefillin* and Bar Mitzvah rites as "Orientalisms" that had no place in the progressive, modern Western world. By the beginning of the twentieth century, Reform had virtually reduced Judaism to little more than ethical monotheism.

But moods change, and in both the Christian world and Reform Judaism, the need for ritual became ever more apparent. The Catholic Church that had once downgraded Jewish ritual and was founded on the notion of abandonment of *mitzvot* and Jewish ritual, created a whole complex of rituals of its own—rituals that even assumed the importance of sacraments (e.g., communion, baptism, confirmation), and developed a system of Canon law that parallels, in a sense, Talmudic law. The Protestant Reformation that shook the foundations of the Roman Catholic world had propagated the core belief that "*sola gratia, sola fide, sola scriptura*, only grace, only faith, only Scripture count." Martin Luther's revolution tended to slight the ritual laws. But it did not take long for the Protestants to reassess the importance of laws and ritual and reverse their negative attitude on the necessity to the preserve ritual observance. Indeed, John Calvin was positively inclined to the Hebrew Bible and law, and as time passed, many Protestant denominations fashioned their own laws and rules.

Reform Judaism has also had a change of heart and has undergone a radical turn to increasing ritual observance. Hebrew has been restored in much of the Reform liturgy; Bar and Bat Mitzvah ceremonies are almost universal in contemporary Reform synagogues; head coverings and *tallit* are now optional in most temples; festivals and *Shabbat* rules and aspects of *kashrut* long since abandoned have been welcomed back into all but the most classical Reform congregations. Clearly, the Reform movement felt something was lacking in the lives of Reform Jews, something tangible and palpable, some element that enriches Jewish life and celebrates the passage of time in a meaningful and spiritual fashion. And that elusive "something" is—ritual.

What, then, are the functions of ritual in our lives? And why do human beings crave rituals? Of course, for the Orthodox, there is no need to justify the observance of the *mitzvot*. God has commanded us to keep them—end of subject! And we are just wasting our time if we seek a reason or a rationale behind the various commandments. As one rabbinic sage put it, "I have passed a decree, I have legislated a law, and you do not have permission to quibble or question its validity." But that is not the end of the matter; nor does it cut off discussion and speculation. In fact, already in the Torah we detect reasons for the various commandments. The Book of Leviticus connects the *mitzvot* to a sense of holiness and the holy way of life: "You shall be holy, for I, the Lord your God, am holy" (Lev 19:2). Later in chapter 20 of Leviticus, the Torah indicates that holiness implies separation from anything that is morally or ritually repugnant or degrades a human being. The rules of *kashrut* as well as laws advocating sexual purity and sanctioning permitted marriages while proscribing others, were designed to achieve that goal. Since the civilizations and life styles of Israel's neighbors sanctioned the most foul and degrading behavior including child sacrifice, sacred prostitution, and incest, we were expected to separate ourselves utterly from those patterns of behavior: "You shall be holy to Me, for I the Lord am holy, and I have set you apart from the other peoples to be Mine" (20:26). God gave us these rules to elevate us above the animal instincts and drives within the human heart. In so doing, God's laws help us to lead the pure and moral life.

The Bible also instructed us that the sense of holiness (*kedushah*) is cultivated by the perception of God in our lives, and many commandments are designed to do just that. The *tzitzit* (fringes on garments and on the *tallit*) are to remind us constantly of the presence of the Divine and to keep us from sinning (Num 15:39). The *tefillin* and the *mezuzah* serve much the same purpose (Exod 13:9, 16), A person who surrounds himself or herself with Godly symbols engenders a mood of reverence and is apt to lead a holier and a more consecrated life (Deut 6:8 and 11:18).

The sages who fashioned the Talmud and Midrash were equally committed to the notion that there is an underlying purpose or teleology (from the Greek, *telos*, "end, purpose, goal") to the laws. Criminal, civil and domestic laws were designed to protect human dignity (*kevod ha-beriyot*), never to embarrass a person (*shelo le-vayesh*), and to improve and repair society (*tikkun ha-olam*). Ritual laws were guided by these norms and goals, as well as by concern for the transcendent command to save a human life (*pikuah nefesh*), and advancing the ways of peace (*darkhei shalom*). Interreligious relations were constantly informed by the need to avoid enmity (*eivah*), and the importance of fostering an atmosphere of good will and peaceful relations (*mipnei darkei shalom*).

Interestingly, scholars and commentators of every generation detected reasons behind virtually all of the numerous *mitzvot* incumbent upon a Jew. Philo of Alexandria, Egypt (first century B.C.E.) was one of the first to search out rationales for the commandments. Saadia Gaon, Yehudah Halevi, Maimonides, Gersonides, Joseph Albo, Samson Raphael Hirsch, Samuel David Luzzatto—virtually all major thinkers and philosophers were convinced that there is a higher purpose, a teleology to the laws. If we fail to understand the underlying purpose to a specific law, that failing is ours, and continued study will ultimately reveal to us God's purpose in commanding a specific behavioral pattern. Maimonides summed up this approach succinctly and movingly: "The commandments are designed to remove injustice, to teach proper morals that will help improve society, and to convey true beliefs which we should acknowledge either on their own merits or because they help remove injustice and promote morals." In a word, *mitzvot* are crafted to improve human character and establish a just, safe, moral, and peaceful society (*Mishneh Torah, Shabbat* 2:3; *Hanukkah* 4:14; *Guide of the Perplexed*, 3:26–50).

Therefore, I think the *first purpose of the commandments and rituals is to help us lead a holy life*, a life separate and apart from the corruption, moral pollution, and coarser aspects of society. When we perform a mitzvah, we recite the blessing formula that includes the phrase, ". . . Who has sanctified us through His commandments." In observing a mitzvah, we, ourselves, become sanctified, our lives take on holiness, and we inject a sense of the sacred to our mundane existence. We are thus ennobled and raised above the animal; we purify ourselves of the dross within us. The rabbis teach us that the *mitzvot* are the antidote to the evil urge we all possess (*yetzer ha-ra*) (*B. Bat.* 16a; *Qidd.* 30b). In one famous and often-cited passage we read: "What does it matter to God whether we slaughter an animal at the front or back of its neck? But the purpose of the *mitzvot* is really to purify human beings" (*Gen. Rab.* 44:1, 4, pp. 424–25 and parallels).

Closely related to the notion of engendering holiness, is the role of *mitzvot* in *developing our ethical sensitivities*. For example, we develop a reverence for life, both animal and human, when we abide by the laws prohibiting cooking a kid in its mother's milk or from taking the eggs in the nest of the mother bird before her eyes. Likewise, we are required to feed our animals before we take our own meals. When we slaughter our meat for food, we are to utilize the most humane, swiftest and most painless method (*shehitah*) lest we cause the animal needless suffering. These rules, that fall under the rubric of *tzaar baalei hayyim*, "causing pain to living creatures," sensitize us to the preciousness of all of God's creatures.

Rituals also teach us discipline: They infuse in us a sense of self-control so that we learn through the discipline of their repetition, that this is proper and that is improper. The sages share an interesting insight into the disciplinary role of *mitzvot*: "A person should not say, 'I really don't like pork; that's why I refuse to eat it.' No, a person should say, 'I really do like pork; it is a delicacy. But what shall I do? My Master has decreed that it is forbidden to us'" (*Sifra Kedoshim* p. 93d). Unquestionably, the individual who abstains from eating non-kosher food that is temptingly delicious learns discipline. The student who goes through college without eating non-kosher food; the soldier who serves in the armed forces and abstains from violating the Sabbath; the athlete who will not compete on *Shabbat* and *Yom Tov*—have displayed a courage of convictions that is to be admired, for they have transcended appetite and risen to a higher level of self-discipline and holy living. And the businessman who has a chance for a killing in a deal but who holds back because the deal violates Jewish ethical norms, is to be admired as a human being whose service of God transcends the thrust for profit and riches.

Yet another important reason for ritual is that *ritual serves as a means of group survival and a bulwark against assimilation*—especially for a small, insignificant, minority people. The *mitzvot* are a means by which to live as Jews: "You shall keep My laws and My rules by which a person shall live" (Lev 18:5). The sages interpreted this verse to mean, "You shall live by these commandments—and not die in performing them." Herein lies the seed of the great rabbinic teaching of *pikuah nefesh*, that one may violate the Sabbath or Yom Kippur or any other ritual rules to save a life because saving a life takes precedence over all else. But it also indicates that the great goal of the commandments is to keep us alive Jewishly (*Num. Rab.* 17:7). The disease of assimilation can only be warded off by a strong vac-

cine of faith in the form of rituals and commandments that clearly differ-
entiate between a Jew and his non-Jewish neighbor, especially in a society
where the Jew remains a small minority. "More than the Jews preserved the
Sabbath," remarked Ahad Ha-Am, "the Sabbath preserved the Jews." It is
unthinkable that Jews could have survived twenty centuries of *Galut* (exile,
Diaspora) had they not carried with them their portable spiritual homeland and the tools of survival. The "portable homeland" is the Torah and
Jewish learning. The tools of survival are the pattern of rituals, the distinctive Jewish way of life that has set us apart from the majority that always
threatens to overwhelm us in one way or another. Our Hebrew language,
diet, customs, rituals, marital patterns, and festivals—all of these elements
serve as a centripetal force countering the powerful centrifugal forces of
assimilation into the mainstream. No other exiled people ever returned
home; none maintained their integrity as a separate and identifiable minority; all integrated and eventually assimilated into the mainstream. But
not the Jews! Even when we constituted a tiny minority, such as in the
medieval Rhineland towns where Rashi flourished or in modern Polish
shtetls, we were able to swim on the wave of the majority without drown-
ing because of the distinctive Jewish way of life. It was only when barriers
came down and Jews cast off their rituals as in Spain during the fourteenth
and fifteenth centuries and in Western Europe after the Emancipation of
the nineteenth century, that the ranks of our people began to display fis-
sures and crumble.

Each festival engenders in our people, young and old, a sense of linkage to a chain of historical connections and memories that has stretched
back over the centuries to scores of different lands. The lighting of the
Hanukkah menorah does not just commemorate a miracle of ancient
days, but marks a miracle that is occurring today, right now, in this land
and in others as well, *ba-yamin ha-heim, u-vazman ha-zeh*. The Passover
Seder does not simply recall the redemption of our Hebrew ancestors from
Egyptian bondage over 3,000 years ago, but is a dramatic presentation
engaging us all—young and old—in a pageant designed to make us feel as
if "we ourselves were liberated from Egypt." Through such rituals we are
linked vertically and horizontally to the Jewish people. Vertically we link
up with the people of Israel in past generations and centuries; horizontally,
we join hearts and souls with fellow Jews living on a half dozen different
continents and in several score lands. And that, I suggest, is a powerful
incentive for Jewish living.

A famous Talmudic parable (*Ber.* 61b) articulates this position quite
strikingly. In the days of the emperor Hadrian (ca. 132–135 C.E.), it was

forbidden to a Jew to teach Torah or practice Jewish rituals such as circumcision or *Shabbat* on penalty of death. The great sage and martyr, Rabbi Akiva, continued to instruct his students secretly knowing full well that he jeopardized his life. His student, Pappos ben Judah, challenged him: "Master, how can you endanger your life by continuing to teach Torah? Don't you know that the study of Torah is punishable by death? Why don't you save your life and forsake this folly?" Rabbi Akiva replied with a parable. "Once there was a fox that was walking on the banks of a river when he noticed a school of little fish scurrying and swimming for their lives to escape the nets of the fishermen. The fox said, 'Foolish fish, why don't you come up on dry land where you will be perfectly safe from your enemies?' The fish replied: 'Fox, they say you are the wisest of the animals but you are not so clever after all, it seems. True, if we come up on dry land we will be safe from the nets and the large fish that feed on us. But how long will we be able to survive without water?' "Yes," observed Akiva, "were we to give up the waters of Torah we would be safe from predators like the Romans. But how long would we be able to survive as Jews?"

There is yet one other important function served by ritual: *ritual answers human beings' profoundest psychological needs.* Every human craves rituals. The earliest, most primitive Neanderthal at the dawn of history, developed rituals for birth and puberty, marriage and death, hunting season and harvesting. Rituals for diet, sex, purity and impurity appear early in the human saga. Human beings chose shamans or witch doctors or magic workers to tame the forces of nature and intercede with the powers that controlled a person's life and fortunes. Rituals are found among people in every continent, in every clime, in every civilization. A human needs rituals to understand and fathom the unknown, the mysteries of life, of nature, of the universe, of death. A human being also craves a direction for living; he or she needs to mark the great life-cycle events and to celebrate the changes of seasons. Curiously, even the so-called secular or nonreligious elements of society inevitably discover there is a universal craving for ritual among their adherents. Consequently, the Masons fashioned a complex and complicated order of rituals, laws and regulations many of which are secret or mystery rites. Even the now defunct, officially atheist Soviet Union's monstrous masters created their rituals, their festivals, their superheroes, and their cult of the personality. Humans, it seems, cannot escape the need for rituals and regulations, for laws and procedures, anymore than a person can shed the craving for food or sex. A human being does not live by bread or oxygen alone.

But I do not want to give the impression that ritual observances constitute the essence of Judaism or that the punctilious adherence to rituals is an end itself. There is always the danger of smug sanctimoniousness inducing us to believe we've performed the external rituals—we can now do no wrong! That is not the way I understand Judaism and it certainly was not the way our prophets and sages conceived of the role and goal of Jewish laws. Perhaps the greatest contribution of our prophets was their insistence that one must serve both God and fellow humans with honesty, integrity, justice and peace; that ritual cannot be a cover for immoral behavior in human relations; that atoning for sins by empty cultic rituals is hypocrisy of the highest order. Isaiah denounced those who trampled God's court in the Temple and who oppressed the underclass of society. He admonished them, "Cleanse and purify yourselves; seek justice, relieve the oppressed, judge the orphan and plead the cause of the widow" (1:16). He rebuked those who had approached Him with their mouths and honored Him with their lips, but "have kept their heart from Me and its worship of Me has been a commandment of men, learned by rote" (29:13). Second Isaiah excoriated the hypocrites who filled the Temple on Yom Kippur and fasted meticulously but who oppressed their laborers, failed to free the prisoners, feed the hungry, shelter the homeless, and clothe the naked (58:2–7). Amos exclaimed, "I loathe your feasts, I spurn your festivals, I am not appeased by your solemn assemblies. If you offer Me burnt offerings—or your meal offerings—I will not accept them . . ." (5:21). We must not conclude that Amos was against the cult. What he did reject were the fraudulent offerings of Israelites who should have been seeking good, not evil and who neglected the establishment of justice and righteousness. Jeremiah, with enormous courage, stood at the gate of the Temple in Jerusalem and demanded of the people: "Mend your ways and your actions and I will let you dwell in this place. Don't put your trust in illusions and say, 'The Temple of the Lord, the Temple of the Lord, the Temple of the Lord are these buildings.' No, if you really mend your ways and actions and execute justice between one man and another; if you do not oppress the stranger, the orphan, and the widow, if you do not shed the blood of the innocent in this place, then I will let you dwell in this place and in this land" (7:3:ff.).

Building on the great imperative, "Justice, justice shall you pursue" (Deut 16:20), the prophets of Israel became the champions of social justice for all—rich and poor, mighty and humble, great and small—but above all, the underclass of society and most especially, the poor, the orphans, the widows, and the strangers. They did not demean ritual but viewed it as inadequate service of God unless accompanied by social righteousness. This prophetic passion spilled over into the other books of the Bible as well. The psalmist caught the prophetic drive for justice: "Who may sojourn in Your tent, who may dwell on Your holy mountain? He who lives without blame, who does what is right, and in his heart acknowledges truth; whose tongue is not given to evil; who has never done harm to his fellow, or borne reproach for [his acts toward] his neighbor (Ps 15; cf. Ps 24). And Job emphasized that his religion was not merely confined to cultic practices alone: "For I saved the poor man who cried out, the orphan who had none to help him. I received the blessing of the lost; I gladdened the heart of the widow. I clothed myself in righteousness and it robed me; justice was my cloak and turban. I was eyes to the blind and feet to the needy, and I looked into the case of the stranger" (29:12–17; cf. 31:5ff.).

Critics of Judaism have claimed since Christianity's early days, that rabbinic Judaism forsook the prophetic impulse and substituted instead legalism and the interminable minutiae of the halakhah, obscuring the spirituality of Judaism in the process. In its early, classical rendition, the Reform movement of Judaism made similar charges and downgraded the role of *mitzvot* while correctly re-emphasizing the higher significance of ethical and moral behavior. But the fact is the sages never overlooked the importance of the spiritual; never downgraded the importance of the ethical. They drew a distinction between *mitzvot bein adam la-Makom*, commandments between a human and God, and *mitzvot bein adam le-haveiro*, commandments between one human and another (*Sifre Deut. Re'eah* 79, p. 9a). Both categories are God's command; both are incumbent upon us all. We are apt to forget that the same God, who insisted we must keep the Sabbath, also requires us to deal honestly and truthfully, fairly and justly with one another; that "the law of the land is law;" that *glatt* kosher money is every bit as important as *glatt* kosher meat. "'If you will heed the Lord your God diligently, doing what is upright in His sight' (Exod 15:26). This refers to business practices and teaches us that whoever conducts his business practices faithfully so that people are pleased with him, we consider him as if he had observed the entire Torah" (*Mek. Vayasa*, 2:96). The sages pondered the traumatic question: Why were the Temples destroyed? They tell us the First Temple was destroyed because the Israelites violated the three cardinal principles of Judaism: they worshipped idols, they committed murder, and they were guilty of sexual immorality. But in the days of the Second Temple, while they were scrupulous not to breech these three basic rules, they were guilty of baseless hatred (*sinat hinam*). This proves that hatred between humans equals the three cardinal sins (*Yoma* 9b). The same Divine laws that insisted we honor God also demanded that we honor each other. There are innumerable *halakhot* designed to protect *kevod ha-beriyot*, human dignity, ranging from the law that prohibits us from humiliating a person publicly to the rule that a husband must provide for his wife's needs according to her customary status. In fact, the law rules that one may violate negative commandments and abstain from positive ones in order to protect one's dignity and honor (*Ber.* 19b).

But I move one step further and stress that the sages considered ethical *mitzvot* even more important than ritual or cultic ones. Rabbi Benjamin ben Yaphet, in the name of Rabbi Eleazar, observed that idolatry is less serious than murder because one may atone for idolatry but never for taking a human life (*Sanh.* 7a; cf. *Sanh.* 27a). Rav Huna taught: "Whoever occupies himself with the study of Torah alone is like a person without God . . . because he should be performing acts of loving kindness" (*Abod. Zar.* 17b). One day, after the destruction of the Second Temple, Rabban Yohanan ben Zakkai and his disciples passed the smoldering ruins. Rabbi Joshua began to weep and he exclaimed, "Woe is us for we have lost our Temple, the source of our lives that atones for our sins!" Rabban Yohanan consoled him and the disciples and stated: "Do not fear. We have another means of atonement to replace it, as Hosea said, 'For I desire mercy and not sacrifice'" (*Abot R. Nat.* A, 4, p. 21 on Hos 6:6). The law of Yom Kippur mandates that for sins committed between a human and God, Yom Kippur may effect atonement. But for sins between one person and another, Yom Kippur is ineffectual until the person begs forgiveness and makes restitution to the victim. It is noteworthy that in the long list of sins for which we atone on Yom Kippur (the *Al Het*), very few are ritual sins, most are sins between humans, and many deal with sins of the tongue and lips such as slander and gossip. The rabbinic ideal for humans is *imitatio Dei*, emulating God: "You shall be I holy for I, the Lord, am holy" (Lev 19:2). "Just as He is compassionate and merciful, so must you be compassionate and merciful . . . Just as He clothes the naked, visits the sick, comforts the mourners and buries the dead, so shall you do the same" (*Sifre Deut. Ekev*, 49, p. 85a; *Sotah* 14a; *Shabb.* 133b and parallels). We are to emulate God's just and moral, kind and compassionate qualities—never His capacity for anger or punishment. Indeed, Maimonides lists these moral *mitzvot* as the most important because they are included in the rubric of love of neighbor (*Mishneh Torah, Avel*, 14:1).

The highest goal of all in rabbinic thinking is to become finer and nobler humans. Hillel taught: "That which is hateful to you, do not do to your fellow human being. That is the essence of the Torah. Now go and study the rest!" (*Shabb.* 31a and parallels). Rabbi Akiva taught: "'You shall love your neighbor as yourself' (Lev 19:18). That is the great and most inclusive principle of the Torah" (*Sifra Kedoshim* p. 89a). "The world stands on three pillars," said Rabban Shimeon ben Gamaliel, "namely, justice, truth and peace" (*Abot* 1:18). And the greatest blessing of all, the aim of all the laws and rules—is a peaceful society. "There is no greater blessing than peace. For all the blessings end in the word, 'shalom'" (*Sifre Num. Naso*, 42, pp. 12b–13a and parallels).

Am I overstating the matter? I think not: An array of distinguished scholars and peerless sages will buttress my thesis. The great Spanish Bible commentator, Rabbi Abraham ibn Ezra, noted, "The essence of the commandments is to make the human heart upright." The eminent Spanish legal scholar and mystic, Nahmanides, cautioned that one can be a scoundrel within the parameters of the Torah if one observes only the rituals and ignores the ethical commandments. The remarkable compendium of German pietism, *Sefer Hasidim*, edited in the thirteenth century, records: "A person must set aside specific times for study of Torah daily . . . but it is better to have a little fear of Heaven than to act like the multitude of wicked people who study all day and fail to live by the teachings of Torah." The famous mystic and philosopher of Prague, Rabbi Isaiah Horowitz, suggested that the ethical way of life means honest behavior, chastity and high and noble character traits. It means that we must love our fellow humans and be beloved of them; we must be persons of peace as well as people of integrity and honor. Rabbi Moses Haim Luzzatto, the renowned Italian mystic and theologian, summed up the ethical duties of humans in these words: "The saintly and pious people direct their deeds to their contemporaries in order to ennoble them and protect them." Rabbi Israel Salanter, distinguished Talmudist and creator of the *Musar* (ethical) school of thought in Eastern Europe, argued that the individual Jew must correct his or her flaws and improve and refine his or her character thereby creating better people. And Rabbi Leo Baeck, German Reform scholar and survivor of the *Shoah*, insisted that in Judaism "there is no piety without fellow humans." So while Jews are bound to the ritual *mitzvot* for all the reasons stated above and more, they are equally required to uphold the ethical and moral commandments.

How do the various movements in Judaism approach ritual today?

Orthodoxy is fervently committed to ritual, espousing the belief that all *mitzvot*—ritual and ethical—are God's commands. However, while most Orthodox Jews adhere scrupulously to rituals including Sabbath and festivals, *kashrut* and Torah study, there is little reinterpretation of laws in the Orthodox world so that some terrible legal anomalies remain unresolved. For example, the tragedy of the *agunah*, the chained woman who may not remarry because she lacks a *get* (religious divorce) due to the absence of her husband or due to his incalcitrance or meanness, is one of the scandals of Orthodoxy. Critics within the movement, such as Bar-Ilan Professor Daniel Sperber, have decried this "paralysis in contemporary halakhah."

Reform has veered back to much ritual observance, restoring long-ignored *mitzvot* such as Hebrew prayers, head-covering at worship, some aspects of *kashrut*, and various elements of Sabbath laws and practices. But the movement's guiding principle is, "individual autonomy"; each person shall decide for himself or herself whether or not to abide by a particular mitzvah. Understandably, this has created a crazy-quilt pattern of observances impelling the Reform scholar, Rabbi W. Gunther Plaut, to deride the anarchy prevalent among Reform Jews.

Conservative Judaism is officially a "halakhic movement," espousing the notion that halakhah has always been reinterpreted in the light of changing ethical values and socio-economic conditions. At the same time, the vast majority of the laity ignores rituals such as *Shabbat*, *Yom Tov*, and *kashrut*, creating a chasm between rabbis and laity, a chasm that has only widened in recent years. Moreover, there seems to be little difference in patterns of observance between Conservative and Reform Jews so that Seminary Professor Neil Gillman speaks of "the myth" of the Conservative movement as a halakhic movement. But despite this regrettably valid criticism, the movement does aspire to higher levels of ritual observance, and none of the Conservative rabbinic or lay leaders would deny the binding nature of the halakhah and the need to convince the laity of the importance of *mitzvot* such as *Shabbat* and *Yom Tov* observance, private and public worship, and *kashrut*.

The Reconstructionist movement, following Rabbi Mordecai M. Kaplan's teachings, considers rituals merely "folkways and customs"—the creation of human beings and society. The past should have a "vote but not a veto," and the will of the people, *vox populi*, should determine which ritual practices to keep, which to reinterpret, and which to discard totally. Understandably, this has led to a chaotic situation of observances, prompting Reconstructionist scholars, Professors Rebecca Alpert and Jacob Staub, to foster the development of a detailed *Reconstructionist Guide to Jewish Practice*.

I believe that we Jews must retain a system of *mitzvot* for all the reasons stated above and more. Rituals are designed to protect and preserve our people and our principles. We are to "erect a fence around the Torah" to preserve and safeguard the garden within (*Abot* 1:1). We transmit our heritage and teachings via ritual *mitzvot*, the tangible expressions of Jewish identity. We pass these ideals on to the next generation so that we might fulfill our mission. Without the system of commandments by which we are to live, Judaism is reduced to a pale imitation of its authentic self; it is transformed into little more than liberal Christianity minus Jesus. At the same time, however, we Jews are equally committed to the ethical and moral commandments. As I have stressed several times before, we are a teleological people, a people with a purpose and a goal. The ultimate purpose to our existence was stated for us long ago in the Book of Exodus (19:6), "You shall be a kingdom of priests and a holy nation." And Second Isaiah formulated it this way (42:6): "Behold I have appointed you as a covenant people, a light of nations." A. D. Gordon rephrased it beautifully when he urged that we are to become a "people created in the image of God." How do we achieve that goal? There are three cardinal virtues the Jewish people are to exemplify, noted the sages (*Yebam.* 79a): "We are to be compassionate, modest, and perform acts of loving kindness." In upholding these ideals, we sanctify the Divine; in acts of *Kiddush ha-Shem*, we strengthen the *Shekhinah*, God's sacred presence that dwells among us, and we fulfill our sacred destiny.

Points to Ponder:
Why Ritual?

1. If, indeed, Judaism is a religion of law, as the author maintains, how can one ignore the laws of Judaism and yet remain a Jew?

2. Do you agree with Saadia's assessment that our people is a people by virtue of the Torah?

3. The author talks of *hiddur mitzvah*, esthetic presentation of the commandments. Do you think that is an important factor in Jewish living and observance? How can it be strengthened?

4. Reform Judaism had long repudiated the need for rituals. The movement has reversed its direction in recent years and is more positively inclined to rituals. How do you interpret this change?

5. Shall we discard a mitzvah if we fail to find a reason for it?

6. The author suggests that one purpose of the *mitzvot* is to develop our ethical sensitivity. What do we do if a mitzvah violates our ethical sensitivities?

7. What do you think of Ahad Ha-Am's statement, that more than the Jews preserved *Shabbat*, *Shabbat* preserved the Jews?

8. The author suggests that ritual links our people horizontally and vertically. Do you consider that analysis still valid? And is that an adequate motivation for ritual observance?

9. Do you agree that "a human being does not live by bread or oxygen alone"?

10. Nahmanides denounced "scoundrels within the purview of the Torah." What does that mean? Do you know such people? Can you give contemporary examples of such behavior?

11. Some people insist, "I do not keep the rituals but I am a good, honest, and decent individual and that is the essence of religion." How do you react to this point of view?

12. Why do you think that most of the sins listed in the *Al Het* prayer of confession for Yom Kippur are sins between one person and another?

13. Imitating God's ways is the goal of Jewish ethics. Does this appeal to your ethical impulses?

14. The author views *mitzvot* as tangible action-symbols of Jewishness and the best means of transmitting Judaism to the next generation. How do you react to this idea?

9

Why Pray?

PRAYER IS as ancient as humanity. From the earliest times, primordial men and women offered prayers: prayers to various deities, prayers to the ancestral spirits, prayers for rain, prayers for good crops, prayers for victory in battle, prayers for good health, and prayers confessing sins. Invariably accompanied by some type of sacrifice, occasionally human, prayers are as universal as humanity. As William James observed, "Prayer . . . is the very soul and essence of religion." Abraham Joshua Heschel described prayer as an ontological necessity—our very being requires us to pray. According to Heschel, "we pray because we cannot help praying."

How did Jewish prayer develop? When did the prayers, as we know them, take shape? We know that the Bible includes a variety of prayers uttered by various persons in quite different circumstances. Professor Moshe Greenberg delineates four categories of prayer that were already fairly standardized in form and content in the Bible: entreaty, confession, thanksgiving, and blessing. Abraham prayed for the healing of the sick Avimelekh and his harem (Gen 20:7, 17). Moses prayed for his sick sister and brother, Miriam and Aaron, that they might be healed of their leprosy (Num 12:13). Isaiah and Jeremiah prayed for the welfare of Judea in its political struggles and Amos, Jonah, and Habakkuk offered prayers on a variety of occasions. Hannah uttered a silent prayer for a child (1 Sam 1:10), and King Hezekiah prayed that God might heal him of his affliction (2 Kgs 20:2 ff.). Joshua and David prayed for victory in battle while Solomon prayed for Divine wisdom. Daniel prayed three times daily facing Jerusalem (Dan 6:11). There were prayers to be recited when bringing the first fruits to the sanctuary (Deut 26:12 ff.) and there were prayers containing blessings and curses. The three-fold priestly blessing is precious to Jews and Christians (Num 6:24–26), and the parental blessing offered to children is still invoked (Gen 48:20). Many of the Psalms are prayers of various types, most notably prayers of praise of God (*halleluyah*). Above all, the ancient Hebrews believed fervently in a God who responds to prayer when offered sincerely and in purity and truth (Pss 65:3; 145:18).

There are several words in Hebrew for "prayer" but the most popularly used term is *tefillah*, and the verb is *le-hitpalel*, a reflexive verb from the root, *p.l.l.* meaning, "to judge," or "to reflect." Hence, prayer in Hebrew seems to suggest self-judgment: when we pray, we come to God for self-judgment to determine whether we are worthy of a Divine response or not. This is quite a different understanding of prayer than that popular among westerners whose term, "prayer" stems from the Latin meaning "to beg." There are, of course, Jewish prayers begging God for forgiveness or begging for specific blessings (*bakashot*), but they are not the most common type of prayer.

The sages described prayer as "the service of the heart" (*Sifre Deut. Ekev* 41, pp. 87–88; *Ta'an.* 2a–b) and they attributed many of the prayers, including the three daily services, to the Patriarchs (*Ber.* 26b). Maimonides, however, takes a more rational-historical view, suggesting that the basis of prayer is in the Torah (Exod 23:25) and some prayers, such as the grace after meals, are indeed biblical, although the time and forms and numbers of most of the prayers are post-Biblical (*Mishneh Torah, Tefillah*, 1:1). No doubt the Psalms formed the core of the earliest prayers and were supplemented by other passages from the Bible such as the *Shema* (Deut 6:4 ff.). According to rabbinic tradition, the Men of the Great Assembly who flourished sometime between the fifth and the second centuries B.C.E. played a substantial role in formulating many prayers (*Meg.* 17b). Each sage in each age added more prayers of his own invention so that, eventually, the *matbea shel tefillah*, "stamp" or "coin" of prayer, began to emerge in a more formal and standardized version or pattern.

In Temple times, these prayers accompanied sacrifices. When the First Temple was destroyed by the Babylonians in 586 B.C.E. and certainly after the destruction of the Second Temple in 70 C.E. by the Romans, prayer services separate and apart from sacrifices were developed. This marked a revolutionary break with the pagan pattern. The earliest prayer service that accompanied Temple daily sacrifices evidently consisted of the *Barekhu* (call to prayer), the *Shema*, readings from the Torah, Psalms, and other blessings culminating in the priestly benediction (*m. Tamid* 5:1). According to Ezra Fleisher, the early prayers were more formalized and structured. The Talmud records that there were booklets of prayers that circulated among the sages and people, but no formal or canonized version of the prayers existed. Indeed, the prayer pattern was quite flexible and very much in flux for several centuries after the Second Temple was destroyed. At Yavneh, around 90 C.E. and for several decades thereafter, concerted efforts were made to crystallize the prayer service and standardize the blessings and prayers. The *Amidah* prayer (literally, "standing" prayer) was the most important prayer crafted by the Talmudic sages and second in importance only to the *Shema*. Similarly, the sages crystallized the three services held daily in the morning, afternoon, and evening. But the process took more than a few centuries as we know from discovery of Genizah fragments of prayers covering several centuries of development.

Such free-spirited and spontaneous approaches to prayer could not go on indefinitely if chaos and anarchy were to be avoided. As the Jewish dispersion widened, the need for a standardized or canonized liturgy became more acute. In 865, Amram Gaon of Sura, Babylonia, sent notes on the order of the prayers, which he called *Seder* (order), to the Jewish community of Lucena, Spain, to guide the members in their search for a proper order of the service. The great philosopher and rabbinic scholar, Saadia Gaon of Sura (882–942), composed his version of the prayers that he called, *Siddur*, with Arabic notes and commentary. Various versions of the prayers were compiled in the Rhineland for Franco-German Jewry in the eleventh century, in Italy, in the Land of Israel in the sixteenth century by the kabbalist school of Rabbi Isaac Luria, and in Hasidic circles in the early nineteenth century in Eastern Europe. And so, the ordering of the prayer service took shape. Each country fashioned its own peculiar liturgy and melodic lines (*nusah*), and *minhagim* or "customs." But the basic *matbea shel tefillah* is essentially the same. Until modern days, a Jew could feel reasonably at home in a synagogue in Yemen or Italy, France or Poland, New York or Jerusalem despite the differences in melodies and wording, especially between Sephardic (Spanish-Portuguese), Middle Eastern (such as found among Jews in the Mediterranean basin and Middle East) and Ashkenazic worship (German, Polish, Austro-Hungarian, Russian), provided he or she knew how to read Hebrew.

The prayers adopted as the official liturgy of Judaism consist of a variety of types. Most of the prayers come from the Psalms or other books of the Bible. Many prayers are praises of God and His holy name. Others are petitionary prayers, asking of God the granting of our request for life, health, food, happiness, prosperity, and peace. Indeed, the nineteen benedictions of the daily *Amidah* are essentially all requests: we ask God to grant us wisdom, forgiveness of sins, redemption from our enemies and restoration to Zion and Jerusalem, healing, blessings for the crops and land, justice and messianic redemption for Israel and the world, and peace for Israel and humanity. Curiously, these requests are eliminated from the

Amidah on Sabbaths and festivals when, perhaps, it is viewed as inappropriate to introduce prayers for personal requests into the liturgy with one exception: the prayer for peace which is never deleted from the services. Some prayers are confessions of sin. Others, notably the *berakhot*, are benedictions to God expressing our gratitude for bread or wine, fruits or vegetables, health or release from peril. In fact, one rabbi suggested that we recite 100 such blessings daily (*Menah.* 43b). There are also prayers that are not really prayers but are affirmations of some basic Jewish beliefs or principles, ideals or standards. The *Shema* is a perfect example: it is a section of the Torah (Deut 6:4 ff.) and it is a statement of belief in one God alone. It is so important and basic, that it is recited several times daily, upon wakening in the morning and retiring at night, and on a person's deathbed. Another such example is a rabbinic prayer, *modim*, recited at each service and acknowledging the existence of God who performs the daily miracles of life, in whose hands are all souls, the source of compassion. And we should not forget that Torah study is an integral part of worship, whether in the reading of the weekly Torah portion on Mondays, Thursdays, and Saturdays, or as a result of the insertion of rabbinic passages for study taken from the Talmud. Study in Judaism is viewed as superior even to prayer. Actually, the study of Torah equals all other *mitzvot*.

Starting from the sixth century or so, poets (*paytanim*) began to insert sacred poems or *piyyutim* (from the Greek, "poetry") into various parts of the service. These insertions, generally the works of synagogue *hazzanim* or cantors, but sometimes the creative genius of great scholars such as Saadia Gaon and Yehudah Halevi, were designed to heighten the sense of awe and spirituality among the worshipers and to showcase various prayers that were considered particularly sacred and vital. Interestingly, Maimonides vehemently objected to *piyyutim*, and in at least three different works, he denounced them as illegal interruptions of the liturgy and poetic nonsense. But the masses overruled the great sage of Fustat, and *piyyutim* are recited in their amplitude in Orthodox congregations, although Reform and Conservative synagogues have shortened, deleted, or replaced many of them, sometimes substituting modern poetic creations.

The liturgy in Judaism developed in tandem with the emergence of the synagogue—one of the more remarkable creations of Judaism and one of its greatest legacies to the western world. Indeed, the synagogue is the oldest extant institution of the western world. Precisely when it originated is shrouded in mystery. Did it develop after the Babylonians destroyed the First Temple and exiled the people to Babylonia? Or are its roots in the Hellenistic period? Or did it not assume the present form until Roman times? The earliest mention of a synagogue is a papyrus from Egypt dating to the third century B.C.E. There is, moreover, abundant epigraphic and archaeological evidence for the existence of synagogues in the Second Temple period. The synagogue was usually called by the Greek name, *synagoge*, house of gathering, or, more commonly in the Diaspora, *proseuche*, house of prayer. There are at least four known synagogues in the Land of Israel that pre-date 70 B.C.E. and the destruction of the Second Temple by the Romans; the oldest is at Gamla and dates from the first century B.C.E. There are numerous remains of synagogues in Israel from after the destruction of the Temple in at least 100 places such as Capernaum, Bet Alpha, and Bet Shean with 30 in the Golan Heights alone. The Diaspora synagogues are older then those in Israel, for the obvious reason that the people of Israel focused on the Temple as the locus of their worship; hence, there was little or no need to develop synagogues, unlike the need in the Diaspora communities. Synagogue ruins have been found in diverse places such as Ostia, Italy, Egypt, Delos, Greece, and Sardis, Turkey. Over 200 identifiable remains have been uncovered from the Greco-Roman period alone. Indeed, Professor Lee Levine's magisterial volume, *The Ancient Synagogue*, runs to 758 pages and only covers the period up to the end of antiquity. The synagogue was designed to supplement and later on to replace the Temple as the focal point of Jewish worship. Once the Second Temple was laid waste, the synagogue became the sole means of religious worship. It alone could fill the people's spiritual need and instill in them the courage to carry on as Jews even without Temple, Jerusalem, and homeland. Had it not been for the synagogue, Israel would have, like so many other captive nations before, disappeared from the stage of history.

The synagogue was a radical institution in several ways. First, it was a place of worship without sacrifices—a striking departure from the norm of the ancient world. Second, it was a democratic institution. Whereas the Temple and the sacrificial cult were in the control of the aristocratic priests who alone could offer the sacrifices and who inherited their office, and the Levites who chanted the Psalms, in the synagogue any lay person who was knowledgeable could lead the service and read the Torah, and every Israelite including the humblest artisan or farmer could serve as the messenger of the community to God. The old caste system of Temple worship was finished once and for all with the emergence of the synagogue, and except in a few minor areas, all distinctions between the priestly caste of *kohanim* or priests and their assistants, the Levites, and the average, ordinary Israelite were abolished. Ironically, as Professor Reuven Kimelman has pointed out, the elements of the Temple discarded by Judaism resurfaced in Christianity—viz., the priestly officiants at the mass to the exclusion of the laity, sacrifice and the communion meal, incense, the altar, and other Temple protocols.

Early on, the functions of the synagogue were delineated, and these were remarkably varied. It quickly became a house of the gathering of the people (*beit knesset*), sometimes for secular and political purposes, a house of worship (*beit tefillah*), and a house of study (*beit midrash*). Seth Schwartz, in his *Imperialism and Jewish Society*, argues that the prayer aspect only assumed prime importance much later on, perhaps as late as the fourth and fifth centuries when the synagogue truly became the central Jewish institution. Curiously, the most popular term for synagogue among Ashkenazi Jews has become, *shul*, school, and similarly among Italian Jews who frequently refer to their synagogue as a *scuola*. Doubtlessly, this is indicative of the primacy of the educational aspect of the synagogue. An ancient inscription from the first century C.E. in Jerusalem provides us with an ample portrait of the role of the synagogue in antiquity. The Theodotus Inscription reads:

> Theodotus, the son of Vettenos, priest and archysynagogos [president], grandson of archysynagogos, built this synagogue for the reading of the Torah and the study of the commandments and a guest house and rooms, and water installations for hosting those from abroad, it having been founded by his fathers, the presbyters [elders] and Simonides.

Other evidence exists indicating that besides being a house of study and prayers, sermons were delivered regularly, a *mikveh* (ritual pool) was installed on the premises, charity monies were collected for the Temple of Jerusalem and for a host of charitable endeavors and stored in the safe of the synagogue, meetings on communal and political matters were convened in the synagogue, rooms were attached as a hostel for wayfarers, and kitchen and communal banquet facilities were also installed. Early on, therefore, the synagogue was a synagogue center—quite a modern concept!

Throughout the ages, little changed in the synagogue. To be sure, the outside architecture reflected the milieu. The thirteenth-century Altneushule in Prague is in the Gothic style. The synagogues in Italy are in the Renaissance, Baroque and Rococo mode. Elsewhere, Romanesque and Moorish architecture prevailed, whereas in Poland, wooden synagogues were popular. Medieval synagogues were often built like stone fortresses, for obvious reasons. The Touro Synagogue of Newport Rhode Island in the United States is in Colonial style. And the Beth Shalom Synagogue in the Philadelphia suburb of Elkins Park is the ultra-modern creation of Frank Lloyd Wright. If the exterior of the synagogue changed, depending on the architectural mood of the day, the interior changed but little. The *bimah* or reading stand was invariably found in the center of the congregation while the *Aron Kodesh* (Holy Ark) was up against the wall in the front, generally on the eastern wall facing the Holy Land.

The importance of the synagogue may be measured by the remarkably potent fact that in the United States alone, according to the 2001 study of the *American Jewish Yearbook*, there were over 3,700 synagogues and 43 percent, or roughly 2.6 million American Jews currently belong to a synagogue. This is in stark contrast to the tens of thousands of women who are members of Hadassah or the several thousand affiliated with the American Jewish Committee or the Anti-Defamation League. They are all wonderfully vital organizations that make substantial contributions to Jewish life. But the masses still view the synagogue as the one and most enduringly authentic institution of Jewish life.

Modernity has challenged our understanding of the nature of prayer and the role of the synagogue in Jewish life. Europe's Enlightenment movement undermined many tenets and principles that had guided Jewish life for centuries. Because of philosophical, theological, and psychological factors, the classical Jewish liturgy just could not satisfy the needs of all but the Orthodox community.

The philosophical problem stems from the very nature of modern thinking. We live in an age of science. After Newton and Copernicus and Einstein, we tend to view the universe as a complex of unchanging, immutable laws of gravity, light, heat, sound, nature, the rotation of the cosmic spheres, and other biological, chemical, and physical phenomena. In such a universe, prayer seems inappropriate and irrelevant; no prayer can affect the cosmos. The very idea of Joshua praying to God to make the sun stand still flies in the face of all we know of the laws of physics and astronomy. Such an intervention into the laws of the spheres should be a physical impossibility. And the notion of praying to God for rain or sunshine or some other manipulation of the natural order seems preposterous to us moderns. Consequently, a petitionary prayer (*bakashah)* would be ludicrous and a laudatory prayer (*tehillah)* would be superfluous.

The theological difficulty is simply this: People no longer believe in a "God who hears our prayers and petitions" (*El shomea tefilot ve-tahanunim*, as the daily *Amidah* puts it) because many accept the notion of a transcendental, rather than an immanent Deity. If we did advocate an immanent concept of the Deity, we would be nudging and badgering Him hourly, daily, much as many high school football and basketball players do prior to their games. But as Einstein suggested, "He [God] does not play dice with the universe." He has better things to do than hearken to the petitions and requests of individual men and women who, in the grand scheme of things, are but flecks on the universal canvas. It is a supreme chutzpah on our part to believe that God is cognizant of or interested in our personal needs and requests or requires our songs of praise. So our fundamental difficulty is not bad prayer but bad theology: Either we arrogantly assume that God is cognizant of our prayers or we ask the impossible of Him when we finally do pray. There are other theological issues of somewhat lesser importance but controversial nonetheless. Most modern Jews reject the traditional notion of resurrection of the dead; of a personal messiah; of a restoration of animal sacrifices in a rebuilt Temple in Jerusalem. Many also spurn the idea that Israel is God's chosen people. These theological qualms, added to the basic one of a God who does or does not respond to human prayers, increased the degree of theological misgivings that have rendered traditional liturgy irrelevant and obsolete for the masses.

The third problem is psychological. We moderns have no feeling of awe or wonder, amazement or reverence. We also lack a sense of gratitude. And since that is what a *berakhah* is all about, is it any wonder that we have trouble reciting blessings or offering thanksgiving? To be sure, we run to ask the rabbi to offer prayers for us when we are in anguish, when a dear one is ill, when we are beleaguered by business or personal problems. And we come in mourning to recite the *Kaddish* or say *Yizkor*, although I detect a decline even in those hallowed practices. But we rarely sing God's praises or thank Him for the miracle of daily life, for significant milestones reached, or rejoice with God in the gift of life. In short, *we are not a praying people because our age is too sophisticated for davening.* Mark Twain observed that Jews are like all other people—only more so. Consequently, Jews lead the way of the sophisticated and set the pace for others.

As Jews entered the modern era, they attempted to meet the challenge of the new thinking established by the Enlightenment in Western Europe and accept the invitation to become equal citizens offered by the Emancipation. A number of modern religious movements emerged in Judaism in an attempt to counter the assaults on Jewish beliefs and practices and reinterpret Jewish norms to make it feasible for the modern Jew to retain Jewish practices while living in the modern world. The Reform movement began in Germany in the early nineteenth century and spread to America somewhat later. It revolutionized the traditional understanding of prayer and the synagogue. Anxious to be accepted into the western world with its stress on reason and rationalism, it sought to extirpate all vestiges of "Orientalism" in Jewish worship and banish every trace of mysticism in obvious emulation of the Protestant service. The interior of the synagogue was changed so that the *bimah* was moved to the front of the synagogue next to the Ark and the rabbi and cantor officiated there rather than in the center of the congregation. A mixed-voice choir and organ were often added to enhance the service and the rabbi preached in the vernacular. The *yarmulke* (head-covering) and *tallit* (prayer shawl) were discarded from most Reform congregations. The traditional *nusah* (liturgy) of the chants was overhauled and western-style musical compositions were introduced. The more traditional, florid cantillations and chants were either revised or discarded completely. Even the amount of Hebrew was severely curtailed so that the *Union Prayer Book* of 1894 was almost entirely in English. It was argued that by praying in the vernacular, Jews would understand their prayers and be inclined to join in public worship. The Reformers also objected to the idea of restoration of the Jewish people to Zion along with the reinstitution of sacrifices in the Temple, so they removed all such references from the service. Likewise, they rejected the notion of a personal messiah and resurrection of the dead and these concepts were similarly expunged. In effect, they abolished the *matbea shel tefillah.*

But the Reform movement learned that these innovations were hardly the panacea for the absence of worshipers and poor attendance at services on Sabbaths and festivals. By the 1970s, the Reform movement totally revised its old *Union Prayer Book* with a series of boldly innovative liturgical works spearheaded by *Gates of Prayer, Shaarei Tefillah,* mostly the creative endeavors of Rabbi Chaim Stern, assisted by Professor Lawrence Hoffman and others. Much of the Hebrew was restored, in keeping with the new turn to tradition of the Reform movement. New prayers were added for special occasions. Long discarded notions such as the yearning to rebuild Zion and support for the State of Israel found their way back into the liturgy. A choice of several different types of services for the Sabbath was offered the worshiper to avoid rendering the prayers stale and repetitive. Most of the Reform congregations adopted the new works; a few of the "classical" Reform temples held on to the *Union Prayer Book.* Nor is the process complete: The Reform movement has recently prepared yet another update of its liturgy exhibiting greater gender sensitivity with a new *Siddur* titled, *Mishkan T'filah.*

The Conservative movement, true to its name, was much more reticent about changing the liturgy. True, men and women sit together, unlike the Orthodox *shuls* where a *mehitzah* (curtain, partition) separates the men from the women; some Conservative synagogues use an organ or mixed-voice choir; many of the prayers are recited in English as well as in Hebrew, and the services have been noticeably shortened. But tampering with the prayers had, until recently, been tightly limited. The three criteria that guided the Liturgy Commission (1946) were: 1. continuity with tradition; 2. relevance to the needs and ideals of our generation; and, 3. intellectual integrity. Consequently, the surgery on the prayers has not been radical until the 1986 *Siddur Sim Shalom*. References to the sacrificial cult were retained, although the verb praying for their restoration was changed to the past tense; here or there a word was inserted or deleted to give the prayers a more universal and less particular flavor; some new poetry and prose material was added; some of the prolix and unintelligible *piyyutim* were shortened or deleted. Material on the Holocaust and the State of Israel was added along with transliterations. Still, dissatisfaction simmered and a new version of the *Siddur Sim Shalom* (1996) was issued that exhibited more radical tendencies and a discernable influence of the women's movement so that the classical rabbinic prayer opening the *Amidah* which refers to the Patriarchs, Abraham, Isaac and Jacob now includes the Matriarchs, Sarah, Rebecca, Rachel and Leah and is gender sensitive in its language.

Rabbi Mordecai M. Kaplan, founder of the Reconstructionist movement, was a religious rationalist who denied supernaturalism and the idea of the chosen people. Consequently, he stripped the references to chosen people from the prayers and introduced a naturalistic-humanistic concept of the Deity in his translations, while he deleted the notion of a personal messiah. Reconstructionists under Dr. Kaplan's guidance strove for intellectual clarity in their prayers as well as rationalism. The first Reconstructionist *Siddur* that served the movement for half a century deleted references to a personal messiah and chosen people in keeping with Kaplan's theological position. However, his love for Hebrew and deep commitment to the Zionist ideal and the rebuilding of the State of Israel made it unthinkable for him to drop these notions and follow the Reform lead. The recently produced prayer book follows the older pattern but has allowed the chosen people concept to creep back into the prayers ever so surreptitiously.

And what have been the results of all this frenetic creativity and radical surgery to our liturgy? Sad to say, Jews still don't pray, despite all our ingenuity, creativity, and gender-sensitive innovations. Solomon Schechter once quipped that in former days when Jews prayed, *one* prayer book sufficed. Now that they no longer pray, we have many different editions of the prayer book. Our synagogues and temples are generally empty except on the High Holidays. Only about eleven percent worships regularly—the lowest percentage of all the American religious groups. And when synagogue seats are, on those rare occasions, filled, they are peopled by silent spectators. The greatest spectator sport of all is not baseball or football but worship. Rabbis orate; cantors chant; choirs and organs make music; but the average Jew remains silent. We have developed what Abraham Joshua Heschel called, "prayer by proxy."

Yet, despite the challenges of modernity, there are Jews who pray daily and fervently, for whom it would be unthinkable to allow a day to pass without donning *tefillin* and *tallit* or a Sabbath without attending services in *shul*. For them, the theological, psychological, and philosophical qualms that roil so many contemporary Jews seem irrelevant. Why? How shall we explain this behavior pattern? The answer is: They believe it is a mitzvah, a positive obligation and duty, a Divine command to pray not once but three times daily and to utter appropriate *berakhot* over foods or drink or when spying a rainbow or meeting a head of state. For people of this mind-set, there is no challenge about relevance of a prayer or whether a prayer satisfies "modern people's" thinking or theology or philosophical orientation. The trappings of worship are unimportant; the beauty of the sanctuary of peripheral interest. Some of the most fervent and passionate prayers have been uttered in the most unpretentious and least esthetic surroundings. Whether there is or isn't a choir or organ is irrelevant, just as the language of prayer is secondary. Even if one is not fluent in Hebrew and can only read by rote, one prays as it is commanded. It is not even an issue whether there is a hearing, responding Deity who harkens to human prayers. There is only one question here: Did or did not God command us to pray? If God did, then the rest follows ineluctably. For the Orthodox Jew, as for the believing Christian or Muslim, there are no theological or philosophical or psychological considerations to be reckoned with, and certainly no irrelevant esthetic considerations such as the beauty of the house of worship, the magnificence of the cantor's voice, or the intellectual and oratorical skills of the preachers. Orthodox Jews are basically untroubled in their liturgical habits. The great Talmudic scholar, Rabbi Joseph B. Soloveitchik, was harshly critical of those who would tamper with the prayers, avowing a belief in their eternal sanctity. Even the liberal Orthodox Rabbi Emanuel Rackman described those who revise the liturgy as "arrogant." If one believes in a commanding God, one prays—period.

How can we get modern Jews who do not subscribe to this fundamentalist view to pray? What steps can we take to cultivate a prayerful attitude among our people? I believe there are several concrete strategies we might adopt to alleviate the problem.

First, technically we must remove the language barrier; we must learn Hebrew, at least sufficiently well to read and understand the basic vocabulary of the prayer book which is not, after all, that extensive. Rabbi Eric Yoffie, president of the Union for Reform Judaism, describes the Hebrew language as "the great democratic tool of Jewish worship." It is a national blight and disgrace that we American Jews, the most educated and learned, cultured and literate community in all Jewish history in secular matters, are so illiterate and ignorant in a Hebraic sense. It is galling to note that the latest editions of the Conservative *Siddur* and *Mahzor* retain transliteration of prayers. After all, Solomon Schechter had launched a campaign to promote Hebrew literacy among Jews almost a century ago. And here we are, still wrestling with Hebrew illiteracy in the twenty-first century! It does not say much for the quality of Hebrew education for children or adults if transliteration and translation of our classics are still *de rigueur*. It is true that halakhah rules that only a few basic prayers must be recited in Hebrew; that even the *Shema* may be recited in any language the person understands best (*m. Sotah* 7:1 & 2; *Shulhan Arukh, Orah Hayim* 101:4). Even the Passover *Haggadah* may be read in the vernacular. Clearly, the sages who laid down these rulings were more concerned with comprehension than with the technical requirement of utilizing Hebrew, the Holy Tongue. But if we cannot read our classics in the original, if we can only study the Bible or read our prayers in translation, what can we expect of our future? Reading in translation, observed Chaim Nachman Bialik, is like kissing a woman through a veil. Too much is lost; too many of the nuances missed. Besides, language is a psychological and sociological element in a civilization that cannot be sufficiently stressed. It is an adhesive glue that causes adherents to cling together. There is no gainsaying the fact that when a Jew walks into a synagogue in Hong Hong or Hawaii, Johannesburg or Jerusalem, he or she is comfortable because the *lingua franca* is the same Hebrew universally. There is also a mystique to language that translation cannot quite convey, no matter how expert. Catholics have discovered this especially since the Latin Mass has been replaced by the vernacular. Somehow, *Kol Nidrei, Kaddish, Shema, Adon Olam*—just to mention a few—never quite touch the heart in translation as in the original Hebrew or Aramaic. So the first priority for us should be, in my view: stamp out Hebrew illiteracy.

Second, we ought not to be dissuaded from revising, shortening, adding to, updating our prayers. After all, the Bible is God's word to humans but the prayers are human's word to God. They are human creations. To be sure, their creators were extraordinarily spiritual men and women who through the ages nurtured and developed a liturgy that has inspired and uplifted Jews for millennia. But they are unequivocally human creations. If prayers are no longer relevant (such as the lengthy sections on animal sacrifices in the Temple era), then they ought to be revised or deleted. If they seem to be discriminatory against people or individuals (such as the blessing "for not having made me a woman"), they need to be revised or excised. Integrity and honesty must be our guides: If we can no longer recite certain prayers because they are obsolete or at variance with our deeply felt convictions, they must be revised or discarded. Samuel David Luzzatto, the encyclopedic nineteenth-century Italian scholar, who was not a religious liberal, wrote in the introduction to his edition of the Roman *Mahzor:* "Our elders did not intend to establish a fixed liturgy that would be as rigid as an unmovable pillar to which no additions or deletions were permitted. They merely wished to give us the basis on which to praise and pray to God . . . ."

Moreover, the *Shulhan Arukh* ruled (*Orah Hayyim* 1:4), "Better fewer prayers with more *kavvanah* (devotion, inwardness, intention) than more prayers with less *kavvanah*" Sometimes repetition is needed to drive home an important lesson to the worshiper. But needless prolixity and repetitiveness can become boring, tedious and counterproductive. Rabbi Soloveitchik would not allow a *hazzan* to repeat any of the Hebrew words in the liturgy. After all, how many times can we praise God and how many adjectives can we invoke in that process? The Talmud records a funny story of a *hazzan* who led the service in the presence of Rabbi Haninah. He piled on the epithets and adjectives of praise to God so extravagantly that Rabbi Haninah chided him sarcastically saying, "And have you exhausted all of the praises of God?" (*Ber.* 33b).

Nor should we, I believe, shy away from novelty and innovations in prayers. Let us recall that the Palestinian prayer tradition was much more creative and innovative than the Babylonian tradition. For example, Rabbi Aha insisted that worshipers should compose a new prayer every day (*y. Ber.* 4:3, 8a). That may be an exaggeration as well as a spiritual impossibility. But it certainly is a challenge to our religious ingenuity as well as a license to free ourselves from some of the limiting restraints of the past. After all, the psalmist on several occasions urged us to "sing a new song unto the Lord" (Pss 96:1 & 149:1). Obviously, *payyetanim* took this seriously and created an enormous body of *piyyutim* that stud the services, especially on the festivals.

At the same time, we must strive to preserve the essential "stamp of prayer" and essence of tradition and beware slavish imitation of the *Zeitgeist*, the mood of the hour and the passing fads and fickle trends. Today's relevancy can be tomorrow's absurdity. Just thumb through some of the "Freedom *Haggadot*" of the 1960s or the loose-leaf *Mahzorim* of those days, and you cannot help but smile at how naively irrelevant and outdated these works which seemed so vital then, appear to us these days. Back in the 1960s and early 1970s, jazz services attracted national attention as synagogues turned to a new style to attract young people. Today, I doubt if any even remember those radical efforts. Moreover, do we really require a new *Siddur* or *Mahzor* or *Haggadah* every five or ten years? Has our understanding of God and humanity and the world so changed that we need to change the liturgy like a suit or dress? Is "political correctness" to be the arbiter of our prayer services? Solomon Schechter wrote that there is something better than modernity, namely eternity. Consequently, I believe it is essential that we curb our creative instincts to the degree that we learn to strike a delicate balance between tradition and change, between the classical model and the latest version.

The great goal of prayer is to develop a reverential, prayerful mood and cultivate, what the sages called, *kavvanah*. This is one of those Hebrew terms not readily translated. Its root meaning is, "direction." When applied to prayer it means, "inwardness, intention, devotion." The goal of all prayers is to heighten the amount of *kavvanah* so that prayer is more than just a chore, more than a mere rote exercise. The sages cautioned us (*Abot* 2:13; *m. Ber.* 4:4) never to allow our prayers to become a load or burden; rather, they should be a spiritual direction or channel to God. Prayer without *kavvanah* is like a body without a soul, runs one aphorism. That charming anthology, *Sefer Hasidim*, edited in Germany around the year 1200, tells of a pious but untutored shepherd who used to pray daily with great fervor and intensity, "God, if You have any sheep I should be most happy to tend them for You." And God took delight in this simple prayer. A sage overheard this simple and naive prayer and was scandalized. He berated the shepherd for his blasphemy and resolved to teach him to recite the *Shema* properly, which he did. A few days later, God came to him in a dream and berated him for ruining the sincere prayer of the humble shepherd. The next day, the sage went to the shepherd, told him of his dream, and urged the shepherd to return to reciting his own little prayer. Although we should sincerely strive for *kavvanah* and freshness in prayer, it is a mistake to argue, "I'll pray when the spirit moves me." As Israel Abrahams, observed, "What can be done at any time and in any manner is apt to be done at no time and in no manner." Yes, we want to avoid rote worship and insipid prayers; but without the framework of liturgy, the chances are we will never be in a prayerful mood except in moments of crisis when "foxhole religion" takes over.

There are several techniques we might apply to deepen our sense of *kavvanah*. For example, the early pietists would prepare themselves for prayers by meditation and study before worship (*m. Ber.* 5:1 & 32a). We should encourage people to study sacred texts or uplifting Torah passages or rabbinic teachings to put them in the mood for worship. Additionally, we must cultivate a special inner mood to enable us to worship. "Know before Whom you stand" is a saying based on the Talmud (*Sanh.* 22a) often found on the top of the Holy Ark in the synagogue. We are to recite the *Amidah*, noted the sages, when in a reverential and serious mood. We must never come to God with impure hands or sullied hearts (Ps 15). And it is wrong of us to seek to use prayers to manipulate the Deity—to extract a sort of quid pro quo bargain and expect Him to reward our fervent prayers (*B. Bat.* 164b & Rashbam ad loc.). Rabbi Isaac Luria, the great sixteenth-century kabbalist, would recite a series of *kavvanot* (meditations) he composed or borrowed from the Zohar and indulge in various spiritual exercises in order to put himself and his disciples in a prayerful mood, and the Hasidic rebbes instruct their disciples to do the same. One cannot just plunge into worship without some spiritual and intellectual preparation.

Additionally, our sages urged that we focus on specific ideas or concepts or geographic places or sacred scenes in order to focus our minds on prayers. "He who prays must direct his heart to heaven," they urge (*Ber.* 31a). "One who prays must imagine that the *Shekhinah* (God's sacred presence) is facing him" (*Sanh.* 32a). The sages suggested that when reciting the *Shema* the worshiper should fix his or her mind on the notion of God in the heavens and earth, east and west, north and south in order to instill a greater sense of Godhood (*Ber.* 13b & Rashi ad loc.). I try to envision the Western Wall when reciting the *Shema* to shut out mental distractions and concentrate on the unity and universality of God. Biofeedback has convinced us that by mentally concentrating on certain images we can raise the body temperature and achieve a higher level of relaxation. So the idea of mental imaging clearly has value in heightening a worshipful mood.

I also believe quite fervently that we must sing; that music, tunes, *niggunim*, melodies are vital to meaningful worship and heightened *kavvanah*. "Sing unto the Lord a new song," urged the psalmist (Pss 96:1 & 149:1). I have found the most uplifting and exhilarating services are participatory services in which all the people join in and blend their voices in song. As Rabbi Eric Yoffie put it, in calling for a revolution in the Reform movement's understanding of prayer, "We yearn to sing to God and let our souls fly free." That is perhaps, the secret of success of Camp Ramah services or Eisner Camp worship or the various Orthodox camps: Children, as well as counselors, enjoy blending their voices in common song. This is not to suggest that we indulge in cheap or vulgar, low-brow tunes. But I do suggest that there are wonderful old as well as new and Israeli tunes of sufficient caliber and attractiveness to encourage congregational participation and chanting. In this regard, Rabbi Shlomo Carlebach deserves much credit for popularizing tunes (many with a Hasidic flavor) that we hear in all kinds of synagogues of the various streams. I have always been affected by the singing in African-American churches where I have truly felt spiritually uplifted. And there are chants and hymns in Catholic and Protestant churches that all but raise the rafters in rollicking rhythm as the congregation joins in. Likewise, nothing can compare to a synagogue service that engages the participation of the bulk of the congregants. Conversely, nothing chills the soul more completely than a service monopolized by the professionals with a deadly silent group of worshipers. So I think that the more we sing at services, the more we seem to enjoy them. The days of the prima donna cantor and soloists, choirs and professionals are over: our people want to, need to sing.

One of the popular challenges to those who advocate prayer is: Are prayers efficacious? Does God answer our prayers? Or are we just praying to ourselves or shouting into the storm? The traditional view, of course, is that God does respond to genuinely sincere prayers. Indeed, the sages teach that God "yearns for the prayers of the righteous." The Bible records God responding to prayers and performing miracles for Moses and Joshua and a variety of prophets. And the Talmud tells of the saintly Honi Ha-Meagel whose prayers were efficacious in bringing rain. But even Maimonides (in his *Guide of the Perplexed*) expressed reservations about this understanding of prayer. He wrote that since God is all-perfect, He is not in need of our prayers which can neither add to nor diminish from His perfection. Hence, worship perfects us—not God. And as I mentioned earlier, modern men and women are generally skeptical that our prayers for rain or sun, victory in war, or healing of the sick are truly effective.

These challenges to our notion of efficacious prayers are grave and weighty. Rabbi Mordecai M. Kaplan, who was a religious naturalist and opposed to anything smacking of supernaturalism or irrational thinking, rejected the view that God can be swayed by our prayers. We pray to our higher selves, he maintained, as we seek to stimulate the latent potential that is within each and every human being. By constantly highlighting values such as love, justice, moral behavior and peace in our prayers, we activate the higher selves within us and impel ourselves to work for the realization of these ideals. But there are shortcomings to this approach to prayer, as Abraham Joshua Heschel noted. This view of prayer reduces it to "solipsism or auto-suggestion." Kaplan's interpretation of the meaning of prayer smacks of anthropolatry or the worship of humans—a form of idolatry, in my judgment.

We might view the value of prayer from a different perspective. There is an increasing body of reputable scientists who believe there is a therapeutic value to prayer; that prayer can affect the worshiper's emotional, psychological, and physical state. The great physiologist, Dr. Alexis Carrel, observed that "certain spiritual activities may cause anatomical as well as functional modifications of the tissues and organs" and prayer is definitely one of those activities. Dr. Larry Dossey and Dr. Jerome Groopman, both eminent physicians and research scientists, invoke the power of prayer in the healing process. The electrical genius, Charles Steinmetz, urged us to study prayer because "it is the greatest power on earth." Doubtlessly, this must be the main cause of the remarkable cures reported at shrines such as Lourdes. The more we have come to appreciate the emotional and psychological factors in human health and disease, the more we have come to appreciate that the spiritual dimension does play a potentially pivotal role in mental and physical health.

Prayers are efficacious if, by enunciating our highest and worthiest ideals and goals, they stimulate the worshiper to action on behalf of those ideals and impel the worshiper to stake his or her very life on achieving those goals. If we articulate constantly in our worship the ideals of just and pure living and a devotion to advancing the cause of a just, righteous, equitable, and peaceful society and world, and that repetition causes us to actively work for those ideals, then we can honestly say that prayer is effective. If prayer changes the pray-er then it works. A Jew prays three times daily (at least) for peace in the world: If thereby the worshiper gives his or her heart and soul to achieve peace, then the prayer has indeed worked its magic. A Jew prays three times daily to "guard my tongue from evil, my lips from speaking guile" and if, as a consequence, the worshiper is impelled to refrain from speaking evil but speaks only good of humans, then we can say unequivocally, that our prayer was, indeed, answered. As one student of prayer phrased it, "The answer to our prayer may be the echo of our resolve."

Finally, much depends on how we view human history over the long range. The cold cynic views the rebirth of the State of Israel in military, economic, and geopolitical terms. The religionist understands this phenomenon as a modern miracle. It is the culmination of 2,000 years of prayers for the return to Zion and the rebuilding of Jerusalem—prayers that have kept alive a people's dreams and hopes and aspirations despite the Diaspora when all facts pointed to a futile and fruitless dream that could never become a reality. Those prayers for Zion rebuilt which were recited daily kept that spark of hope alive for a people long dispersed, who had never even seen the Holy Land, much less dwelled in it. The victory of a poorly armed, untrained rabble out of a population of some 600,000 Jews against the well-equipped armies of six or seven Arab countries in the 1948 War for Independence may be analyzed by the cool military experts and secular Zionists as the triumph of a united and well-motivated people's army against inept and divided Arab forces. But the person of faith and prayerfulness conceives of this victory against all odds as truly a miracle: the Divine response to the heartfelt worship of millions of Jews all over the world, in dozens of lands spanning close to 20 centuries. In this sense, prayer may be seen as effective and answered.

Having said all this, I return to the troubling question that is probably on the mind of most readers: What if a Jew does not believe that God commanded that we pray regularly? How, then, is prayer possible? I respond: You have to start praying in order to learn how to pray and enjoy involvement in prayerful experiences. It is like swimming: You have to plunge in and do it in order to learn; it cannot be grasped merely by reading a textbook or taking a seminar. Naturally, the would-be worshiper must master the basic skills of Hebrew of the prayer book as well as the melodies and architecture of the prayer services. Get the experience of prayer and the rest will follow; start gradually and build up the prayer immersion, step by step, "here a little, there a little," as Isaiah put it, adding to the time and exposure. As the prayer experience deepens, the worshiper begins to sense a psychological and sociological force that is potent beyond our comprehension.

Psychologically, prayer puts us in touch with the Transcendent, coupling us to the element of Divinity in the universe. And that is a connection all humans, at some point or other, crave and seek. Prayer activates the latent good in humans and society; it has the power to affect, as the kabbalists believe, the very cosmos. We cultivate through prayer humility, gratitude, a sense of awe—an appreciation that there is something beyond the material, something that transcends the merely human. When we pray fervently, we should do so as if every word is weighed and there is a Divine Listener. But we cannot just plunge into a service for Rosh Hashanah or Yom Kippur without proper preparation anymore than one can attend an opera for the first time and expect to be exhilarated. Of course many people are "bored" or "turned off" at High Holiday services. Small wonder: they are the longest services of the year; they are replete with liturgy, prayers, melodies, *piyyutim*, and lengthy sermons. The person who never enters a synagogue the rest of the year is, to say the least, ill-prepared for such a massive dose of worship. But those who are not just casual dabblers in the prayer service and frequent the synagogue on Sabbaths and festivals can find proper inspiration and participation on the High Holidays. The prayer experience is not just a passing flirtation; it is a constant and passionate love affair.

Sociologically, prayer unites us with fellow Jews and eases our sense of isolation and spiritual loneliness. There is no substitute for communal prayer; the *minyan* (quorum of ten worshipers) is an especially potent amalgam that binds us closer to one another. The sages understood this phenomenon. They stressed the superiority of communal prayer over individual prayer, noting that God's *Shekhinah* is present in a *minyan*. Certainly an individual may pray privately (even as we do on our bed before sleep when we recite the *Shema*). The *tzaddikim* among the kabbalists and Hasidim often prefer private devotions. A beautiful Midrash expresses this idea most tellingly (*Mid. Pss.* 4, p. 46):

> God said to Israel, "I bade you pray in the synagogue. If that is impossible, then pray at home. If not at home, then pray in the field or in bed. If this is impossible then pray in your heart."

But public prayer is deemed superior both by halakhah and sentiment. Public prayer is one of the most potent forces for group survival, for each Jew identifies himself with his or her fellow worshiper horizontally in the contemporary Jewish world and vertically in the communities of past and future eras. As we blend our voices and hearts in worship, as we rub shoulders with our fellow-Jew, we forge a chain with the Jewish people and its traditions that no force can tear asunder, even as we fashion the links to the future. When Hillel admonished us, "Do not separate yourself from the community" (*Abot* 2:4), he undoubtedly had the notion of communal prayer in mind. If we understand the abiding value of prayer in this light, I believe more Jews will be inclined and inspired to join together with the community of worshipers.

Still, prayer will pose a problem for many if not most Jews. Perhaps it would help to remember the teaching of the Tzanzer Rebbe who was asked, "What does the Rebbe do before he prays?" He replied, "I pray that I may be able to pray." We need to approach the problem of prayer with more reverence, humility, and introspection and pray that God may enable us to pray. And maybe, just maybe, we will then be able to ignite our souls to pray.

Points to Ponder:
Why Pray?

1. Contrast the Hebrew notion of *tefillah* as self-judgment with the Latin notion of prayer as begging. Which one speaks to you?

2. Until modern days, a Jew could feel at home in a synagogue anywhere in the world. What elements were common to all synagogues and what snapped the threads of unity?

3. Why do you think *berakhot* and prayers of praise are the most common Hebrew prayers?

4. The author writes that had it not been for the synagogue, the people of Israel would have disappeared. What elements of the synagogue have served as a preservative?

5. What are the three main functions of the synagogue? How has there been a shift in the importance of one over the other?

6. How is it that the exterior of the synagogue changed radically over the ages but the interior remained constant until fairly recently?

7. What are the challenges that make prayer problematic for the modern Jew? Do you sense those difficulties when you try to pray? Try to compose your own prayers to mark special moments.

8. How do you feel about praying in the vernacular? Is Hebrew a must in worship?

9. Schechter quipped that when Jews prayed, one prayer book sufficed; now that they don't pray, we have many prayer books. Heschel has derided "prayer by proxy." What is your view of these critiques?

10. Orthodox worship has been unyieldingly traditional and Orthodox synagogues are generally crowded with young people as well as older ones. Reform and Conservative synagogues have made radical changes in the prayer services and are not overly crowded. What do you say to this phenomenon?

11. *Kavvanah* is essential in prayer, but we cannot always achieve it. What techniques do you adopt to heighten your sense of *kavvanah*?

12. Do you see pitfalls and dangers in shaping prayers to fit the fads and spirit of the times?

13. The author believes fervently in the value of singing our prayers. How do you feel about singing at services? What types of tunes do you prefer to enrich the experience?

14. Do you believe that prayers are efficacious?

10

Why Eretz Yisrael?

WHAT IS a land? What is a country? To many, it merely means a geographic designation, a place where one lives, works, marries, procreates, and dies. To many, it is merely a slice of earth and soil, of hills and valleys, of lakes and rivers. It is a place where one raises cattle or crops; where one builds cities and towns, villages and hamlets; where one gives birth to a family and watches children grow; where one works and sweats to eke out a living and then, in the fullness of times, where one dies. To some people, a land is sacred. To some people a country is holy. Sir Isaiah Berlin has written that Israel has always had more history than geography. Very true: But for the Jew, there is a land, a country that is special and holy; its very soil is sacred. It is the place where the Jewish nation was born; where the forefathers inhabited and built and cherished and loved; where the prophets of Israel prophesied, the kings reigned, the sages interpreted and the judges legislated. It is the place that Jews lost at least twice to enemies, but which they never despaired of seeing again. It is the homeland, the fatherland, the center of the Jew's universe and of humanity's as well. That land is the Land of Eretz Yisrael, and only the people of Israel has displayed such fervently consuming devotion and attachment to a tiny sliver of rock and soil and desert on the Mediterranean between Egypt and Mesopotamia.

> They say that there is a land—a land drunk with sunshine. Where is that land? Where is that sunshine? (Saul Tchernichowsky)

The claim of the people of Israel to the land of Israel, or as it was originally named, the land of Canaan, dates back to the days of the Patriarchs and Matriarchs, some fourteen centuries before the Common Era. God told Abraham, "Go forth from your native land and from your father's house to the land that I will show you" (Gen 12:1). This Divine promise was reiterated several times to Abraham and Sarah as well as to their heirs. God spoke similarly to Isaac in a vision: "Reside in this land and I will be with you and bless you; I will assign all these lands to you and your offspring, fulfilling the oath that I swore to your father Abraham. I will make your descendants as numerous as the stars of heaven, and give your descendants all these lands . . ." (Gen 26:3–4). Once again, God reiterated His promise to Jacob, the third of the Patriarchs and the antecedent of the twelve tribes of Israel: "I am the Lord, the God of your father Abraham and the God of Isaac: the ground on which you are lying I will assign to you and your offspring" (Gen 28:13).

So precious was this Promised Land to our forefathers that they insisted on being buried in its soil, a custom pious Jews observe until this day. Abraham purchased the burial plot at Machpelah at Hebron for his cherished wife, Sarah (Gen 23:1 ff.). Indeed, we read in the Torah that Jacob commanded his children to carry his body from Egypt back to Eretz Yisrael for burial in the family sepulcher (Gen 47:29–31). Joseph did likewise: He commanded his family to bury him not in the tombs of the kings and nobles of Egypt where he was entitled to be buried as prime minister of the land, but, rather, in the humble burial ground of his ancestors in Canaan (Gen 50:24–26).

To enslaved Israelite exiles in Egypt, the thought of a promised land where freedom and prosperity were to be found was truly an inspiring dream. The Hebrews, who were compelled to serve as slaves in building the royal storehouses and cities of Pharaoh, must have pined away their hearts as they groaned under the rigor of slave labor and dreamt of a better life in the land where their ancestors had dwelled in freedom and comparative security. All that was necessary to ignite this spark of hope into a burning flame was a charismatic leader and spokesman. Moses filled this role brilliantly. He was charged by God to declare to the Hebrews that God had not forsaken them: "I will take you out of the misery of Egypt into the land of the Canaanites, Hittites, Amorites, Perizzites, Hivites and Jebusites, to the land flowing with milk and honey" (Exod 3:17). The image of that land propelled the people relentlessly onward through forty years of wandering in the Sinai, as they battled against natural and human enemies as well as the enemies within their own ranks and their own indecisiveness and rebelliousness. The promised land was to be not just a land flowing with milk and honey but a land of wheat and barley, of grapes and figs and pomegranates, a land of olive trees, and a land from whose mountains they would one day mine iron and copper (Deut 8:8–9; 31:20). But more: it would be *"admat kodesh*, a holy soil" (Zech 2:16), a sacred land whose inhabitants must be holy and free from the pollution of the pagan native peoples and the surrounding corrupt civilizations of the day. This would be a land whose inhabitants would be "plucked up and cast away" for immoral practices and degenerate ways (Deut 11:11–12, 16–17). Moses warned the children of Israel in bluntly picturesque language that this is a land that will "vomit forth its immoral inhabitants" (Lev 18:25; 26:32–33), for this land is God's own special land.

The Book of Joshua informs us that the brilliant general and successor to Moses, Joshua ben Nun, led the people in the bloody and prolonged conquest of the Promised Land. We read of the destruction of Canaanite fortresses of Ai, Hatzor, Jericho and others. Archaeological evidence point to massive destruction and burning of these fortified cities around the year 1200 B.C.E., and the great archaeologist, William Foxwell Albright, has even set the dates of their destruction to the year. Contemporary archaeologists are more skeptical of these conclusions. But clearly, Hebrews did infiltrate and conquer the land partially, although the more-or-less complete capture of Canaan did not come about until the time of Kings David and Solomon. It was David who united the northern and southern territories of Israel and Judah around 1000 B.C.E., and it was his son, Solomon, who expanded the border of his nation as far south as Etzion Gever, presumably near today's port city, Eilat, on the Red Sea.

But borders shifted in various eras so that the boundaries of Eretz Yisrael were never really fixed. One biblical source places the western border from the Nile to the Euphrates (Gen 15:18) whereas yet another source (Num 34:5) locates it from Wadi El Arish eastward—180 miles east of the Nile! The Gaza area was in the hands of the Philistines for some 600 years and then was controlled by Egypt. Additionally, the borders shifted under the monarchy and later during the Second Commonwealth, as a glance at any biblical atlas will confirm. Those ultra-nationalists in Israel who demand a return to *Eretz Yisrael ha-sheleimah*, the borders of a complete and greater land of Israel, betray an ignorance of the historical geography of Eretz Yisrael.

When we turn to Israel's prophets, we detect a constant theme that runs through their oracles and writings: the people's disobedience to God's laws and the justly deserved punishment that will follow unless the people engage in *teshuvah*, repentance. The prophets witnessed the moral and ethical failings of the people, from the top echelon down to the common folk. They observed their countrymen worshiping fetishes and perverting justice; cheating foreigners and oppressing the poor, the widows, the orphans; defrauding people in business and enslaving their fellow citizens; and lying and slandering. They were absolutely convinced that this state of affairs could not continue and would eventually lead to disaster and national calamity (Isa 8:8, 20–24; Jer 7:1–7; 25:1–5, 8–9; Hos 10:13). Some of these prophets had actually witnessed the destruction of the northern kingdom of Israel, whose capitol was located at Samaria, in 722 B.C.E; all were painfully cognizant of that tragedy. The conquering Assyrians finished off that kingdom ruthlessly and utterly, exiling the ten tribes to various places in the Assyrian empire where they ultimately disappeared from the pages of history and assimilated into the majority pagan populations. That terrible lesson was not lost on Hosea and Amos, Isaiah and Jeremiah who warned that a similar national disaster would strike the southern kingdom of Judah if it did not mend its ways and learn from the tragic experience of its northern brothers and sisters. Jeremiah warned the people not to rely on their special relationship to God; not to believe that no invaders could capture the sacred land and sacrosanct Temple in Jerusalem; that the people were immune by Divine fiat to any foreign conqueror. This smugness and complacency would not prevail and, although it broke Jeremiah's heart to say so, he announced (and was almost lynched for his opinions) that this nation was finished; this people would march off to exile and this Temple—the Lord's house—would be burned and shattered unless they repented.

The prophets taught that the exile from the land would serve to purify the people and show them the error of their ways so that when they would return home—and they would return one day—they would be a better people for the experience (Hos 3:4–5; Isa 40:1–5). And in the end of days, *aharit ha-yamim*, the land of Israel would play a glorious role not just for the Jewish people but for the world at large as well. Here is one of the paradoxes of the prophets: In their supremely ethereal moment of universalism when their visions and dreams encompassed the entire world and all of the nations, they reflected on the narrow and nationalistic fate of a particular people and a specific land. In Isaiah's greatest prophecy on the end of days, he proclaimed:

> In the days to come, the Mount of the Lord's House shall stand firm above the mountains and tower above the hills; and all the nations shall gaze on it with joy, and the many peoples shall go and say, "Come, let us go up to the Mount of the Lord, to the House of the God of Jacob; that He may instruct us in His ways, and that we may walk in His paths." For Torah shall come forth from Zion, the word of the Lord from Jerusalem . . . And they shall beat their swords into plowshares and their spears into pruning hooks. Nation shall not take up sword against nation; they shall never again learn war (Isa 2:1–5).

Never again will this people be plucked from their land; never again will they experience the darkness of exile; Jerusalem will become the center of light to the entire world (Jer 3:17 ff.; Amos 9:13 ff.).

Unfortunately, the prophets were devastatingly correct: The people were exiled to Babylonia and the Temple and capitol, Jerusalem, were destroyed in 586 B.C.E. by Nebuchadnezzar and the Babylonian armies. The Book of Lamentations describes graphically the horror of the siege and the calamity that awaited the fractious people. As the exiles marched off to a strange land, their hearts broke, and their eyes flowed with tears as they bitterly bade farewell to their homeland. Jeremiah depicts Mother Rachel weeping over her departing children as they passed her tomb on the outskirts of Bethlehem (Jer 31:14–16). "How can we sing a song of the Lord on alien soil?" they wondered (Ps 137:4). Yet, they would never forget Zion: It would remain uppermost in their minds and hearts and souls. "If I forget you, O Jerusalem, let my right hand wither; let my tongue stick to my palate if I cease to think of you, if I do not keep Jerusalem in memory even at my happiest hour" (Ps 137:5). This became a sort of motto of the Jewish people throughout the ages; it was the byword that inspired us and encouraged us and nurtured within our spirits the conviction that no matter what would happen, no matter to which land or continent we would be scattered, no matter how bitter our fate and lot, someday we would return.

And we did return. Jeremiah and Ezekiel and Deutero-Isaiah imbued hope within the hearts of the people, and in but fifty years after the exile to Babylonia, Cyrus, the Persian conqueror of the Babylonian empire, issued a decree allowing the Jews to return and rebuild their shattered and desolate land. And so, in 537 B.C.E., some 42,360 exiles did return to reclaim the ruined country, plant fields, construct houses, fashion a new society, and rebuild the Temple in Jerusalem. Under the leadership of Ezra the scribe and Nehemiah the governor, the Second Commonwealth was born, at first modestly and almost pitifully. But later, it blossomed and flourished and grew into a great and glorious commonwealth.

The Second Commonwealth was a period of unusual creativity and spiritual-cultural brilliance. The three pilgrim festivals, Passover, Sukkot and Shavuot, mentioned in the Torah (Exod 23:14–17; Deut 26:3–10) as occasions for pilgrims to visit Jerusalem with sacrificial offerings became magnets for Jews throughout the Mediterranean basin. The first-century historian, Josephus, described in glowing terms how tens of thousands of pilgrims crammed the Temple courts, offering their sacrifices and prayers, fraternizing with brethren from various lands, and enjoying the spiritual and physical beauty of the Holy City made ever more magnificent by King Herod the Great. Those were the days in which much of the Wisdom Literature and the Apocrypha were composed and edited. Those were the days when the Maccabees revolted against their Syrian-Greek masters and succeeded in freeing their land from the yoke of the pagans. Those were the days of the early academies and the teachers of the *Torah she-b'al peh*— the Oral Torah that ultimately crystallized into the Mishnah, the first great code of the rabbis' oral interpretations of the written Torah. Those were the days of the birth of a new faith that was to become the nemesis of Judaism, namely, Christianity.

Sadly, the people were torn by inner dissension and factionalism; rival parties and sects struggled with each other and even warred against one another constantly, oblivious to the dangers of inner division that only weakened them and enabled the mighty Roman Empire to divide and conquer them. As a result, in the year 70 C.E., the war party prevailed and a suicidal battle against the mightiest military force of the day was launched, ending in the destruction of the nation, the burning of Jerusalem and its sacred Temple, and the murder, enslavement and exile of tens of thousands of Judeans. This time, unlike the first destruction of 586, a substantial population of Jews was allowed to remain, rebuild the shattered land, and reconstitute the Sanhedrin—the highest court of the people—that both legislated and interpreted the oral law for all of the Jewish people. Their task was to encourage the people to serve God without the Temple, prevent emigration, restore the lost dignity of the people, and keep the flame of Jewish learning and living alive. The challenge became even more acute after the ill-fated and insanely ruinous Bar Kokhba rebellion in which a messianic pretender, Simon Bar Koziba, challenged the might of Rome yet again in a bloody confrontation that lasted from 132–135 and drowned the already wounded nation in a blood bath. The land was ravished and ruined; the towns and cities were shattered; the farms were destroyed; tens of thousand were killed and exiled. Jerusalem was plowed under and renamed, Aelia Capitolina, and Jews were barred from setting foot on its Temple mount. Now the task of the sages was even more daunting than before as they sought to discourage emigration and somehow encourage efforts to rebuild from the ruins. Gedaliah Alon has shown how a series of far-reaching laws was enacted to further these goals including the prohibition against raising small animals that defoliated the already ruined agriculture and the ban against importing glass from foreign pagan manufacturers in order to stimulate local manufacture. Even divorce law reflected this concern so that if a husband wanted to move to

Israel and the wife refused, he might divorce her. Conversely, if she wanted to move to Israel and he refused, she might demand a divorce (*m. Ketub.* 13:11). Likewise, in civil law, if one wanted to purchase a house in Israel, it is permitted to draw up the bill of sale on *Shabbat*, opined one sage. This was a bit too radical for the rest of his colleagues: "On *Shabbat* you say! That would not be permissible even to buy property in Israel. But follow Rava's view and let the purchaser authorize a gentile intermediary to handle the sale for him even on *Shabbat*" (*Git.* 8b; *B. Qama* 80b). Thus, in laws and ordinances, the sages strove mightily to reconstruct out of the ashes a viable and vibrant nation.

But the sages did not just confine their efforts to bolster Zion in legal matters alone. Their sermons and homilies reflected their deep concern for the future of their land; they never missed an opportunity to extol the land, to praise its soil and climate, to laud its special spirituality and sanctity. Israel is the holiest of lands and higher in elevation than any other land (*m. Kelim* 1:6 ff; *Qidd.* 69b). Ten measures of wisdom fell to the world and Eretz Yisrael received nine. Ten measures of beauty fell to the world and Jerusalem received nine (*Qidd.* 49b). Rabbi Shimon ben Yohai preached in a sermon, "God tested all of the lands and could find not a single place worthy of the Children of Israel except the Land of Israel (*Lev. Rab.* 13:2, pp. 273f.). The sages noted that only in the Land of Israel could a Jew perform all the *mitzvot*, notably agricultural laws that are not observed in the Diaspora. That is why, they observed, dwelling in the land of Israel (*yishuv Eretz Yisrael*) is the equivalent of observing all of the commandments (*Sotah* 14a; *Sifre Deut. R'eah* 80, p. 91b). They extolled the spirituality of the land of Israel to the point of observing that there is no Torah like that of Israel, where even the ordinary conversation of people is rich with Torah insights and the very air of the land makes one wise (*B. Bat.* 158b). There is a funny story in the Talmud about Rabbi Zeira who left Babylonia to settle in Israel and fasted one hundred days to forget all the foolishness he had learned in the schools of Babylonia in order to begin afresh with the teachings of the Palestinian academies (*B. Metzia* 85a). God's *Shekhinah*, His sacred presence, is only found in Eretz Yisrael, according to some of the sages. And to drive home the point, some insisted: "Whoever dwells outside of Eretz Yisrael it is as if he worships idols" (*Ketub.* 110b). David Ben-Gurion, Israel's first Prime Minister and a rabid secularist-Socialist, was fond of quoting this passage as he goaded the Orthodox Jews to leave the Diaspora and settle in Israel.

The liturgy of the Jewish people reflects the deeply felt passion for Eretz Yisrael. For example, all prayers of Diaspora Jews are to be directed towards the Land of Israel. In the land itself, all prayers are to be directed towards Jerusalem. And in Jerusalem, all prayers are to be directed towards the Temple mount. The prayer book is studded with references to and prayers for the welfare of Eretz Yisrael and Jerusalem—prayers that are intended to stimulate *ahavat Zion*, love of Zion, and the will to, one day, return to land of the forefathers and foremothers. In the daily *Amidah*, we recite the tenth blessing that reads: "Sound the great shofar to herald our freedom, raise high the banner to gather all exiles. Gather the dispersed from the four corners of the earth." The fourteenth blessing states: "And unto Jerusalem Your city may You return, God, in mercy . . . praised be You who rebuilds Jerusalem." The seventeenth blessing begins, "And may our eyes witness Your return in compassion to Zion, O God." Before the *Shema* we pray: "Bring us safely from the four corners of the earth and lead us in dignity to our holy land." The third blessing in the grace after meals reads: "Rebuild Jerusalem Your city in compassion." And we complete the two most significant services of the year, Yom Kippur and the Passover Seder, with identical words, "Next year in Jerusalem!" The seventh of the wedding blessings expresses the hope (the text is taken from Jeremiah) that "once again there will be heard in the cities and streets of Judea and Jerusalem the voice of gladness and rejoicing, the voice of the groom and the bride." Every wedding ceremony ends with the breaking of the glass under foot, generally interpreted to be a reminder of the shattering of the Temple of Jerusalem by the Romans. All of these liturgical and poetic devices were crafted in order to perpetuate in the hearts and souls of Jews a loyalty to and love for Eretz Yisrael.

The middle ages were in many ways a dark era for our people. Yet, there was always the light of Zion in their souls and lives. Though most were far removed by time and space, the people's attachment to the soil of the ancestral land was undiminished; the flame of Zion and Jerusalem burned in the hearts of Jews in Poland and Italy, Germany and Spain, France and England, Iraq and Yemen—in fact in every land of their dispersion. Love for Zion was injected into poetry and prose, philosophy and theology, art and architecture. Yehudah Halevi (c. 1075–c. 1141) summoned both his philosophical muse and his poetic muse in the service of Zion. In his famous philosophical treatise, *The Kuzari*, he imagines a dialogue between the King of the Khazars and the Jewish sage. The sage extols lavishly the virtues and mystical value of the Holy Land and the special spiritual blessings accrued to those who are living there. The king gently rebukes the sage stating that if things are so remarkable there what are you doing here, in exile? Abashed, the sage replies, "You have embarrassed me,

O King of the Khazars. I pledge and resolve that before the year is out, I will go and settle in the Holy Land." Many of Halevi's great poems deal with love for Zion. None is more celebrated than this beloved poem:

> My heart is in the East and I am in the uttermost West,
> How can I find savor in my food? How shall it be sweet to me?
> How shall I render my vows and my pledges,
> While yet Zion lies beneath the fetters of Edom and I
> in Arab chains?
> A light thing it would seem to leave all the good things of Spain,
> Seeing how precious in my eyes it is to behold the dust of Your
> desolate sanctuary.

These sentiments were not mere mouthing: In a heart–rending scene, Halevi describes how he tore himself away from his family and beloved grandson, from all of the riches and honors of his beloved Spain, and undertook the arduous journey to the Promised Land where, according to legend, he was murdered by an Arab horseman.

But Yehudah Halevi was not alone in his yearning for and settling in Eretz Yisrael. In 1210, three-hundred French and English rabbis ascended to the Land under the most primitive and challenging conditions. Moses ben Nahman, better know as Nahmanides, settled in Israel after his public debate before the King of Spain in 1264. He reorganized the Jewish community of Jerusalem, establishing a yeshivah and a synagogue that stills bears his illustrious name. Rabbi Ovadiah Bertinoro, the peerless commentator on the Mishnah, forsook his native Italy for Eretz Yisrael in the fifteenth century, leaving for us some fascinatingly illuminating letters of his travels and the state of affairs in the Holy Land at that time. In the sixteenth century, Turkish leader, Don Joseph Nasi, Duke of Naxos, aided by his eminent mother-in-law, Donna Gracia Mendes, attempted to revitalize the Tiberias community by developing the silk industry. In the sixteenth and seventeenth centuries, dozens of mystics flooded the little community of Safed in the Galilee, fashioning the world's most fertile and creative center of Kabbalah. Led by remarkable spiritual personalities such as Rabbis Moses Cordovero, Isaac Luria, Joseph Karo, Israel Najara, Solomon Alkabetz, and Haim Vital Calabrese, Safed was propelled into preeminence, and its sages and poets exerted a lasting influence on Jewish religion and culture. Hasidic rebbes settled in Israel in the nineteenth century, especially in Jerusalem. In short, the mystical-poetic longings of Jews for a return to the homeland energized them to undertake the arduous and dangerous trip and live under the most primitive and inhospitable conditions, forced to contend with murderous Arabs and plagues—conditions that would have deterred all but the very strongest.

The legal scholars and Talmudists had their say, as well, in evaluating the importance of return to the Holy Land. Maimonides does not, interestingly, list the emigration to Eretz Yisrael as one of the 613 commandments. His family had fled the intolerant Arab sect, the Almohades, who had conquered Spain and essentially outlawed the practice of Judaism. After harrowing travels across North Africa, they finally arrived in Acre in Eretz Yisrael in 1165–66. But the Crusaders were in control of the land at that time and Jewish life was impossible, forcing the family to settle in Egypt where they established their extraordinary family dynasty. Was it a sense of guilt and frustration that dissuaded Maimonides from listing emigration to Israel as a mitzvah? At any rate, Nahmanides did not agree with him and listed *aliyah* to Israel as a mitzvah of the Torah, settling, as previously noted, in Jerusalem, with the Crusaders having been expelled by the Muslims.

But I do not want to give the reader the impression that Zion always bested the Diaspora in importance and influence. Even in Talmudic times, there were Babylonian sages who insisted that one should never leave Babylonia even to settle in Israel for Babylonian scholars were superior to their Israeli counterparts. The bitterly fought battle between Saadia Gaon of Sura, Babylonia, and Ben Meir of the Jerusalem academy in the tenth century is another case in point. True, they were fighting for hegemony: which of the two communities would prevail and set the religious standards (including dates for the holidays). But Saadia was certainly correct in demeaning the scholarship level of the Palestinian schools for they were clearly not in the same league with him. Saadia moved the debate a step further into the liturgy. His prayer book does not include the preliminary phrase before the *Shema*, "Lead us in dignity to our holy land." Nor does Saadia conclude his version of the Passover *Haggadah* with the phrase, "Next year in Jerusalem!" In truth, the academies of North Africa, Babylonia and Spain had eclipsed their Palestinian counterparts.

Despite these temporary setbacks, it was always Jerusalem and Zion, far from body but near within the soul of the Jew; always that love and loyalty holding firm, withstanding all pressures and temptations to forget or deny or downplay their significance. In truth, the Land of Israel never fully lost its Jewish presence, except possibly during the Crusades, when the Crusaders brutally massacred the Jews. But some, such as the Zinati family of Pekiin in the upper Galilee (whom I met years ago), maintain that there was a Jewish presence in their town from the time of the Roman conquest of Jerusalem right down to the present. At any rate, Jews yearned to pray at the Wailing Wall—now called the Western Wall—the last remnant of the outer wall of the Temple, preserved by the Romans as a reminder of the disastrous defeat of Judea in the Roman wars. And always, the Jews preserved in their dreams and fantasies the expectation of a messiah who would come and lead them back to Zion, restoring the ancient glory of the House of David, and ushering in a new age of peace.

The story of the revival of the Jewish homeland and the Zionist movement is both inspiring and amazing. The nineteenth century was the era of "the springtime of nations," the rebirth of old nationalisms, and the return of ancient peoples to the stage of history. In this spirit, the Jewish people, like the Italians and the French, the Hungarians and the Poles that fashioned new nations out of the wreck of old empires, sought to return to their ancient land. Already in America during the first half of the nineteenth century, Major Mordecai M. Noah, politician, playwright, editor and grand mountebank, urged the return of his Jewish brethren to Zion. The Hovevei Zion (Lovers of Zion) movement in Eastern Europe in the 1880's galvanized some to support this goal and inspired young members of a group called Bilu to actually move to the malaria-infested, sadly neglected country, then part of the Ottoman Empire, to try their hand at agriculture and other pursuits. But their efforts languished; they needed desperately a charismatic figure.

That charismatic figure was an assimilated Jew from Hungary, turned journalist and playwright in Austria, Dr. Theodor Herzl. Herzl was shocked into identification with the Jewish people by the Dreyfus trial in which he witnessed naked and lethal anti-Semitism in France, the center of liberalism and among the first nations of Europe to emancipate its Jews. He wrote his famous tract, *Der Judenstaat* (*The Jewish State*) in 1896, arguing that anti-Semitism is a disease and the only cure for it is to evacuate the Jews from Europe and other lands of oppression and bring them to their own homeland in Palestine so that they might become a normal people. Derided as either a lunatic or fool, he convened the first Zionist Congress in Basle in 1897. The Congress focused media attention on the issues and made of Herzl a celebrity. I never fail to well up with emotion when I read his diary entry concerning the Congress—an entry that is remarkably prophetic: "Summing up the Basle Congress in one sentence—which I will be careful not to utter in public—I declare: In Basle I founded the Jewish state. If I were to say it aloud today, I would be answered with laughter. Perhaps in five years, certainly in fifty years, everyone will acknowledge it." True to his prediction, the State of Israel was born in 1948. In Israel

Zangwill's words, "The land without a people awaited the people without a land."

But it was not an easily won victory. Herzl encountered all sorts of opposition from within the Jewish world. The rich and powerful Jews and advocates of assimilation were embarrassed by this new Jewish nationalism. The left-wing Communists and anarchists, Yiddish-Socialists and Bundists were equally outraged. The Reform movement opposed Zionism as a betrayal of the universal mission of Israel. In fact, the first Congress was to have been held in Munich, but the Munich rabbis protested and forced its removal to Basle. Ironically, it was in Munich that the Nazi party was born some years later. Many in the Orthodox Jewish world were equally negative on Zionism, arguing that only the messiah could bring the Jews back to their ancient home. Eventually, most of world Jewry, including Orthodox, Conservative, and Reform, joined the ranks of the Zionist movement and remain firmly behind the Jewish state. The Balfour Declaration of 1917 expressed British support for the creation of a Jewish national home in Palestine and the League of Nations ratified the mandate in 1922. But the British severed trans-Jordan from the mandate, leaving a truncated Jewish state of the original area.

In 1947, the United Nations—in what was undoubtedly a momentary flicker of conscience precipitated by the Holocaust—voted to partition the land into an Arab and a Jewish state so that the Jewish portion was now but 24 percent of the original plan. The Jews accepted; the Arabs rejected the plan, and when the state was proclaimed in 1948, five Arab armies plus Palestinian Arab irregulars invaded the new nation to strangle it at birth. It was a desperate struggle of 600,000 ill-armed Jews against overwhelming odds. The Jews prevailed but Arab hostility smoldered and no peace treaty was ever concluded. The Israelis were forced to fight major wars in 1956, 1967, 1993, plus less formal battles and unceasing campaigns to curb terrorism that has plagued the nation all these years and has taken a bloody toll. In the wake of the Oslo accords, the Arabs launched a bloody *intifada* (uprising) including suicide bombings that further bled the Jewish nation as well as the Arabs. With it all, the State has grown by 2006 to over 5.3 million Jews and over 1.2 million Arabs—almost as many Jews as in the United States. If present trends continue, Sergio della Pergola, the Hebrew University's eminent demographer, estimates that by 2020, more Jews will live in Israel than in the Diaspora for the first time since Roman days. The rebirth of the ancient homeland along with the revival of the Hebrew language as a living tongue are unprecedented events in human history and really, in my view, nothing short of miraculous. Let us remember: No other ancient nation survived conquest and exile. No other ancient nation reconstituted itself as a free and independent nation. And no other ancient language that died ages ago has ever been resurrected. But we did the impossible, perhaps because we really meant it when we sang, "If I forget you, O Jerusalem, let my right hand wither."

Where shall we stand in this post-Zionist era? How should we contemporary Jews relate to the State of Israel? And what place should Israel occupy in our hearts and lives?

First, I really do believe that Israel is more than just a Middle-Eastern state, more than just another geo-political entity. It is a holy land: indeed, for us, *the* Holy Land. As such, the role of a holy land is to shape our history, Jewish history, and eventually world history. Consequently, certain norms and standards have to be cherished there. Those norms and standards are what we call Torah values because, as Isaiah envisioned matters, "out of Zion shall go forth Torah." But as Rabbi Mordecai M. Kaplan argued, before the Torah can go forth from Zion, we must put the Torah back into Zion. I do not imply an endorsement for a theocratic state, a nation run by mullahs and ayatollahs. But even David Ben-Gurion insisted that the standards of Jewish marriage and status as traditionally defined must be maintained by the Jewish state if we are to avoid fragmentation and disintegration. We Americans especially, rightly fear a union of synagogue and state; but at the same time, we want Jewish moral, ethical and religious values to be part of the warp and woof of that state. We do not want to witness the emergence of a nation of "Hebrew-speaking *goyim*," in Chaim Nachman Bialik's colorful phrase. We are a teleological people; the State of Israel is a teleological nation. By this I imply that we were placed on earth by God for a higher purpose, a mission, a role. And that purpose is to live the Godly life, to champion justice and freedom, human rights and compassion, and work ceaselessly to foster peace among all nations and peoples. "Zion shall be redeemed through judgment, her repentant ones through righteousness," proclaimed Isaiah (1:27). The State of Israel must be a laboratory of such values and a light and an exemplar to the nations. Ahad Ha-Am hoped that Eretz Yisrael would be the "spiritual center" of world Jewry. Consequently, it is imperative that Jewish education in the State of Israel stress Jewish history, the Bible, rabbinic literature and Jewish ethical values as an integral part of the curriculum of every single Jewish student. If we fail in this area, we will fail to create a nation that lights up the world.

How to maintain a state that is free and accepting of all religious variations, that recognizes equally all forms of religious pluralism both within and without Judaism, that is not a theocracy, and yet preserves Jewish moral and ethical values is a thorny dilemma, I admit. The return of the Jewish people to sovereignty in its own land has challenged us as never before since Roman days. Will we wield power in a just and equitable fashion? Will we treat all citizens of all faiths and ethnic backgrounds fairly and decently? On the whole, the state has passed the test under the most trying and taxing circumstances. Are there inequities? Is there room for improvement? Of course: but I should like to point out that no other nation on earth has ever fought wars, absorbed several million immigrants of varied colors and cultures from perhaps 100 nations, built a thriving state with a robust economy and lively arts and creative scientific and technological sectors—and all in less than six decades. I am certain that Israel can—with intelligence, good will and hard effort—solve that dilemma once the problems of physical survival in a very rough neighborhood are resolved.

Second, we view Israel as the haven of refuge for Jews who—to put it starkly—were unwanted, persecuted, or murdered elsewhere. Israel has become the home for the survivors of the Holocaust, the flotsam and jetsam of European Jewry, the refugees from Arab persecution, the Jews of the former Soviet Union, the Ethiopian Jews, Jews from the former Iron Curtain nations, and from other places where they were simply not welcome, although they had lived there for many centuries. For them, Israel is home; the right of return for all and any Jews has made it feasible for millions, "brands plucked from the fire," to rebuild shattered lives and sink roots in a homeland. Regrettably, I have not detected among Christian scholars and theologians with whom I speak, sufficient appreciation of this fact. And the fact is: Had there been a "State of Israel" in the 1930s and 1940s, we would not have lost one-third of world Jewry.

Third, we detect in the State of Israel "*reshit tzemihat geulateinu,* the beginning of the sprouting of our redemption," as the official prayer for the State of Israel puts it. Many in the world of religious Jews are wrestling with the theological and religious implications of the reborn nation. Is the state God's will? Is this, indeed the Third Commonwealth predicted by the prophets? Are we witnessing the sprouts and shoots of redemption? These are thorny and complex matters and I am deeply ambivalent about their resolution. But I do believe fervently that Israel is the *nehama purta,* the tiny balm of comfort after our grievous losses during the Second World War. It gives us hope that out of the black and bleak yesteryears we Jews can rebuild and refashion our lives and take command of our destiny at long last. And that, in my judgment, is a necessary element of messianic salvation. But this explains why Jews are so perturbed when Israel is criticized and so horrified when the nation is endangered. I do not believe we could handle emotionally another *Shoah* that would end the State of Israel and slaughter or exile its population who would hardly fare well at the hands of Arab conquerors. We just have to reflect on events in Lebanon some years back or in today's Iraq to imagine what fate would befall our brothers and sisters in Israel if, God forbid, Israel should lose a battle. And that is why we Jews are so passionate about the security of Israel.

Fourth, we view Israel as the only place on earth where a Jew can live a full, untrammeled, unrestricted, richly Jewish life. It is a place where normal and complete Jewish living is perfectly natural; where Hebrew is the language of the land, and the Bible is the basic textbook and guidebook for the people; where one can keep *Shabbat* and *Yom Tov* openly and unabashedly; where no one assails a yarmulke-toting Jew or a Hasidic type; where offices close on Jewish festivals and workers are not penalized or threatened because they opt to observe the occasions. Hence, we should view *aliyah* as a mitzvah, not so much in the sense of a Divine commandment, but rather as a good, worthy, and honorable deed and noble enterprise.

Fifth, we ought to make it clear that we Diaspora Jews have been around for a long time—at least since the sixth century B.C.E.—and we have been generally more numerous and often more creative than Israel's Jewry. After all, the Talmud of Babylonia was created outside of Israel and is the more authoritative of the two *Talmudim*. Spanish and Portuguese Jewry in their Golden Age, Italian Jewry in its Silver Age, Polish Jewry in its heyday of rabbinic creativity, Franco-German Jewry in the days of Rashi and the Tosafist School, were every bit the equal of Eretz Yisrael in cultural and religious creativity. It does no good to disparage the Diaspora, as the old Socialist-Zionists used to do regularly. For better or for worse, we have to live with the reality of twin foci of Jewish communities: Israel and the Diaspora. The rabbis uttered a strange statement: They tell us, "God bestowed merit [*tzedakah*] on Israel by scattering the Jewish people among the nations of the world" (*Pesah.* 87b). The usual interpretation is that God scattered us so that we might teach the gentiles and convert them to monotheism and moral living. But Rashi offers a remarkable insight in his comment on the passage, suggesting that God scattered us among the nations so that we would not be concentrated in one place and thereby make it easy for enemies to erase us once and for all.

At the same time that we venerate the Land of Israel, we must beware what the iconoclastic Israeli philosopher, Yeshaiah Leibowitz, termed, "the idolatry of land." He was disturbed that many Israelis, as well as Diaspora

Jews, had turned the land into a kind of totem and the Western Wall into a shrine. But we Jews are a transnational people; we have flourished without a land longer than we possessed that land. We are, as Abraham Joshua Heschel put it, a religion of time rather than space. And that has enabled us to survive, as well as the fact that our Torah could be carried to any and every nation and continent and sustain us in the face of overwhelming odds. Had we been a land-locked people, we never would have made it to this point in time. To those ultra-nationalists who regard every inch of Eretz Yisrael as sacred and therefore non-negotiable, I say: lives are more important than land and souls more precious than soil. If we can trade land for peace and in the process save Israeli lives, I see the choice as clearly demarcated.

We Jews of Israel and the Diaspora are partners in this great enterprise we call, "Judaism." But we do not have the right, I think, to dictate to the Israelis what policies to follow or reject. I am infuriated when Jews in New York or Boston, Chicago or Los Angeles, instruct the Israeli government on how to deal with the Arabs and criticize the government sharply and publicly for policies they find abhorrent. There is a simple way to become a legitimate critic of the Israeli government: Go and settle there, serve in the army, put your life and your family's life on the line; accept the problems and challenges of Israeli living; and vote in its elections. Long-distance super-patriots are illegitimate, in my view. Likewise, it ill suits Israelis to demean Jews living outside of the land who are trying their best to lead Jewish lives and bolster world Jewry and at the same time harness vital support for the State of Israel, without which, I fear, it could not exist.

The reality is: we need both partners. Herzl's thesis that we can cure anti-Semitism by creating a Jewish state and removing Jews from the lands of the haters has proved wrong. First, most Jews have not willingly opted to go to Israel—certainly not from lands of freedom. Second, anti-Semitism has now been diverted in large part from world Jewry and has been focused on Israel. This is especially true of Muslim nations; but it is lamentably, also the case of European nations who, we thought, might have learned their lesson from the *Shoah*. We need to be—as once we were—in symbiotic relationship: Israel nurturing Diaspora Jewry and being nurtured in kind; Diaspora Jews feeding from and being enriched by Israel and sustaining and enriching Israel in return. We need a partnership that transcends borders and boundaries but unites hearts and souls and engages minds and intellects. Rav Kook wrote that the Temple of Jerusalem was destroyed by the Romans as a result of causeless hatred. He suggested that the Third Commonwealth could be built by causeless love. With love between Israel and the centers of world Jewry and by strengthening each other, we help sustain and enrich the Jewish world.

Points to Ponder:
Why Eretz Yisrael?

1. The claim of the Jewish people to the land stems from God's promise to the Patriarchs and Matriarchs. Do you accept the Divine promise as a valid claim? If you do not accept it, what right do the Jewish people have to Eretz Yisrael?

2. Do you endorse the notion that the land of Israel is a "holy land"?

3. How do you feel about the use of violence by fanatical groups to return to the ancient boundaries of the land of Israel?

4. How did the Jewish people keep alive hopes to return to the land?

5. The sages were of the opinion that baseless hatred caused the destruction of the Second Temple. Do you see parallels in the contemporary State of Israel?

6. The author states that sentiments of love for the Holy Land were not mere mouthing. How so?

7. Why does Maimonides not list *aliyah* to Israel as a mitzvah whereas Nahmanides does so?

8. There were times when Diaspora Jewry outshone Jewry of Eretz Yisrael. How so?

9. Do you agree that the story of the revival of the Jewish homeland and Zionist movement is both inspiring and amazing?

10. Do you concur that the State of Israel must be more than just another state? How do you interpret Bialik's phrase, "Hebrew-speaking *goyim*"?

11. Are we asking too much of the State of Israel by holding it to higher standards? Would it not be better if the State became, as some have demanded, a "normal" nation?

12. How can Israel resolve the dilemma of remaining a free nation that accepts varieties of religious pluralism and yet is a "Jewish" nation? Can religious values be part of the fabric of Israel without endangering democratic values? Or are democracy and Judaism incompatible, as some have insisted?

13. Do you consider the State of Israel to be the beginning of messianic redemption? Are we guilty of "the idolatry of land"?

14. The author argues that Israel is the only place where a Jew can live a full, unrestricted Jewish life. Do you agree with this view?

15. How can world Jewry and Israeli Jewry forge a strong and enriching partnership?

11

Tolerance? Pluralism? Which?

A MAN WAS walking on the Golden Gate Bridge in San Francisco some time ago when he spotted a man perched on the edge about to jump. He rushed over to him:

"Stop!" he cried. "Are you a person of religious faith?"

"Yes," he replied.

"So am I," he responded. "Are you a Catholic or Protestant, a Jew or a Muslim?"

"I'm a Protestant," he answered.

"So am I." "Are you a Methodist or Episcopalian, a Baptist or a Lutheran?"

"I'm a Baptist," he stated.

"So am I," he said. "Are you a Southern or a Northern Baptist?"

"I'm a Northern Baptist," he said.

"So am I." "Are you Great Lakes Regional Council 1879 or 1911?" he asked.

"Great Lakes Region 1879," he responded.

"Die heretic!" And he pushed him off.

The point of this zany story is this: Lamentably, we live in an age that is increasingly intolerant of religious differences; an age that views the "other" as either an outright heretic or as blind to the truth; an age in which persecution for religious beliefs and practices has once again reared its potentially lethal head. We are currently witnessing nations and religious groups that are increasingly intolerant of dissent or different views; that pit one religion or one subculture of a religion against another; that highlight one cult or group within a single religion battling another within the same religious group, and even sanction murder in the name of the "true faith" or the "true interpretation" of the faith. In Iraq today, the picture is particularly bloody and grim as Shiites and Sunnis murder each other, and both assault Kurds. Ironically, they are all fellow Muslims! One can well imagine what would happen if these groups gained control over non-Muslims. The incrementally ugly face of intolerant Islam, especially in the Wahhabi version of extremist Islam cultivated in Saudi Arabia, has spread a dangerous poison around the world and threatens the very stability of society. Samuel Huntington's thesis of a "clash of civilizations," to which I referred earlier, may not be so far from the truth: A clash between the Muslim world and the West seems to be escalating.

But it is not just Islam that has turned ugly. Many Americans are uncomfortable with developments in our own America. Certain fundamentalist or extremist Protestant groups, most notably among the Evangelical sects, have sharpened the religious differences and set back both dialogue and religious tolerance, wiping out much of the progress in interreligious tolerance and understanding that has evolved so successfully in the last two centuries. Some Protestant sects denounce the other Christian faith groups as heretical and "anti-Christ"; others have intruded their religious dogmas and practices into the public square to the point of opposing politicians over issues that, many insist, belong in the private realm of belief and not in the public arena. Consequently, prayer in the public schools and in public institutions, and the debate over the legitimacy of abortion, as well as the teachings of "creationism" and other such religiously slanted doctrines, have become hot-button issues in political campaigns and litmus tests for both public office and judicial appointments. *Polarization* rather than *pluralism* seems to be the mood of the hour in the United States as well as in other nations. Quite frankly, I find it frightening.

People such as Arnold Toynbee have suggested that this mood of intolerance is the legacy of monotheism. Monotheistic faiths tend to be intolerant because their very essence is the belief in one and only one God to the exclusion of all others. A faith predicated on the notion that all other gods are false and illegitimate considers it perfectly proper and legal to persecute, uproot and eradicate the other faiths that possess no "theological legitimacy" and therefore no validity for existence. A polytheistic faith is by nature tolerant because it tolerates a hundred different gods, so what difference if there are one or two more in the pantheon? Toynbee and others have taken this tack, extolling the virtues of polytheistic faiths such as Hinduism. Well, Hinduism turned out to be less benevolently inclined than Toynbee would have us believe, as evidenced by the brutality and bloody battles between various sects of Hindus, not to mention the Hindu assaults against Muslims, who have been attacked and slaughtered in modern-day India. Religious intolerance certainly seems not to be the monopoly of any one, particular faith group. Jonathan Swift's words seem as apt today as when he uttered them: "We have just enough religion to make us hate one another, but not enough to love one another."

I think it is important for us to define the key terms or concepts involved in this issue. These two basic concepts are: "tolerance" and "pluralism," and they are very different.

Religious tolerance is a system wherein the powerful majority religious system considers itself correct and tolerates the existence of other religious systems it believes erroneous, inherently false or in error. Religious pluralism, on the other hand, views other religious positions as possibly erroneous or not but extends to them the freedom, respect, and equal opportunity to make their case publicly and unimpeded in the free market of ideas. "Weak" pluralism preaches that only one faith possesses the truth but allows others to propagate their views freely and openly. "Strong" pluralism preaches that we have all got the truth or at least some part of the truth, so that every group may freely practice its particular brand of religion.

The question I want to deal with in this chapter is: Is Judaism tolerant of diverse points of view within itself? Is it accepting of pluralistic positions? And how does Judaism view other faith groups?

Internally, within itself, Judaism is rather tolerant and even pluralistic when it comes to theology—to what a Jew ought to believe. The tent of Jewish theology is broad and wide and high. It is not systematic but organismic, by which I mean that it neither follows a set order nor fits into readily identifiable categories. It is so flexible that it embraces the most diverse opinions and viewpoints. True, there are a few inviolate principles and unimpeachable tenets. For example, the belief in one God may never be diluted: It is essential. Another matter is the acknowledgement of Jesus as the messiah or Son of God. If one has accepted either the messiahship or divinity of Jesus, one has crossed the Rubicon and left Judaism behind.

At the same time, varied and variegated voices have been heard in Judaism since antiquity. The biblical world was hardly monolithic: God's words were articulated by priests and prophets, sages and poets, kings and warriors, lawgivers and judges. Rabbinic tradition is richly variegated; it is a cacophony of robust and often conflicting ideas and arguments, viewpoints and themes. The Talmud and Midrash are replete with varied opinions and contrapuntal themes. Every page of the Talmud reflects the healthy degree of dissent and differing views that marked rabbinic Judaism as open to numerous ideas and opinions.

This mosaic of opinions was perpetuated in the middle ages. Jewish theology remained flexible and fluid; its exponents included Maimonides and others who were indebted to Aristotle, as well as Solomon Ibn

Gabirol and Yehudah Halevi and others who followed the thinking of Plato. Apart from these approaches, the mystical school—especially the Kabbalah—was equally honored and influential in various circles and in numerous countries of Jewish settlement. The Zohar and the teachings of the Lurianic School of mystics captured the fancy of theologians for several generations and even spread to Christian circles. Varied concepts of God co-existed in classical Judaism and the modern philosophies of God include the rationalistic, non-supernatural approach of Mordecai M. Kaplan as well as the neo-Hasidic, mystical concept of God advocated by Abraham J. Heschel, with both great thinkers coexisting within Judaism, and, indeed, on the same faculty for many years at the Jewish Theological Seminary of America.

But let me be more specific and cite four areas of Jewish beliefs where the remarkably flexible approach is readily seen: God, Revelation, Messiah, and Afterlife.

Is anything more basic to a religion than its concept of God? Yet, in Judaism we find a curiously broad range of concepts of the Deity. For example, the Midrash records that at the Sea of Reeds, God appeared as a warrior to the people, but at Sinai, He appeared as an old man full of compassion. Abraham perceived God on a mountain; Isaac experienced God in a field; and Jacob viewed God in a tent. In modern terms, Abraham's God was transcendental, Isaac's was the God of nature, and Jacob's God was viewed in immanent relationship. Isaiah conceived of God from the perspective of an urbane city dweller; Ezekiel conceived of God from the perspective of a country lad. Rabbi Levi taught: "Why is it written, 'The voice of the Lord is power?' (Ps 29:4). It should have been written, 'The voice of the Lord is His power.' The reason is, had it been His full power that the people heard at Mount Sinai, the world would not have been able to stand. Hence, God's revelation at Sinai was perceived by each person according to his or her own spiritual power: the young people according to their power; the elders according to their power; and the little ones according to their power" (*Ex. Rab.* 5:9 and many parallels). As we noted in our discussion of the God idea in Judaism, the concept of an omnipotent God coexists side by side with the notion of a finite or limited deity. So to speak of Judaism as insisting upon one concept of God betrays an ignorance of the sources.

Revelation is another of Judaism's basic tenets. Indeed, it is one of the few authentic dogmas of the faith. Yet, it is a remarkably flexible dogma. For example, the maximum approach to revelation of Rabbi Akiva and his disciples informs us that the entire written Torah was revealed to Moses as well as the entire oral Torah and even the future decisions and interpretations of the Torah in the various academies and *yeshivot*. The minimal approach of Rabbi Yishmael and his followers insisted that only the general rules were given at Sinai. Subsequently, generations of prophets and sages filled in the rest (*Hag.* 6a and many parallels).

The belief in the messiah is another cardinal teaching of Judaism, although it is not a dogma. The range of imaginative speculation about the nature of the messiah and redemption is staggering. Rabbi Akiva believed passionately in a personal messiah who would lead Israel to victory over the Roman enemies, and he endorsed Shimeon ben Koziba (Bar Kokhba) as the promised savior. But Rabbi Hillel, who lived in the fourth century, insisted that there is no personal messiah for Israel, as they had already enjoyed messianic blessings in King Hezekiah's time. Mar Samuel went a step further: He rejected all the fanciful descriptions of the days of messiah and declared, "There is no difference between this world and the days of the messiah except that political tyranny and oppression will disappear" (*Sanh.* 99a; *Ber.* 34b).

Judaism certainly affirms a belief in the afterlife—*olam ha-ba*. It, too, is one of the dogmas of the faith. But the range of interpretations of what that means is astounding.

Some sages maintained the most sensuous and gross notions of Heaven and Hell complete with banquets of the finest delicacies in Heaven and the harshest and cruelest punishments imaginable in Hell. Conversely, Rav insisted that in Paradise, there is neither eating nor drinking nor copulating, but the righteous sit around God's table and enjoy the *Shekhinah*, the Divine Presence. Rabbi Shimeon ben Lakish went further proclaiming that there is no Hell in the afterlife, but God will remove the sun from its sheath to heal the righteous and judge the wicked.

The French-Jewish philosopher, Emanuel Levinas, was quite correct in stating, "The fact that tolerance can be inherent in religion without religion losing its exclusivity is perhaps the meaning of Judaism, which is a religion of tolerance." I would go further and argue that Jewish theology is broad and inclusively *pluralistic*—not merely tolerant. There are very few limits to theological speculation and opinions. This diverse pattern continued right down through the Middle Ages so that we encounter Jewish rationalists and mystics, literalists and allegorists. Rarely have religious fanatics persecuted theologians for "unorthodox" or "heretical" views. The burning of Maimonides' *Guide of the Perplexed* by Provençal fundamentalists in the thirteenth century was an aberration. The *herem* (excommunication) pronounced against Spinoza by terrified ex-Marranos in seventeenth-century Amsterdam was hardly typical of Judaism.

I think we can all agree that theology in Judaism is clearly pluralistic. But Judaism is not a religion of *creed* so much as one of *deed*. "It is not the theory that counts but the action," taught the sages. We are a religion of halakhah—of laws. And it is the nature of law to be decisive and final, lest we encourage anarchy. So I ask: Is halakhah tolerant? Is it pluralistic?

The answer is: Yes, to a certain degree even Jewish law is tolerant and perhaps even a bit pluralistic. It is definitely not monolithic. Avi Sagi wrote that Judaism is built on a "culture of debate" and therefore tolerates and even encourages differences of views in the search for truth. Nothing is more illustrative of this insight than the famous debate between the schools of Shammai and Hillel described in the Talmud (*Eruv.* 13b). We read there:

> For three years Beit Shammai and Beit Hillel debated. Beit Shammai said, "The halakhah is according to us." Beit Hillel said, "The halakhah is according to us." A *Bat Kol* [echo of a Divine voice] went forth from heaven and proclaimed, "Both these and those are the words of the living God, but the halakhah is according to Beit Hillel." But if both are the words of the living God, why was Beit Hillel deemed worthy of having the law set according to them? Because they were gentle and tolerant, they cite both their views as well as Beit Shammai's, and they cite Shammai's first.

We derive many principles from this famous debate. We learn the importance of human reason in searching for the truth in law, as in other areas of life; we learn that that search for truth is often discordant and fractious; that the process is tough and challenging; that differences of opinion do not negate legitimacy. And we also learn that character is an important factor in deciding the law, that not all is "divinely ordained," as fundamentalists would have us believe, for Hillel was "gentle and tolerant"—necessary qualities, we are informed, in arriving at the final legal ruling.

The halakhic system allowed room for differences in practice. We know, for example, that the followers of Shammai and of Hillel differed over marital rules and definitions of bastardy and they disagreed over the laws of purity of utensils. Yet, the Talmud informs us they did marry among one another and they did eat of each other's food (*m. Yev.* 1:4 and *Gemara* 14b ff.). There were substantial differences in legal practices both in the realm of secular and religious laws between Palestinian Jewry and Babylonian Jewry. For example, the Babylonian Talmud developed evasions of the restrictions against charging interest through the devise of legal fictions; the Palestinian Talmud adamantly refused any such relaxation of the biblical prohibition.

There were also striking differences in the liturgical patterns between the two major communities in the texts of the *Amidah*, the grace after meals, the Passover Seder and others. Many of these differences have been preserved long after the academies voted on the so-called "final" text of the liturgy. We can observe these differences today by simply visiting Ashkenazic and Sephardic congregations and comparing. The first thing that strikes the visitor is the fact that the pronunciation of Hebrew is remarkably different. The *nusah* (sacred liturgical music) is radically different, and the Torah and Haftarah cantillations are not at all similar. Additionally, there are totally different *piyyutim* (sacred poems) recited in the services of the Ashkenazim and Sephardim.

Yet another significant and lasting factor that has made for a degree of tolerance and even pluralism in halakhic observance is *minhag*, custom, the power of which is still potent. The Mishnah and Babylonian Talmud stress the importance of *minhag ha-makom*—local custom—as a major factor in legal procedures. The Talmud of Eretz Yisrael went even further, ruling that "custom nullifies law" (*m. B. Metzia* 7:1, 9:1 and many parallels; *y. B. Metzia* 7:1, 11a). Let me cite several examples.

Variations based on custom abound in food and dress. For example, by custom, Sephardim eat legumes such as peas and beans as well as rice on Pesah while Ashkenazim shun such foods. The Satmar Hasidim, following the view of Maimonides, will eat only *glatt* kosher meat, that is, meat from animals whose lungs are smooth and free of any lesions. They introduced this standard of *kashrut* observance into the United States after World Was II as Hungarian Hasidim found refuge in this country. Some of the most eminent decisors and Talmudists such as Rabbi Moshe Feinstein opposed this practice. In fact, Rabbi Feinstein's son-in-law, Professor Moshe Tendler of Yeshiva University, informed me many years ago that there were *shohetim* (ritual slaughterers) who did not slaughter *glatt* meat whose slaughtering Rabbi Feinstein accepted and there were *glatt* kosher slaughterers whose slaughtering he refused to trust. Despite his, and others' opposition, *glatt* kosher won out and has become the benchmark of *kashrut* in most of the Jewish world.

The pattern of head coverings for married women provides another illuminating example of variety of custom within the halakhah. Rabbinic law provided that married women must cover their heads as a sign of *tzeniut*, modesty or chastity, especially in public. But what constitutes proper covering? In the Middle Ages, women used hoods or cowls or kerchiefs.

At the time of the Renaissance in Europe, the newly fashionable French wigs had begun to attract the fashion-conscious Jewish women of Italy, prompting their rabbis to take up the question of whether a wig satisfied the halakhic requirement to cover the head or not. The generally liberal Italian rabbis prohibited such wigs as a violation of the spirit—if not the letter—of the law, because the wigs were even more alluring than many women's natural hair. At most, they allowed women to wear such wigs provided they covered them up with kerchiefs or scarves. But today there are still varied patterns of observance in the Ashkenazic Orthodox communities. Some ultra-Orthodox women prefer *sheitels* (wigs); some prefer kerchiefs. The *sheitels* of some Orthodox women are even more alluring than their natural hair. Others don hats that look like bonnets or pillboxes and are specially made by shops that cater to the younger, more modern Orthodox crowd. Sephardic women, on the other hand, rarely wear wigs, preferring hats or kerchiefs or no head coverings at all.

Another striking cultural difference in custom is the issue of polygamy. Ashkenazim were allowed to practice polygamy until around the year 1000 when the famous Rabbenu Gershom of Mayence prohibited it. His decision undoubtedly was affected by the Christian milieu in which he lived where polygamy was illegal. But Sephardim who lived in polygamous Muslim countries were allowed to have more than one wife until the creation of the State of Israel when the Sephardic rabbis, prodded by the laws of the new nation, joined their Ashkenazic brethren in prohibiting the practice.

Surely the reader must be wondering by now how two or more scholars can disagree over a legal ruling and come to quite opposite conclusions and yet achieve legitimacy under the doctrine of, "Both these and those are the words of the living God"? The Talmud and Midrash attempted to answer this question, offering several interpretations. One view is that inherent in the Torah given at Sinai are multiple interpretations that often are opposed to each other. But they all stem from one shepherd, the Master of all, and that is why they are all considered Torah. Another view holds that it was God's will that there be as many as 49 different interpretations of a biblical law and that every expositor of the law is fulfilling the Divine mandate, so that when the majority rules, God's will is done. Rashi suggests, somewhat differently, "We must not assume that one person is lying in presenting his ruling as the will of God, for each one follows his own view quite legitimately; one allows and one prohibits; one draws the analogy one way, the other draws it another way." And he adds: "And yet, we may say, 'Both these and those are the words of the living God.' There are times when this reason is appropriate, and there are times when the other reason is appropriate. For the line of reasoning will change with altering circumstances with but the slightest change." The Maharal of Prague took the view that it is impossible for the sages to be of one opinion and not to dispute matters of law even as they differ in intellect. The meaning of the phrase, "Both these and those are the words of the living God" is that both views are equally valid from each one's point of view. Rabbi Shmuel Edels cited the view of the Talmud (*Shabb.* 88b) that the Divine voice of God at Sinai was split into various voices so that all opinions derive ultimately from God's own words. "God wanted us to add, from human intelligence, laws and prohibitions to those already given in the Torah. This is the way we 'magnify and glorify His Torah' (Isa 42:21) . . . And lest you argue, 'Who appointed puny humans to make themselves partners of God who gave us the Torah and *mitzvot*, by adding a new Torah and *mitzvot*?' God responds to this by citing the verse from Isaiah, as if to say, 'Just the opposite! The Holy One, blessed be He, wants this to happen.'"

Among modern rabbinic scholars, I want to cite two views on this issue. Rabbi Yehiel Epstein wrote that our Torah is referred to as a "song" and the beauty of a song is that it blends different voices. This is the essence of its pleasantness. His son, Rabbi Barukh Epstein, took a different tack. He noted that out of the clash of different opinions and views that are often antithetical to one another, there emerge different positions "and from these clashes emerges the truth of the law." "It is the will of God that sages differ in their opinions in order to clarify the matter," he wrote.

To be sure, there are limits to varieties of interpretations and rulings and once the majority establishes the law, then dissent becomes deviancy. That is the nature of legal systems; otherwise, we end up in chaos. The sages were terribly worried that constant bickering and debates over legal rulings could lead to two *torot* instead of one (*Sotah* 47b). But clearly, *within* Judaism there is much leeway for varying opinions in theology and, yes, even in halakhah. Internally, then, Judaism was definitely tolerant of dissent and opposition, and even accepting of a measure of pluralism.

What, however, of Judaism externally? What of its views of and attitudes to other faith groups? Was it—is it—tolerant and possibly even pluralistic?

Unquestionably, Judaism was absolutely intolerant of paganism and polytheism. Pagans were viewed as possessing neither God nor morals; neither laws of civilized behavior nor respect for human dignity. We were commanded by the Torah to uproot idolatry and never tolerate it in our land. We certainly could never tolerate faiths that practiced human sacrifice or incest or sexual depravity as part and parcel of their cult. Tolerance and pluralism are not to be confused with relativism. Relativism means that all faiths and all religions are *equally valid* no matter what their laws and norms demand. We rejected and still reject that approach because there are, simply put, faiths that are illegitimate and evil. A religion that requires human sacrifices (as among the Phoenicians or Aztecs) can never be tolerated. A religion that practices incest, sexual immorality or sacred or temple prostitution as integral to its cult (such as among the Egyptians and Canaanites) cannot be legitimized in our view of civilized living.

But Judaism offered such pagans a chance for "salvation." It insisted that if they wanted to live among us, pagans had to accept the seven laws of Noah, the so-called Noahide laws. These include six negative commandments: No idol worship, no blaspheming God, no murder, no stealing, no sexual immorality, no eating the limb of living animals. The positive commandment is the establishment of courts of justice and law in every community. Whoever keeps these seven laws, declared the Talmud and Tosefta, is deemed one of the *tzaddikim*, righteous people of the nations and is assured that he or she "has a portion in the age to come" (*Sanh.* 105a; *t. Sanh.* 13:2, p. 434). Maimonides codifies this view into law, referring to such people as *hasidei umot ha-olam* (pious ones of the nations) and worthy of life eternal. I wonder how many other faiths came to such a conclusion already in the second century C.E. and, even more remarkably, in the twelfth century C.E. at one of the darkest moments in European medieval religious history?

What of Judaism's attitude toward other monotheistic faiths? That is a much more complex and complicated issue.

Islam is viewed by virtually all of the Jewish theologians, philosophers and sages as a monotheistic faith. There are some sharp criticisms of Islam and Muhammad in Jewish sources, but no one suggests that Islam is less than a pure, monotheistic religion.

The attitude of Judaism towards Christianity is much more murky and ambivalent. Many early scholars and rabbis considered Christianity less than a monotheistic faith. Some even insisted it to be a form of idolatry. Why? For one, the association of Jesus with God, or as the Son of God, suggests a dilution of the monotheistic principle. Additionally, the use of icons and statues in Christian worship suggests idolatry. The issue of the messiahship of Jesus is a side issue and not relevant to the matter of monotheism, though it certainly tinged Jewish attitudes toward Christianity with a negative hue. But early on, economic factors came into play and forced a reevaluation of Judaism's view of Christianity. The

Talmud had prohibited business dealings with pagans on their festivals, going so far as to proscribe such dealings three days before their festivals. Psychological factors were the motivating force in these rulings. The sages did not want to do business with pagans on their sacred days because such deals might give them pleasure and impel them to offer a sacrifice to their gods in gratitude (*m. Avod. Zar.* 1:1 & *Gemara*). This was a feasible policy in Babylonia with its huge Jewish population who could forgo business with pagans on the specified days of their holidays. But it created an impossible situation in Christian Europe where Jews were such a tiny minority in France, Germany, Italy, and elsewhere and where international fairs were a vital source of revenues. Consequently, the school of the Tosafists alleviated or relaxed the restrictions by removing Christians from the category of pagans. In other words, since Christians "in our days" are not analogous to the pagans "in their time," we may do business with them on Christmas or Easter or any of the other Christian holidays and attend their international fairs to engage in commerce. Furthermore, since Jews in the Rhineland and Champagne regions depended for their livelihood on the wine industry, it became imperative for them to allow Christian workers to handle the grapes and process the juice. Talmudic law prohibited the use of wine handled by pagans, since pagans poured out libations to the gods from their wine. But if Christians are not pagans, then we may allow them to handle the grapes and the juice during the processing without rendering the wine unfit for Jewish use or sales. The rabbis boldly reinterpreted Talmudic laws, concluding that "today's Muslims and Christians are not to be considered pagans," in order to permit Jews to earn a living in the Christian world.

Rabbi Menahem Meiri of Perpignon went even further: He created a new category of non-Jews who stood on a higher plane than those who observed the seven Noahide laws. He defined Christians and Muslims as "*umot ha-gedurot bedarkhei ha-datot ve-nimusim*, people who are regulated by the laws and norms of religion" and are certainly not pagans. In fact, as Professor Moshe Habertal has shown in a meticulous analysis of his writings, Meiri removed all of the prohibitions against dealing with non-Jews and ruled that we are to relate to non-Jews who are regulated by the laws of religion as we would with fellow-Jews. His relaxation of the ancient regulations was a minority opinion, but his views about Christians would serve as a vital foundation on which later scholars would shape their conception of Christianity. It was a precedent for the creation of a new relationship between Judaism and other monotheistic faiths.

In short, we find in Judaism tolerance of other monotheistic faiths, at the very least, and pluralism of sorts, at the most. We detect what Avi Sagi describes, "sprouts and shoots" of religious tolerance and, yes, even pluralism within the Jewish tradition. And those sprouts and shoots were sufficiently vigorous to flourish and grow into a life-giving tree. The fuller foliation of religious pluralism in Judaism would not blossom until the eighteenth century when the German Talmudic sage, Rabbi Jacob Emden, and the famous German-Jewish philosopher and leader of the Jewish Enlightenment, Moses Mendelssohn, would advocate this position clearly and consistently.

The Jewish people has never been a majority population in any land since Roman times so that much of this material has remained theoretical for centuries. But the birth of the State of Israel has focused the spotlight on the question as never before in twenty centuries. How shall a Jewish government deal with non-Jewish populations? How shall it relate to diverse faith groups? And how shall the government handle non-Orthodox Jewish groups? On the whole, the Israeli government has dealt fairly with non-Jewish faith groups, protecting their sacred places, guaranteeing their right of free worship, and subsidizing various educational and religious projects, and providing equal medical care. There are, of course, tensions and rough spots. But what nation, even among democracies, is free of such conflicts? After all, America hardly lacks for church-state points of tension and friction. But there are enough precedents, I think, for the Israeli government to reach out beyond mere tolerance of the "other" to full-blown pluralism.

Isaiah Berlin wrote about political pluralism: "Pluralism is the conception that there are many different ends that men may seek and still be fully rational, fully men, capable of understanding each other and sympathizing and deriving light from each other." Cross-pollination of ideas and beliefs enriches a society, I think. Frequently, such a process is fractious and raucous. Salman Rushdie suggested that this is for the good: "I think that democracy, freedom, art, literature—these are not tea parties, you know? These are turbulent, brawling, arguing, abrasive things. I've always seen the work of the imagination and the world of the intellect as being turbulent places. And you know, out of turbulence come sparks, which are sometimes creative and sometimes not. But without that turbulence, in a calm sea, nothing happens." We have to learn to live with differences if we are to survive as humans. "Pluralism is the will of God," wrote Abraham Joshua Heschel. I suppose he was right: Why else would God have tolerated so many diverse faiths and creeds and philosophies and political systems for so very long? Until the messiah comes and makes of us truly one world and one human race, we shall just have to learn to live and let live and get along with each other despite our differences, finding mutual enrichment in our variations and diversities.

Points to Ponder:
Tolerance? Pluralism? Which?

1. Do you perceive greater or less religious intolerance these days? What do you see as the causes?

2. The author cites Jonathan Swift's comment that we have just enough religion to make us hate one another but not enough to love one another. Do you think this view is still valid today?

3. What is the difference between tolerance and pluralism?

4. Emanuel Levinas stated that Judaism is a religion of tolerance. Do you agree?

5. What lessons do you derive from the debates between the schools of Hillel and Shammai that a *Bat Kol* declared are the words of the living God?

6. Can you cite examples of tolerance or pluralism in halakhic practice?

7. Can you cite examples of customs affected by the country and milieu in which Jews lived?

8. Are there limitations to variations in halakhic practice? When does dissent become deviancy?

9. What are the implications of the Noahide laws for humanity? What of the teaching that the righteous or pious of all nations have a portion in the afterlife?

10. How did economic factors affect our view of other faiths?

11. How has the rebirth of the State of Israel refocused our perception of other faiths?

12. Pluralism is the will of God, suggested Heschel. Do you agree? And can there be religious peace without pluralism?

12

Why Evil?

A HASIDIC TALE: A tailor who was normally a pious and quietly accepting individual had been so severely tried that he challenged God one Yom Kippur. "Dear God," he intoned, "I know You are all-wise and all-just but I have a number of grievances. Why did You take my wife in childbirth leaving me with ten little orphans? Why did You allow the angel of death to smite the blacksmith with typhoid leaving a widow and six children? Why did You permit the pogrom last Easter in which twelve of my townsfolk were slaughtered like chickens? I'll tell You what, dear God. You forgive my little jokes on You and I'll forgive Your great big ones on me." The rebbe overheard his dialogue and chided him, "You let God off too easily."

This charmingly profound tale showcases one of the oldest and most vexing problems of religion: Why is there evil in this world? How could a good God who is all-wise, all-compassionate, all-just, and all-powerful permit unspeakable evil? Archibald MacLeish formulated the paradox well in his play, "JB," a modern paraphrase of the Book of Job, the Bible's classic tale of the suffering of a good and righteous man. "If God is good He is not God; if He is God, He is not good." Ever since the unspeakable horrors of Auschwitz and the Holocaust, the question has assumed an even more profound dimension. How could a good God have tolerated the bestiality of the Holocaust? Where was God when six million Jews, including over one million innocent children, were done to death so cruelly and methodically? A school of Christian theologians emerged out of the chaos of the Second World War known as, "The Death of God" school (borrowing a term from Nietzsche). In Jewish circles, theologians like Richard Rubenstein, especially in his major work, *After Auschwitz*, denied that we could ever again believe in a God who intervenes in human history. The God we thought we knew died in Auschwitz. Abraham Joshua Heschel, who lost most of his family in the Holocaust, denied that God died there, argued instead that it was man who died there. And Eli Wiesel, survivor of Buchenwald concentration camp, has also wrestled with the problem conceding that he can no longer worship God the way he did as a young Hasid in Eastern Europe.

The disastrous tsunami that obliterated over 200,000 people in South East Asia and left millions homeless focused our attention on this challenge as did the calamitous hurricane and flood that wiped out New Orleans and left much of southern Mississippi devastated as well. A slew of sermons, newspaper articles and essays followed in the wake of these calamities of 2005, further expanding the literature dealing with the eternal riddle, "Why such suffering?"

Such philosophical questioning is hardly new to the twentieth century. It is as old as the first suffering human on earth. Human beings confront three types of evil: natural, such as earthquakes; moral, such as wars; and metaphysical, such as crippling or fatal accidents. The sages formulated the problem in the phrase, "*tzaddik ve-ra lo, rasha ve-tov lo*—the righteous person who has it bad and the evil person who has it good," or as we would say, "Why do the wicked prosper and the righteous suffer?" Abraham challenged God over the impending destruction of Sodom and Gomorrah: "Shall You slay the righteous along with the wicked? Shall not the Judge of all the earth do justice?" (Gen 18:23–25). Jeremiah questioned God in frank terms, "I know that You are just and that You deal justly. But why is the way of the wicked successful?"(Jer 12:1–2). Habakkuk, Jeremiah's younger contemporary, assailed God on a national and international level, wondering why wicked nations seem to ride roughshod over the righteous ones (1:13 ff.). Malachi wondered, "Where is the God of justice?" (2:17). The Psalms are replete with challenges to God's justice and questions about evil (Pss 10, 44, 73, 82, 94). "How long, Lord, shall the wicked exult? . . . They slay the widow and stranger and murder the orphans and say, 'the Lord will not see, neither will the God of Jacob give heed'" (94:3 ff). And Qohelet (Ecclesiastes) morosely observed that "in the place of judgment there was wickedness and in the place of righteousness, wrong" (3:16 ff). He noted "the tears of the oppressed, with none to comfort them; and power in the hand of the oppressors with none to comfort them" (4:1 ff.), cynically concluding that it is all the same for the righteous and the wicked for they all end up in the same place: the grave (3:19 ff.; 9:2).

But no Biblical character, perhaps no character in all literature, articulated this metaphysical issue better than Job. Job was the pious man, the good husband and father, the loyal child of God who treated his workers fairly and compassionately, who gave charity to the poor and sought justice at the gate. And with it all, he was grievously afflicted, sorely tested physically and emotionally, losing his children and forsaken by his wife, smitten by a loathsome disease so that he repelled human company. And still he does not cry out and curse God, although he does demand some kind of explanation. He is convinced that, "It is all one, I say, the blameless and the wicked He destroys alike . . . . The land is given over to the hand of the evildoer" (9:22–24—a passage described by Dr. Heschel as the most depressing in the Bible). He wonders "why the wicked live on, reach old age hale and hearty?" (21:7), steadfastly maintaining his integrity while refusing to concede that his own sins have caused his suffering (27:2 ff.). Job mightily challenged God's goodness and demanded a response to his challenge.

The sages of old also raised the issue of human suffering in a number of contexts. They were, naturally, deeply troubled by the suffering the nation endured first under the Greeks and then, most lethally, under the Romans against whom they rebelled in the Great War from 67–73 C.E. with the disaster of 70 when the Temple was destroyed and the people shattered and exiled. The rabbis could not fathom how God could have allowed a pagan nation to destroy His sacred house and so cruelly crush His chosen people. It was an echo of the lament of the prophets who witnessed the destruction of the First Temple in 586 B.C.E. and subsequent exile by the Babylonians. But the rabbis were not averse to challenge God's justice as this remarkable Talmudic dialogue indicates (*Yoma* 69b):

> The men of the Great Assembly were so named because they restored the crown of Torah to its rightful place. How so? Moses prayed to God, "The great, mighty and awesome God" (Deut 10:17). Along came Jeremiah and said: "Pagans are smashing through His Temple. Where is His awesomeness?" So he deleted the adjective, "awesome" (Jer 32:18). Along came Daniel and said: "Pagans are enslaving our children. Where is His might?" So he deleted the adjective, "mighty" (Dan 9:4). Along came the men of the Great Assembly and said, "Just the opposite! Were it not for His might and awesomeness, how could this nation ever survive among the pagan nations?" And they restored the full text of the prayer.

This unusually candid text displays the frankness and courage of the sages in challenging God's justice. But it also indicates for us how highly they prized honesty in prayer: They would not countenance reciting prayer formulas that violated their conscience and flew in the face of reality and human experience.

The sages were also perplexed by the suffering of pious individuals who were smitten with illness or suffering, financial ruin or personal tragedy. The pious and humble Nahum of Gamzo was afflicted with a variety of troubles for no apparent reason. When challenged by his disciples as to the cause of his calamities, he pointed to an old sin of omission in dealing with a starving man (*Ta'an* 21a). Rabbi Akiva and a number of his colleagues were cruelly martyred under the Roman emperor Hadrian in 135 C.E. and their deaths raised the old issue of the suffering of the righteous and the prosperity of the wicked. A famous legend (*Menah.* 29b) has Moses going "back into the future," where, to his horror, he witnesses the flesh of the scourged and martyred Rabbi Akiva being sold in the market. Moses queries God, "Is this Torah and its reward?" God rebuffed his challenged by demanding his silence. Another challenge to God's justice was launched by the enigmatic Rabbi Elisha ben Abuya whose faith in Divine justice cracked, we are told in one source, when he witnessed a child whose father had sent him climbing a tree to take the eggs from a nest. The father also admonished him to follow the biblical commandment to send away the mother bird before destroying the nest. The child followed his father's instructions to the letter and, to the horror of all, a branch broke, the boy tumbled to he ground and died of a broken neck. When Elisha witnessed this, he bitterly mused that the child had performed two *mitzvot* for which the promised biblical reward is long life: honoring parents and sending away the mother bird from the nest. Instead, the life of the innocent child was snuffed out. And we are then told that Elisha cried out, "There is neither justice nor a Judge in the world," and he became a heretic (*Hul.* 142a; *Qidd.* 39b; *Hag.* 15a).

Various religions and diverse philosophers have endeavored to respond to this ferocious challenge and to justify God's ways to humans, an exercise called "theodicy." Milton's *Paradise Lost* is an attempt to justify Gods' ways to humanity. In the wake of the calamitous Lisbon earthquake that killed tens of thousands, some revived the philosophic view of Leibniz who attempted to justify God, arguing that, "All is for the best in this best of all possible worlds." Voltaire scorned his puny efforts and lampooned him in his wicked satire, *Candide*, familiar to many in the musical version by Leonard Bernstein. Pagan religions attributed evil to evil deities and fate. Zoroastrianism crafted a concept of dual gods: Ahurmazda, the god of light and good, versus, Ahriman, the god of darkness and evil. The two deities are constantly battling each other for supremacy. Christianity laid the source of evil at the foot of Satan and original sin caused by Adam and Eve in the Garden of Eden and transmitted through the generations.

Islam fatalistically considers evil the will of God. Some faiths insist that evil is the neutral force, the force of inertia in nature; that it is the absence of good. Buddhism preaches that evil is merely an illusion; that if we rid ourselves of passion we will conquer evil. Philosophers draw a distinction between moral, natural and metaphysical evils. Human beings themselves are responsible for moral evils such as crime and warfare. Natural evils such as earthquakes are part of the scheme of imperfect nature. And metaphysical evils such as terrible accidents that kill or cripple are merely matters of chance, the roll of the dice. Indeed, Jewish philosophers such as Philo and Maimonides took this path.

But this metaphysical "randomness" is hardly a comforting thought for the husband whose young wife has just been destroyed by cancer leaving behind motherless infants; or for the parents whose precious child has been snuffed out by a car as he rode his bike to the store; or for the family literally blown apart by a terrorist bomb. As for the theory that evil is merely illusory, the last thing one might argue with a suffering victim is that his or her suffering and anguish are all an illusion. To argue that illness and suffering and murder at the hands of terrorists and madmen are illusions is an insult to the victims and the survivors alike. To maintain that all is the will of God is to ascribe to the Deity base and unworthy actions, actions that demean God and diminish Gods' glory. Has not God better things to do than smite little babes? Is God like the pagan deity Moloch whose power depended on the sacrifices of children?

To these timelessly tormenting challenges Judaism offers a variety of responses. First, Judaism at least in Biblical times insisted that all was created by God at the birth of the universe, even the snake who, by seducing Eve to eat of the fruit of the tree of knowledge, was the source of human depravity and universal evil. Isaiah makes this clear in two famous verses (45:6–7) proclaiming that "God creates light and darkness, makes good and evil alike." Similarly, the author of Lamentations (3:38) insists, "Does not evil proceed from on High?" (reading the sentence interrogatively). And Amos also argues (3:6), "Shall the shofar be sounded in the city and the people not tremble? Shall evil befall a city and the Lord has not caused it?" Satan, the messenger of God to cause evil in the world, challenges God to a bet that he can cause Job to sin, as we read in the prose prologue to the book, and God accepts the challenge. But clearly, Satan, the messenger of evil, is a Divine creation.

Second, the Bible knows of a belief in an afterlife—how could it not, just from contact with Egyptian culture and religion?–and explicitly rejects it. Thus, the psalmists proclaim any number of times that, "The dead cannot praise God, nor those who go down to Hades" (115:17; cf. 6:6). Job forcefully denies an afterlife several times and is unchallenged by his friends in this: "If a person dies shall he live again?"(14:14; cf. 7:9 ff. & 7:15 ff.). King Hezekiah, smitten with a seemingly incurable disease, begs God to spare his life, arguing passionately, "The living, only the living can praise You" (Isa 38:18 ff.). It is only at the end of the Biblical period, in Maccabean times, that the notion of resurrection and afterlife began to take hold (Dan 12:2 ff.).

Third, the Bible is crystal clear that punishment is the result of sin; that the person who suffers must have committed some transgressions, whether wittingly or unintentionally. This is the thrust of the arguments of Job's friends Eliphaz, Bildad and Zophar. "Remember, I pray you, who ever perished being innocent? Or where were the upright destroyed?" (Job 4:7; 8:3 ff.; 11:13 ff.). Moreover, the earlier theological view was that the punishment of sinners continues down through the ages; that children pay for parental sins. This is clearly stated in the Ten Commandments: "Do not bow down to idols and do not worship them for I the Lord your God am a passionate God who visits the sins of the fathers on the children to the third and fourth generation to those who hate Me. But I show kindness to thousands of those who love Me and keep My commandments" (Exod 20:4–5). But the Prophets Jeremiah and Ezekiel were obviously troubled by this "vertical punishment" and collective guilt and both reinterpreted it radically. Both declared, quoting a popular proverb, "No longer shall it be said, 'the fathers have eaten sour grapes and the children's teeth will be set on edge'; but each person will die for his own sin" (Jer 31:28; Ezek 18:2 ff.).

Fourth, the Bible insists that evil-doers are punished and righteous people are rewarded in the here and now. This position is stated frequently in the Psalms and Proverbs. "Behold the righteous shall be rewarded on earth, how much more the wicked and the sinner" for "evil pursues the sinners while the righteous shall be rewarded with good" (Prov 11:31; 13:21).

> "Evil shall kill the wicked and they that hate the righteous shall be held guilty, but the Lord redeems the person of His servants and none of those who take refuge in Him shall be judged guilty" (Ps 34:22 f.).
>
> "The wicked may sprout like the grass and the workers of sin may flourish only to be destroyed forever" (Ps 92:8).

But Job cuts the nexus between sin and punishment, for clearly, as we are told in the prologue, he has *not* sinned! It was all a metaphysical test, a bet between God and one of his surrogates, Satan. So the God speeches introduce a new solution to the problem—a solution that really is no solution, namely, it is all a mystery and part of the Divine plan that mere humans cannot fathom:

> Where were you when I laid the foundations of the earth? Tell Me, if you have any understanding. Who marked out its measure, if you know it, who stretched the plumb line upon it? Upon what were the earth's pillars sunk; who laid down its cornerstone, when the morning stars sang together and all the sons of men shouted for joy? (Job 38:4ff).

Robert Gordis formulated the proposition this way: Just as there is an order to the physical world that humans cannot fully grasp, so, too, there is an order to the moral world that remains equally elusive.

Yet another view of the function of evil in the world is injected by Elihu, the fourth friend of Job. Elihu argues that suffering is a discipline and a warning; it purifies a human being (Job 33:16 ff.; cf. 5:17). This position is advocated in several passages in Psalms and Proverbs. "Fortunate is the person whom God chastens" (Ps 94:12). "The person God loves He reproves" (Prov 3:12). But this was clearly not the popularly accepted viewpoint.

One final position should be mentioned. The notion that God hides His presence; that He is, as it were, in eclipse when unspeakable evil rages in the world and humanity is particularly depraved is suggested in any number of Biblical passages. "When Israel will one day go straying after foreign gods I will be furious with them on that day and will abandon them and hide My presence from them. . . ." (Deut 31:17 ff). "Why, Lord, do You forsake my person? Why do You hide Your presence from me?" (Ps 88:15). "Surely You are a God who hides Himself, O God of Israel, the savior" (Isa 45:15; cf. 57:17). This notion of a God "in eclipse" or a God who "hides His presence" has had an impact on the thinking of some modern thinkers including Martin Buber and Irving Greenberg. But it begs the question: Why should God tolerate such monstrous evil that He is compelled to withdraw from this world and cut off relations with humanity? What does He gain by His withdrawal? If anything, He worsens the human situation!

Rabbinic Judaism expanded on these biblical foundations in approaching the issue of evil. The sages wrestled mightily with the issue.

They interpreted the puzzling request of Moses (Exod 33:18), "Oh, Let me behold Your Presence!" to mean, "Why do some righteous people enjoy goodness and others suffer? Why are there some wicked people who enjoy blessings and prosper and others suffer?" They offered a variety of conflicting answers: "A righteous son of an evil person suffers for his parent's sins," or, "A righteous person who suffers is not a perfect saint" (*Ber.* 7a). Clearly, the sages believed that suffering is normally the punishment for sin in keeping with their concept of *sekhar ve-onesh*, reward and punishment. Some sages taught that the righteous are cut down prematurely lest they sin, while the wicked are given long life in the hope that they might produce righteous progeny. Moreover, they taught that a person is rewarded or punished in equal measure with the measure of sin or virtue exhibited by the individual, *midah ke-neged midah*, "measure for measure." This view is clearly articulated in the *Musaf* prayer of the festivals, where the text reads, "Because of our sins we were exiled from our land." Human sins cause God to withdraw His *Shekhinah*, His sacred presence from society, because God and depravity cannot dwell together. That is the way the sages interpreted the Biblical notion of a Deity who hides or conceals His presence. "The enemy (Satan or the Angel of Death) only comes because of sin or transgressions" (*Mek. Vayasa*, 2:129). "The sword comes to the world because of delay of justice, perversion of justice and interpreting the Torah improperly. Wild beasts come to the world because of false oaths and the profanation of God's name (*hillul ha-Shem*). Exile results from idolatry, sexual immorality and bloodshed, as well as neglect of the sabbatical year laws" (*Abot* 5:8, 9).

Furthermore, punishment was seen as a collective phenomenon; it affected the people horizontally and vertically; it extended to contemporaries who may be perfectly innocent, as well as succeeding generations. Infant mortality rates were appallingly high until fairly recently. The sages were perplexed by the death of innocent babies and infants. Indeed, several sages including Rabbi Akiva, Rabbi Meir and Rabbi Abahu are recorded as having lost children. Rabbi Yohanan said in the name of Rabbi Yose that children suffer and die for parental sins. And Yehudah bar Nahmani argued that "great men are caught up in the sins of contemporaries" and suffer with them (*Ber.* 5a–b; *Ketub.* 8b; *Shabb.* 33b). To be sure, there is some truth to this. Children do suffer mentally and physically for parental sins such as drug use, and a corrosive environment and upbringing can warp a child's development forever. And individuals who are perfectly innocent and even saintly do pay the price of the folly of their perverse and sinful contemporaries. "Once permission is given to the Angel of Death to do his bloody work," comment the sages, "he does not distinguish between the righteous and the wicked." The sinful appeasement by Chamberlain and colleagues in 1938 led to the unspeakable horrors of the Second World War and the Holocaust in which at least fifty-million innocent and even saintly people were annihilated in the maelstrom. But not all the sages agreed with this notion of collective punishment. They argued that, "God does not do justice unjustly"; an all-good God is incapable of perverting justice and truth. The ancient Aramaic translation of the Bible, the *Targum* of Onkelos, translated the verse, "who visits the sins of the fathers on the third and fourth generation," to mean only when the succeeding generations continue in the path of wickedness. Other sages agreed that only when the children follow the wicked ways are parental punishments added to their own; that the idea of children dying for parental sins is odious. Rava stated bluntly: "The life-span of children and the ability to earn a living do not depend on virtue but are just a matter of luck (*mazal*)" (*Moed Qatan* 28a). The rabbis knew the book of Job; they understood that there is such a thing as a blameless person who is punished unjustly. There is a fascinating debate in the Talmud (*Shabb.* 55a–b) over the question: "Is there the punishment of death without sin?" The opening argument presented by Rav Ami and a number of sages is that there is no death without sin: If a person is smitten and dies, he or she must have sinned. But the conclusion of the debate is quite different. The Talmud rules against Rav Ami: Death is not necessarily caused by sin. The ultimate lesson of Job's saga is accepted and endorsed by the sages.

Another important teaching of the sages is that God is not necessarily the source of every evil; that forces beyond the Deity may be responsible. The sages did believe that God created in humanity two instincts: the *yetzer tov* (good instinct) and the *yetzer ha-ra* (evil instinct), and these two drives in a human are in constant battle for dominance. In that sense, both good and evil owe their genesis to the creation of Adam and Eve, although this is not synonymous with the Christian doctrine of original sin, despite Reinhold Niebuhr's assertion to the contrary. But the rabbis were clearly uneasy with the teaching of Isaiah that, "God creates light and darkness, good and evil." To ascribe to an all-good God the creation of evil was clearly repugnant. As the Midrash phrases it, "God does not associate Himself with evil but with good" (*Gen. Rab.* 3:5, p. 23). Consequently, in editing the *Siddur,* they changed the morning blessing to read, "God who creates light and darkness, Who makes peace and creates *everything.*" Obviously they read the verse in Lamentations 3:38 declaratively, "Evil does not proceed from on High" because, "Humans are born to do evil as surely as the sparks fly upward" (Job 5:7).

A rare view found in rabbinic literature is that evil is an illusion; that it really is an aspect of good and that ultimately things turn out to be just fine. There are several stories about the legendary saint, Nahum of Gamzo, who suffered a good deal despite his virtues. In a number of instances, however, everything turned out for the best, prompting him to declare, "*Gam zo le-tovah*—even this is for the best" (*Ta'an.* 21a). But this is a somewhat isolated opinion and is essentially ignored by the vast majority of sages.

Yet another response to the challenge, "Why Evil?" is that evil and suffering serve a pedagogic purpose. Borrowing the teachings of Elihu in the book of Job (33:16–17) as well as the statements found in Psalms 11:5 and Proverbs 3:12, some sages insisted that suffering chastens and refines us; it teaches us to scrutinize our deeds and mend our ways; it is both a test and a warning. "If a person sees that he or she is suffering, let that person scrutinize his or her deeds . . . If there is no cause, the person may be certain that these are chastisements indicative of God's love" (*Ber.* 5a; *Sanh.* 101a). All well and good, but it seems to me that God has a more efficient and less anguishing means to test human faith and assure our integrity than through grievous suffering and agonizing losses.

Another rabbinic interpretation is that God suffers with us in our pain—that God is an empathetic Deity who feels keenly our agonies. The rabbis taught that God's *Shekhinah* went into exile when Israel was exiled from the Holy Land. Based on texts in Isaiah 63:9 and Psalms 91:15, "I am with him in his sorrow," the rabbis deduce this remarkable teaching of an empathetic deity. If Israel is exiled, persecuted, dispersed, tortured, killed, God, so to speak, endures the very same agony with the people (*Hag.* 5b; *Meg.* 29a; *Ta'an.* 16a). In a remarkably bold and even anthropomorphic image, Rabbi Meir depicts God crying out in empathy with sinners who are executed for their crimes and, all the more for the innocent sufferers, "My head aches and is shamed! My arms ache and are humiliated!" (*m. Sanh.* 6:5). Philosopher Josiah Royce staked out this position in dealing with evil: "You are truly one with God . . . when you suffer; *your sufferings are God's sufferings*, not his external work, not his external penalty, not the fruit of his neglect, but identically his own personal woe." Abraham Joshua Heschel adopted a similar stance in his study of the prophets of Israel; he describes the prophetic notion of the Deity as a God of pathos who suffers intensely with His people, Israel. But this begs the question: Why should God want any suffering in the first place whether His people's or humanity's or His own? Why not nip it in the bud before it becomes an endemic pain? If God is so aggrieved by suffering, why would He want to inflict it on His children, the human race? Is this the only way for God to teach His children?

The conclusion of the Book of Job is that there is a Divine mystery to human events known only to God. This position elicited limited resonance in rabbinic circles. Rabbi Yanai was one sage who took this tack and taught, "It is not within our capacity to explain the suffering of the righteous or the success of the wicked" (*Abot* 4:15). Evidently few sages were content with this response because the sentiment it expresses appears but rarely in rabbinic literature. Perhaps they understood that the wife whose husband has been murdered by a Roman soldier and the parent whose infant has just died of plague are hardly comforted by the thought that it is all a Divine mystery. Most people scorn mysteries and prefer rational explanations, I think.

The most popular and amply discussed view of the answer to evil was developed by the sages after the Maccabean revolt. The answer they articulated was that salvation lies *not in this life but in the next*, in *olam ha-ba*, the age or world to come (*olam* has both spatial and temporal meanings). Judaism, which had rejected this response to the challenge, "Why evil?" in Biblical days, shifted completely to the camp affirming an afterlife. Simply put: The evil-doers will be punished in the next life while the righteous will be rewarded there. The historian, Josephus Flavius, an eyewitness to the destruction of the Second Temple, as well as The New Testament, inform us that one of the major differences between the Pharisees and the Sadducees was that the Sadducees denied an afterlife while the Pharisees believed in both an afterlife and in bodily resurrection. Pharisaic Judaism emerged triumphant from the sectarian struggles and following the destruction of the Temple, it imprinted its version of the faith on Judaism forever. Resurrection of the dead became a dogma and is incorporated in the daily *Amidah* of the liturgy. The belief in an afterlife also took on the semblance of a dogma: "All Israel has a portion in the age to come" (*Abot* 1:1, prologue). "The righteous of all nations have a portion in the age to come" (*t. Sanh.* 13:2, p. 434). The rabbis developed a theology of personal and national suffering predicated on this belief. Rabbi Shimeon ben Yohai taught: "Precious is suffering (*yissurim*) because there are three gifts that are acquired through suffering namely, Torah, the Land of Israel, and the next life" (*Mek. Bahodesh*, 2:279 ff.). "Thus did Moses speak to Israel: 'You see wicked people prospering in this life for what seems a day or two of success. But in the end they will regret it . . . And if you see righteous people suffering in this life for what seems two or three days of suffering, in the end they will rejoice . . .'" (*Sifre Deut. Reah* par. 53, pp. 86a–b). We suffer in this life so that we may be privileged to enter "a world that is totally good" (*Qidd.* 39b; *Gen. Rab.* 9:8, p. 72; 33:1, p. 299). A passage in the Midrash (*Sifre Deut. Ve'ethanan* par. 32, p. 73b) explores the issue of affliction and the afterlife at great length:

> A person should rejoice in his or her suffering more than in good received because if a person enjoys good things all his days his sins are not forgiven. By what agency are his sins forgiven? Through suffering. Rabbi Eliezer ben Jacob cited the verse (Prov 3:12), "Whomever God loves He reproves, as a father is appeased by a son." What enables a son to appease his father? The answer is suffering . . . Rabbi Yose the son of Rabbi Yehudah said, Precious is suffering because the Name of God fuses with the person who is afflicted with suffering, as it is written, (Deut 8:5), "The Lord your God punishes you." . . . Rabbi Nehemiah said, Precious is suffering for just as sacrifices atone so does suffering atone . . . Rabbi Akiva said, Precious is suffering.

Clearly, rabbinic Judaism's response to human suffering and national tragedy was primarily focused on the next life: The wicked individuals and nations may prosper and triumph in this world, but they will receive their just desserts in the next. Conversely, righteous individuals and decent nations may be crushed and oppressed in this life, but great rewards await them in the next. Some would argue that this makes Judaism an otherworldly religion. But that is an incorrect understanding of this profound doctrine. Judaism insists that the enjoyment of life is in the here and now, not in the next life, and it encourages every human being to enjoy life to the fullest and taste all the legitimate pleasures available to us. At the same time, overwhelmed by the tragedy of Israel's fate among the nations as well as confounded by the dilemma of the suffering of the innocent and the righteous, Judaism amplified the nation of *olam ha-ba* to the fullest.

Jewish philosophers also wrestled with this painful dilemma of how can a good God create monstrous evil. Yehudah Halevi (c. 1075–c.1141) wrote in his *Kuzari* (3:11, pp. 155 ff.,) that "the pious person is so deeply convinced of the justice of God's judgment that he finds in this belief protection and help from the miseries and trouble of this world . . . ." He believes that the world is not mere chance or accident and that "there is a wisdom which I am unable to grasp and that I must submit to the Rock whose doing is perfect." Whoever gains this solid conviction will agree with Nahum of Gamzo that all this is for the best and he will then spend the rest of his life in happiness and lightly bear the tribulations; he'll be conscious of the sins of which he is cleansed by those tribulations, glad to have paid his debts while looking forward to the reward and retribution awaiting him in the next life when he will "connect with the Divine Force in the world."

Saadia Gaon (882–942) in his *Emunot Ve-Deot* (5:3, ed. Rosenblatt, pp. 213 ff.) viewed suffering as trials that God inflicts to test humans to ascertain if they can endure them "in order to compensate them for these trials later on with good." This applies to guiltless people and even children. Suffering is a discipline akin to a father who flogs his child to keep him or her from harm (Deut 8:5; Prov 3:12). "God's original purpose in creating the next world was to grant us the greatest possible good, for favors conferred on humans by way of compensation are even more highly praised than those conferred upon them purely as an act of grace." And why do the wicked linger? Saadia offers six answers: because of pious offspring; to encourage them to repent; to compensate for their few good deeds; to add greater punishment; to utilize them as Divine instruments; in response to the petition of virtuous people.

Maimonides (1135–1204) dealt with the problem of evil in several places, most notably in his *Guide of the Perplexed* (3:10–12, 51). He wrote, "That which appears evil is in reality the absence of some condition or of one of its beneficial aspects." For example, death is evil for a human being; it is the absence of life. Similarly, illness, poverty and ignorance are evil because they represent the absence of positive elements. Since God and all His works are absolutely good, "God cannot be described as the source of evil or that His primary intention is to do evil." He merely creates existence and "since existence is good it follows that evils are the absence of various qualities that are not active forces in life." The various evils that humans inflict on one another stem from evil intention, lust, perverted opinions or misguided religious beliefs and these all stem from ignorance. The absence of wisdom is analogous to a blind man who constantly stumbles, injuring himself and his fellow human as well for "wisdom is to humans as the power of sight to the eye." The person who believes that the amount of evil in this world outweighs the good is in error because he or she judges the whole universe by the plight of one person. If that person would but observe the entire universe, he or she would realize that "he is but a tiny part of it and the truth would be known to him. But he must realize that most of the evils that afflict humans are due to themselves—that is, the flaws and defects in humans." Maimonides listed three types of evil that befall humanity. The first results from the imperfect nature of human beings who are, after all, but flesh and blood and subject to illness and deformities. The second class of evils is that which humans bring upon each other, such as aggressive force. The third type is the most common and comprises evil for which humans alone are responsible and stems from human vices such as lust for food and drink and sex. When we find a pious person who is afflicted, it is because he has neglected to reflect on God and seek to know Him, "for no evil can befall a person who constantly walks with God." To be sure, "sometimes a righteous person suffers and an evil person prospers, but that is mere chance and not God's will. Clearly, we ourselves are the cause of God's hiding His face and we are the ones who draw a curtain between humanity and God . . . But the person who does not separate from God and causes Him to dwell in his or her heart will never come to grief."

The kabbalistic approach to the issue of evil was quite different. As Professor Gershom Scholem has noted, Kabbalah was heavily influenced by the old pagan school of Gnosticism that was laden with mythology and presented a dualistic notion of divinity, viewing evil as a separate entity from the deity. The kabbbalists did not go quite that far, of course, lest they be accused of diluting Jewish monotheism. But they certainly stressed the independent existence of evil and cultivated the notion of original sin that had been all but discarded in rabbinic Judaism although it would become a centerpiece of Christianity. The early kabbbalists viewed evil as the absence of good but after the appearance of the Zohar, evil was considered to be an existential reality, the *Sitra Ahra*, or "other side," the realm of Satan. Evil is the exact opposite parallel of the Divine *sefirot* (emanations); it constantly is engaged in a struggle to overwhelm the *Shekhinah* (Zohar 1:204b). Evil emerged from God's quality of strict justice and the debris of creation; it is not a separate creation but a messenger of God's power. Evil in this world is not God's doing but the effect of the force for evil. The primeval snake had copulated with Eve and infused in her the pollution of sin and the serpent is still actively striving to seduce humanity to evil ways, assisted by demonic forces such as Lilith and Samael. But human actions have cosmic power: Sins strengthen the *Sitra Ahra*, whereas the performance of *mitzvot* protects the *Shekhinah* and subdues the *Sitra Ahra*.

The kabbalistic school of the great sixteenth-century Safed mystic, Rabbi Isaac Luria, reinterpreted these ideas in such a way that, as Isaiah Tishby has noted, it dangerously approached the old pagan dualism of the Gnostic school. Luria's views, stripped of the heavy mythology are these: When God created the universe He had to withdraw or contract from it to allow human and animal life to exist in the vacuum left behind (*tzimtzum*).

In doing so, the vessels of the world cracked and these cracks constitute the evil in the world with which we are all so familiar. Additionally, Divine sparks (*nitzotzot*) were scattered throughout the world and are encased in shells (*kelipot*) of sin. It is the human task to repair the damage to the world (*tikkun*), cut away the husks of sin, and reunite the Divine sparks with the Divine Source, the Infinite or *Ein Sof*. In a word, humanity is given an unprecedented charge to conquer all forms of evil through virtuous actions, study of Torah, and performance of *mitzvot*. This challenge to humanity is unprecedented in its scope. Followers of Luria carried his views to even greater lengths. Some of the kabbbalists such as Rabbis Isaiah Horowitz and Moshe Haim Luzzatto stressed the notion of the original sin of Adam and Eve—a notion that had been essentially ignored by mainstream Judaism, became a cornerstone of Christian faith, and reentered Judaism via the mystics. In short, humankind has been permanently stained by the sin of Adam and Eve, and especially Eve who copulated with the snake who injected in her the pollution of sin (*zuhamah*). This is the source of evil in the world and the only way to expunge the stain is by *mitzvot* and sincere engagement in the process of *tikkun ha-olam*—mending, healing and improving the world. Hasidism borrowed many of these notions in building its theology and dealing with the issue of evil in the world. Rabbi Levi Yitzhak of Berdichev, an early Hasidic master, stated his understanding of evil beautifully when he prayed, "Master of the Universe, I do not know why I suffer but at least let me know that I suffer for Your sake."

I turn now to some of the modern Jewish thinkers and their approach to the issue. Clearly the Holocaust has shaped the thinking of contemporary rabbis and philosophers. The Satmar Rebbe blamed the sins of the modern Jews who chose Reform or assimilation for the tragedy of the Holocaust. Martin Buber believed that evil is the not-yet holy. Eliezer Berkovits argued that the Holocaust was "an absolute injustice countenanced by God" and not the result of human sin. He found his only consolation for that tragedy in the creation of the State of Israel. Robert Gordis noted that suffering is a moral discipline that spurs us on to creative achievement. But in the last analysis, he conceded that the moral order, like the natural order of the cosmos remains a mystery. Abraham Joshua Heschel considered evil a mystery that we simply cannot fathom: Evil is the result of man's disobedience to God. All of history is a mixture of good and evil; man's task is to separate the two because on that depends redemption. Heschel added, "At the end of days, evil will be conquered by one; in historic times evils must be conquered one by one." Rabbi Joseph B. Soloveitchik maintained that we see but a small fraction of the cosmos in our petty suffering, for we are but a small patch on the great tapestry of the universe. Irving Greenberg writes of evil as the result of God concealing His face from humanity. And of course there are many fundamentalists who simply believe that reward and punishment are deferred to *olam ha-ba*—the next world.

The naturalist philosopher, Rabbi Mordecai M. Kaplan, followed a radically different route proposing that we deal with the issue of evil by accepting the notion of a finite Deity. That means that we humans must act to transform this world into a better place and religion's role is to point the way to transcending those evils. But even Kaplan admitted that in the final analysis "we must be satisfied with a modest fare of faith" in confronting the challenge of human suffering. Rabbi Richard Rubenstein went even further by arguing that since Auschwitz he cannot believe in a "God of history who chose Jews because then God must have willed six million to slaughter." Rubenstein rejects Divine involvement in human history and he writes pessimistically that, "We are alone in a silent, unfeeling cosmos" for "the thread uniting God and man, heaven and earth, has been broken," although more recently, he has backtracked from this extreme position.

Where does that leave us modern Jews and how are we to sort out these contrary approaches? I believe that most modern Jews reject the dogma of reward and punishment in the next life. They certainly are appalled by the notion that punishment is the result of sin because too many innocents, including over a million children in the Holocaust, have been obliterated. And the notion that evil is an illusion or delusion or the not-yet sanctified is hardly comforting to grieving parents or the young widow or the family whose loved one has fallen in combat. We must agree with the kabbalists, I think, that evil is painfully real and a continuing existential threat to all of us as individuals and as a collective. Nor is the theory of "chastisements of love" very consoling. Are there no better ways for God to instruct us than by inflicting suffering? As to God's eclipse at times of enormous suffering, is that not the proper moment for the Deity to reveal His power rather than withdraw?

I prefer a concept of a self-limiting or finite God. I do not suggest that God is limited in His powers; I suggest that God has *chosen to limit His powers*—leaving the rest to us. After all, if God is omnipotent then He alone has the capacity to restrict His power in this world. With this concept of a Deity, we can now approach the three types of evil in a way that might satisfy the modern Jew. Events of natural evils, then, we may view as a reflection of the fact that the universe is still evolving, still developing. The movement of tectonic plates that causes terrible earthquakes and tsunamis, the explosion of a mighty volcano that incinerates thousands—these and similar natural disasters are reminders that the cosmos is still evolving, that the cracks from the Creation, as Rabbi Isaac Luria insisted, are still not healed or repaired. God did not create these tragedies; He contracted into Himself and withdrew at the Creation leaving a universe still very much in flux, still expanding, still evolving. That is perhaps the way we should understand the daily prayer that, "God renews each day the Creation of the universe."

As to metaphysical evil such as accidents, there are those who insist, "No person cuts his finger unless it was decreed in heaven." But I think few of us find solace in this notion of God who micro-manages the universe and delights in smiting humans. Rather, we might recall Rava's remarkable statement that everything depends on *mazal*, on luck. There is an element of randomness in life; chance is still a potent factor in existence. This, too, is the result of God's *tzimtzum*—His contraction and withdrawal from the universe.

Third is the matter of moral evil such as crime, violence and warfare. A self-limiting deity has left it up to humanity to choose freely, good or evil, life or death. If God had predetermined everything (*bashert*, as they say in Yiddish), we would be robots and not humans. Moreover, how can there be human culpability if all is set on High? Rabbi Akiva phrased the paradox well: "Everything is foreseen but free will is given" (*Abot* 3:15). We have the choice; we pay a high price for that choice when we go the way of evil. At the same time, God challenges us to choose good, rather than evil, life rather than death and to engage in the process of *tikkun ha-olam*, healing, repairing, improving, mending the cracked and fractured society and world in which we live. We cannot palm off on God the results of our human follies. They remain our responsibility and ours alone. *God has deliberately withdrawn from our world to leave it up to us whether we will create a paradise or a hell.*

In the final analysis, the challenge of evil can only be met by a sense that there is the mysterious or unfathomable in human existence and we ought to be humble enough to admit this. After all, when Moses challenged God to reveal the mysteries of divinity all he was able to perceive was a glimpse of the Divine, the afterglow of God's presence. Were we to know God's will we would ourselves be God and that is clearly an impossibility. In the face of overwhelming calamity and personal tragedy the first inclination is to assert, "There is no God!" But that is precisely the time to *use* not *lose* faith. Religion has been described as the worst possible cloak but the best possible armor. In moments of tragedy and loss, we are called upon to arm ourselves with its teachings of faith in the face of all challenges. We may not all be capable of proclaiming with Job, "The Lord has given and the Lord has taken, blessed be the name of the Lord." And we may not be courageous enough in the face of overwhelming tragedy to concur with Job, "Though He slay me, yet will I hope in Him." Perhaps we might be strong and brave enough to join with Job in affirming, "For I know that my Redeemer lives, though He be the last to arise on earth." This would require Kierkegaard's leap of faith and I believe such are the moments when we must leap. We might reflect on a remarkable tale about the early Hasidic master, Rabbi Nahman of Bratslav, who died in 1814. He was so revered by his followers, that they never elected a successor. His home in Uman, Russia, became a shrine of sorts and, until this day, Hasidim make pilgrimages there to pray at his grave. His "throne" was an object of veneration for many years, but the Communist government severely limited access to the town. Finally, the Hasidim hit on a plan: They would smuggle out the throne, piece by piece, to the land of Israel. They knew that discovery by the authorities might result in prison sentences, but they proceeded with their plans. Finally, after many months, the throne was totally removed, reassembled in Jerusalem's Meah Shearim section in the *shtiebel* of the Bratslaver Hasidim, and placed in a glass enclosure for all to see and honor. On the top of the glass is an inscription—a quote from Rabbi Nahman in a peculiar blend of Hebrew and Yiddish: "For heaven's sake, Jews, do not despair!" That statement has become a sort of unofficial slogan or motto of the group. It is a suitable and hopeful slogan for all of us as we all, inevitably, must face some crises and tragedies in our lives. "For heaven's sake, Jews, do not despair!"

Points to Ponder:
Why Evil?

1. How has the Holocaust changed your thinking about God, good, and evil?

2. Various commentators on the tsunami of 2004, the floods in New Orleans, and the stroke that cut down Prime Minister Ariel Sharon, have interpreted these events as Divine punishment for sins. How do you react to these comments?

3. It was only at the end of the biblical period and in rabbinic times that the afterlife was accepted as an answer to human suffering. Why do you think this was so?

4. The author notes that Job cut the nexus between sin and punishment. The Talmud endorses this position. What are the implications for our understanding of good, evil, and human suffering?

5. Is there justification for the belief in collective punishment of contemporaries and successors?

6. How do you react to Rava's statement that life-span and livelihood are a matter of *mazal*?

7. Job concluded that evil remains a mystery and Rabbi Yanai agreed that it is not within our capacity to explain why righteous people suffer and wicked ones prosper. Are you content with this approach to the problem of evil?

8. Given the Jewish stress on reward and punishment in the afterlife, doesn't that suggest that Judaism is an other-worldly faith?

9. The Kabbalah stresses that evil is quite real and potent. Do you agree? And is this not a challenge to the unity of God?

10. Does the concept of a finite Deity appeal to you and does it help you to better deal with the issue of human suffering and evil?

11. How do you understand Akiva's paradox that everything is foreseen yet free will is given?

12. The author suggests that religion is the worst possible cloak but the best possible armor. Do you agree or disagree with this statement?

13. Do you find the belief in an afterlife a satisfactory response to the problem of evil? Or is it all a pious myth and a fairytale for the credulous, as some would have us believe?

13

Can We Repair the World?

THE SHIBBOLETH of the hour in many circles—Jewish and non-Jewish—is, *tikkun ha-olam*, "mending, repairing, healing the world," or as I prefer to translate the phrase, "improving society." Everyone seems to be invoking the concept as it has captured the imagination of politicians and theologians, writers and scholars, social activists and religious leaders in Jewish and Christian circles. I was pleased and surprised to watch former New York Governor Mario Cuomo (a Roman Catholic) on national television discuss at length and with great sensitivity the notion of *tikkun ha-olam* in addressing some of our contemporary dilemmas. The 2005 meeting of the International Council of Christians and Jews held in Chicago that I attended was devoted to the subject, "Healing the World—Working Together: Religion in Global Society." It was curiously refreshing listening to papers and speeches by both Christians and Jews devoted to this ancient Jewish notion. Several significant Catholic and Protestant theological and social actions statements cite the Jewish concept in fashioning their philosophy of social justice and activism. A recent volume edited by Sister Mary Boys for the Christian Scholars Group, *Seeing Judaism Anew*, contains an entire section titled, "Christians Should Work with Jews for the Healing of the World."

What is this notion? Where did it come from? How has it evolved into a virtual synonym for social actions statements? And how can it affect the thinking and acting of today's Jews?

The term is not found in the Bible, but the concepts of social justice and activism are certainly biblical. The best champions of the idea of *tzedek u-mishpat*, "righteousness and justice" (the phrase appears some sixty times in the Bible), were Israel's prophets. They were the zealous defenders of the weaklings and underclass of society: the foreigner, the widow, the orphan, the poor, the oppressed and downtrodden. Amos, Hosea, Isaiah, Jeremiah and others put their lives on the line on more than one occasion as they faced down kings and nobles, land owners and aristocrats, in demanding freedom, justice, righteousness, compassion, equity, and kindness for the weaklings of the world. But they never developed a crystallized concept or abstract notion of social justice. It was left to the sages of the Talmud and *Midrashim* to crystallize those norms and apply them to specific situations.

Curiously, the term *tikkun ha-olam* appears almost entirely in the fourth and fifth chapters of tractate *Gittin* in the Talmud, a tractate that deals essentially with divorce law. This leads me to conclude that originally, the principle was applied to marriage and divorce matters in an attempt to protect women from unscrupulous, recalcitrant or thuggish husbands. For example, the Mishnah (*Git.* 4:3) records the following *takkanah* (ordinance):

> Originally, the *beit din* [religious court] would hear a divorce case in another community and annul it. Rabban Gamaliel the elder ordained that courts should no longer follow this pattern in order to improve society [*mipnei tikkun ha-olam*]. Originally, they used to write only the husband's and the wife's name and the name of his town and her town. Rabban Gamaliel the elder ordained that they must write his name and all the names by which he was known, the wife's name and all the names by which she was known in order to improve society.

What was behind Rabban Gamaliel's *takkanot*? He was afraid that the husband might impugn the *get* (religious divorce) in another community or might claim that the name indicated in the *get* was not his, thereby nullifying the document. The results of such unscrupulous actions could be disastrous: they might lead to bastard children if the woman innocently remarried, or the status of a chained woman (*agunah*), who may not remarry for lack of a *get*. To forestall such tragedies and improve society, Rabban Gamaliel acted boldly.

The principle of *tikkun ha-olam* was expanded into the economic and commercial realms as well. Perhaps the most famous case deals with the sabbatical year when all debts were cancelled in keeping with the biblical injunction (Deut 15:1–3). But this meant that poor people who needed to borrow money would be turned down by creditors as the sabbatical year approached, for they realized that any debts owed them would be wiped out in accord with biblical law. This refusal to extend credit violated another biblical law that states, we must not close our hands or harden our hearts to the requests for loans from the poor (Deut 15:9–10). How to resolve this clash of legal principles? Hillel adopted by *takkanah* the technique of *prozbol*, a Greek legal concept that empowered the *beit din* itself to collect the debts in the sabbatical year rather than the creditor thereby circumventing the prohibition and freeing up loans for the needy. His reason? For the sake of improving society we allow this legal fiction.

The sages also applied the principle of *tikkun ha-olam* in the realm of both criminal and civil law. Let me cite one illustration that has a strangely contemporary ring: the case of medical malpractice. The sages passed an ordinance by which we do not hold a physician guilty of malpractice if his mistakes were made innocently and without malice. Why did they pass this ordinance? They explained: *mipnei tikkun ha-olam*, for the sake of improving society, because if we were to hold the physician liable, no physician would ever want to practice the profession for fear of frivolous law suits.

Then something strange happened: the concept seems to disappear; the term slips out of sight. This remarkably flexible and far-reaching legal norm is nowhere to be seen in rabbinic discussions (except in quotes of the Talmudic debates on divorce), in philosophical writings or in the liturgy. But in the third century C.E., it does reappear, once and only once, in the well-known *Aleinu* prayer attributed to Rav, one of the architects of the Babylonian Talmud, or to his school of liturgists. Whether Rav actually composed the prayer is moot: many scholars maintain the prayer preceded him by several centuries and may have actually been used in the Temple service in Jerusalem; others detect *Aleinu*'s roots in early mystical writings. At any rate, the prayer is ascribed rightly or wrongly to Rav and it reads:

> We therefore hope in You, O Lord our God that we may speedily see Your glorious power, when all the abominations will be re-moved from the earth and all the idols will be abolished; when the world will be mended and improved under the kingship of the Almighty, and all creatures will call upon Your name and the wicked will turn to You.

In other words, we pray that God will mend and improve the world by establishing His kingship on earth (*le-takken olam be-malkhut Shaddai*). So here we once again encounter the concept of *tikkun* but in a totally different context. In the Talmud, the courts were the agents of affecting *tikkun ha-olam*; in the *Aleinu* prayer, it is God and the context is an es-chatological one, that is, a supernatural, Divine intervention in human history that will revolutionize this world by *tikkun* in the end of days. Thus, the responsibility has been shifted from human agency to God. The *Aleinu* prayer became so popular with the people, that it was introduced in the daily, Sabbath, and festival services as the concluding prayer sometime around 1300, and is still sung to a robust tune in virtually all synagogues around the world. Apart from this one synagogue prayer, however, the concept of *tikkun* seems to disappear from the liturgy.

Tikkun was resurrected with the advent of the Zohar and the new system of Kabbalah that appeared in the thirteenth century in Spain as a consequence of the writings and impact of Rabbi Moses de Leon. The Zohar (which he evidently edited, palming it off as an ancient work by Rabbi Shimeon ben Yohai) frequently uses the term *tikkun*, in a variety of contexts, to mean, repair or restoration or amendment. In the words of Isaiah Tishby, "It became the central concept in the history of Kabbalah." How so? The Zohar teaches that every mitzvah we humans perform has cosmic importance so that when we study Torah or observe the *Shabbat* or say our prayers, we help unite the *sefirot*, the ten emanations of the Divine, and restore the world to its pristine state, ending all divisions so that all existence is united with God. Our act of *tikkun* brings down the Divine flow from heaven to earth radiating bliss throughout the *sefirot* and all areas of existence even to the lowest creatures. To give but one example, the Zohar teaches that public prayer in the synagogue is particularly effective in this process of *tikkun*; consequently, the synagogue should be a "replica of the heavenly Temple in all of its beauty and esthetics so that the house of prayer might achieve true *tikkunim* and unite the *Shekhinah* [i.e., Israel, the feminine aspect of the Deity] with its husband, *Tiferet* [i.e., God, literally, "beauty"]." In sum, the Zohar introduced a startlingly new meaning to the concept of *tikkun* and saturated it with mythology: The actions of humans can repair the flaws in the universe, reunite the various *sefirot*, and help restore the cosmic balance. *Tikkun ha-olam*, repair of *this* world by rabbinic sages and judges, has been replaced or superseded by mystical *tikkun olamot, other-worldly* repair of worlds.

Rabbi Isaac Luria and the Safed school of kabbalists raised these notions to new heights. Luria taught that the creation of the world had left scattered sparks of the Divine concealed in the shell (*kelipah*) of sin. It is the human task and mission to redeem those holy sparks and lift them on high to restore them to their source. This is achieved through observance of *mitzvot* and righteous actions so that the ultimate messianic redemption depends on human performance. Luria viewed Israel's dispersion in the Diaspora as a sacred mission to gather up those sparks and return them to God and as an opportunity to rectify Adam's original sin and repair the universe via deeds. Lurianic Kabbalah is saturated with ancient mythology and has been labeled by the great modern master of Jewish mysticism, Gershom Scholem, "one of the greatest paradoxes in the entire history of

Judaism." It also helped introduce into Judaism the concept of *gilgul ha-nefesh*, the reincarnation or transmigration of the soul from body to body. But the novelty of the Lurianic approach is that it elevates the role of human beings far beyond that envisioned by the Talmudic sages who devised the concept. It is now within the hands of every man and woman to lift the sparks and redeem the upper and lower worlds by our own actions—actions that bring *tikkun* to the universe. The Lurianic concepts captured the minds and hearts of theologians and mystics, including the eminent legal scholar and author of the *Shulhan Arukh* (*Code of Jewish Law*), Rabbi Joseph Karo. In the opinion of Joseph Dan, it "became the national theology of Judaism for several generations."

One of the advocates of this philosophy was the great eighteenth-century moralist, theologian, poet and kabbalist, Rabbi Moses Hayyim Luzzatto of Padua. Luzzatto, considered by many to be one of the fathers of the Hebrew renaissance, was accused of being a follower of the false messiah, Shabbatai Zevi and, evidently, even fancied himself to be the messiah. As a consequence, he was hounded out of Italy and his writings were burned as heretical. Luzzatto wrote that evil came into this world in the wake of Adam's sin. The struggle with sin or the *Sitra Ahra* (other side) is constant and *tikkun* or repair is the only way to subdue sin and destroy it completely. *Tikkun* is achieved through deed and thought and the study of the sacred books of the Jews, especially the Zohar. Luzzatto assigned a significant role to the Jewish people whom he describes as "God's partners in affecting the repair needed to bring completion to creation" and restoring its pristine harmony. The *tzaddik* (saintly leader) fulfills a special mission in accomplishing the *tikkun ha-shalem* (complete restoration) by "repairing the creation and removing all separation between God and humans." Israel can hasten the coming of the messiah by lifting the world to greater heights. The messiah will bring the great *tikkun* of body and soul that is essential for repairing the world corrupted by Adam's sin and restore the world and the *sefirot* to their primordial state of perfection. This doctrine would form a crucial component of the Hasidic movement that was to be launched not long after Luzzatto's death.

The Hasidic movement that began towards the end of the eighteenth century in Poland and the Ukraine borrowed many of the elements of Kabbalah. The Hasidic writers rarely use the term, *tikkun ha-olam*; but they talk a great deal about *tikkunim*, by which they mean the healing or improvement of the soul, raising the upper world, and elevating the souls of the departed thereby ending their painful *gilgul* or process of transmigration. We achieve *tikkun* of our souls by studying sacred texts, by praying with *kavvanah* (inwardness, intention) and *hitlahavut* (flaming fervor), and by cultivating the qualities of humility and stoic acceptance of suffering. Rabbi Nahman of Bratslav, for example, recommended the study of the *Shulkhan Arukh* because, "It provides great *tikkun*, purifying all the impairments one has caused by his sins . . . and it enables us to distinguish between good and evil, which is the essence of all *tikkunim*."

But we also achieve *tikkunim* by consecrating the mundane acts of eating and drinking, singing and dancing. The *tzaddik* or *rebbe*—the charismatic leader of the group—is essential to this process. His fervent clinging to the Divine; his prayers; his teachings; his daily *tikkunim* and spiritual exercises; his *kavvanot* (meditations); his good deeds; his intercession for the people with God—all of these activities benefit Jews throughout the world and could usher in the coming of the messiah. The danger of such an attitude towards the charismatic *rebbe* are painfully apparent in the messianic cult that has developed around the late Rabbi Menachem Mendel Schneerson, the Lubavitcher Rebbe, who is viewed by many of his followers as the messiah even though he has been dead since 1994. Many find it both ludicrous and embarrassing to read signs in America and Israel with his picture on them and the emblazoned words, "Long live our master and teacher, the king Messiah, Rabbi Menachem Mendel Schneerson!"

Rabbi Israel Salanter, the founder of the nineteenth-century Musar or ethical movement, was not a Hasid but sought to revitalize Jewish ethical behavior that, in his eyes, had been neglected by East European Jews of the time, even in the yeshivah world. Salanter held a pessimistic view of human nature, which he believed was tainted and corrupted by Adam's sin. He was not so much concerned with repairing flaws in the world as in repairing human flaws, refining character and creating better people. Rather than seeking *tikkun ha-olam*, a phrase he does not use, Salanter sought *tikkun ha-yetzer*, improving instincts, and *tikkun ha-middot*, improving moral traits. "A human was not created to completely repair his inner forces," he wrote, "but rather he must make a start by repairing his external forces as perfectly as possible until he has a powerful effect on his inner forces and then the Holy One will aid him in conquering once and for all his evil urge if he fails to do so on his own." The Musar *yeshivot* took Salanter's teachings to heart and the curriculum of those schools included lectures on ethical behavior and the study of classic texts on morality, along with the standard study of Talmud and law codes.

After Salanter, the concept of *tikkun ha-olam* faded once again except in esoteric kabbalistic circles or in Talmud studies in *yeshivot*. Then, quite unexpectedly, it resurfaced in the middle of the twentieth century. Philosopher Martin Buber, who was heavily influenced by Hasidism, wrote that the purpose of Israel and humanity is "the building of peace" and "the people of Israel was charged to lead the way to righteousness and justice." He mused that inertia "is the root of all evil" and humanity must pierce the shell or crust wrapped around the good. Humans are God's partners in this process of piercing evil to reveal the good "for it is man's task on earth to establish God's power on earth." Similarly, Abraham Joshua Heschel suggested that, "Man's task is to make the world worthy of redemption" and his "faith and his works are preparation for the ultimate redemption." Neither of them actually used the term, *tikkun ha-olam*, but the concept is embedded in their thinking and writings.

Emil Fackenheim, Reform rabbi and philosophy professor, devoted an entire book to the question and titled it, *To Mend the World*. In it, he wrote of the "rupture" created by the Holocaust and the need for *tikkun*. For Jews to affect *tikkun* they must recover Jewish tradition; they must strengthen and cherish the State of Israel, for that is part of the *tikkun* process. *Tikkun*, like recovery from an illness, takes time. Moreover, there is a fragmentariness that attaches to these recoveries making them forever incomplete. But if left unmended, he was convinced this rupture could haunt Jewish-Christian relations forever. Consequently, Jews must rebuild even if the repairing of our fractured world is fragmentary, precarious and incomplete, for "*tikkun olam* depends on Jewish collective, particular response to history."

Another Reform rabbi and professor of philosophy, Eugene Borowitz, has also adopted the concept of *tikkun* in his more recent writings. He notes that since the Holocaust, the most universal Jewish response has been to act to frustrate the goals of the Nazis and prevent its repetition. Negatively, that means opposing evil wherever one sees it; positively, it means fostering goodness. Borowitz notes: "Today's *tikkun olam* has little or nothing to do with halakhic adjustments or mystical intentions. Rather, it summons us to Jewish ethical duty, most often of a universal cast—but in keeping with our intensified postmodern particularity; it legitimates this remnant of modernity by cloaking it in a classic Jewish term." Professor Arthur Green, one of the leading experts on mysticism and Hasidism, goes one step further: he writes that, "In contemporary usage it [*tikkun ha-olam*] refers to the betterment of the world, including the relief of human suffering, the achievement of peace and mutual respect among peoples, and the protections of the planet from destruction." For Jews, *tikkun* implies a program of "activism for political and social change."

Strangely, fewer Orthodox rabbis and thinkers seem attracted to the notion than non-Orthodox ones. An Orthodox rabbi and theologian who does take up the theme is Rabbi Irving Greenberg who writes fervently and eloquently about the significance of *tikkun ha-olam*. He defines it to mean "the arrival of the messianic kingdom—when the actual legal, political, social institutions in the world will be structured so that each human being will be sustained and treated as if he or she is an image of God." He argues (much as Rabbi Salanter had before) that *tikkun ha-adam*, the improvement of humanity is essential to this process, and Jews have a special role as a "goading minority" to bring out the best in humans. In his, *For the Sake of Heaven and Earth*, Greenberg suggests that "Christianity is another one of the particular covenants that God has called into being in order to engage more and more humans in the process of *tikkun olam*." Greenberg writes of a self-limiting Deity who makes room for humans to affect *tikkun olam*, a Deity who has chosen people for a mission to bring God's blessings to the world and stimulate people to *tikkun olam,* for that is the role of religions.

British Jewry's Chief Rabbi Jonathan Sacks has also cited the concept, stating that what stands before us today is "the great challenge of *tikkun*, that we, in a secular age, should become role models for 'spirituality'" and that "we, in a relativistic age, should be able to teach people once again to hear the objective 'Thou shalt' and 'Thou shalt not.'" In his recent volume, *To Heal a Fractured World*, Sacks advances the view that the Jewish religion expects its adherents to actively work for *tikkun* of society and the world for the benefit of all peoples—not merely Jews.

Interestingly, the contemporary religious movements in Judaism have taken up the theme of *tikkun ha-olam* and incorporated it into their pronouncements on social justice. In fact, for the Reform and Conservative movements, it has become virtually synonymous with their social action agenda. Their youth groups support charitable endeavors under the same title and their social justice committees invariably adopt the title, "*Tikkun Olam* Committee."

The Reform movement did not utilize the term in its liberal social justice platforms in 1885, 1937 and 1976. But in its "Ten Principles of Reform Judaism" that was issued in 1999, the term is incorporated unequivocally. The passage on social justice reads: "We bring Torah into the world when we strive to fulfill the highest ethical mandates in our relationships with others and with all of God's creatures. Partners with God in *tikkun olam*, repairing the world, we are called to help bring nearer the messianic age . . . In doing so, we reaffirm social action and social justice as a central prophetic focus of traditional Reform belief and practices."

The Conservative movement has turned to the concept in its social justice platforms as well. *Emet Ve-Emunah: The Statement of Principles of Conservative Judaism*, issued in 1988, utilizes the term in several contexts. In its section on social justice, the document states: "Involvement in this world as expressed in the prayer *Aleinu* reflects our concern for all people and our impulse to mend and improve the world under God's Kingship." In a later section, the statement reads: "There is an unfinished agenda before us: *le-takken olam be-malkhut Shaddai*, to mend and improve the world under God's Kingship" so that we must "take action to fulfill the call of our tradition to advance the cause of justice, freedom, and peace."

Ironically, The Reconstructionist movement has also named its program of social action *Tikkun Olam*. I say "ironically" because the movement is the most rational and anti-supernatural of all the contemporary Jewish religious groups. Its remarkable founder, Rabbi Mordecai M. Kaplan, disdained mysticism and Kabbalah, frequently dubbing them "theurgy" or "magic." Consequently, I find it bizarrely amusing that his movement should adopt a kabbalistic concept.

Not all observers are convinced that this new metamorphosis of *tikkun ha-olam* is valid or even beneficial. Some believe it exalts human freedom and the idea of partnership with God to the point of arrogance in our relationship with the natural world. It seems to glorify human power and excessive optimism about the role of technology in solving human problems, engendering possible difficulties in areas such as genetic engineering. Others, like Rabbi Arnold J. Wolf, decry it as a rank superstition that has been preempted to sanction an ultra-liberal agenda. He suggests that, "This strange notion has become a huge umbrella under which our petty moral concerns and political panaceas can come in out of the rain."

Despite the misgivings of critics, I find that the concept of humans being challenged to improve society and mend and heal the fractured world in which we live to be both exciting and stimulating. After all, God did place us humans on this planet "to till it and tend it" (Gen 2:15). The Midrash offers a remarkable charge to us. We are told that when God created Adam, He gave him a tour of the Garden of Eden to see the beautiful trees and plants. "See my works—how beautiful and praiseworthy they all are. Everything I have created, I have created for you. Take care lest you spoil and destroy My world because if you do, there is no one who can repair it after you." The sages describe our role as that of "partners with

God in creating the world" (*Shabb.* 119b). As such, we are charged with a daunting responsibility to ourselves, to our posterity and our planet.

The Midrash suggests a remarkable insight into the nature of life on Planet Earth. It tells us that all things God has created during the six days of creation need *tikkun*—improvement, completion, finishing. The mustard needs sweetening, the vegetables need processing, the wheat needs to be ground, even the human being needs to be improved and completed via the process of *tikkun* (*Gen. Rab.* 11:6, p. 95). Certainly we should strip the mythological elements out of the concept of *tikkun*. But I see nothing arrogant or haughty in this notion. On the contrary, I view this as both humbling and challenging. Are we humans up to this task, this mission, this demand that we must repair and finish, mend and improve ourselves and our world? Are we faithful stewards of this world in which we have been implanted, prepared to protect and defend its natural resources, its earth and streams, its land and soil, its air and environment? Will we safeguard the survival of God's creatures—the unnumbered species of animals and birds, fish and plants, that He placed in Eden for a blessing and which we humans have so recklessly endangered or annihilated?

Moreover, Judaism is a faith that rejects quietism. And we reject the ideal of turning the other cheek to evildoers. We have learned from long and bitter experience that he who turns the other cheek gets slapped twice. As I mentioned in an earlier chapter, Leo Tolstoy, in his celebrated essay, "My Religion," describes his religious belief as consisting of submission to Jesus' tenet, "Resist not evil or the evil man." But this is not the Jewish way! I think Abraham Joshua Heschel aptly described our position when he stated that Judaism decries subversive inactivity. We are only too familiar with a world that faces evil without a murmur of protest. Hitler, in referring to the slaughter of over a million Armenians by the Turks in the early part of the twentieth century, is reported to have asked cynically, "Who remembers the Armenians?" That genocide went unnoticed and seemed to give a green light to the Nazi program of extermination. We saw the results of such policies in the 1930s and reaped a bitter harvest of death and destruction. We witnessed a silent and indifferent world standing indolently by while six million of our people were murdered. More recently, who lifted a finger when a million or more were annihilated in Cambodia? Or when 800,000 Tutsis were slaughtered in Rwanda as the UN personnel stood by indolently? Or when thousands were massacred in the former Yugoslavia—in the heart of Christian Europe? Or when genocide unfolded in the Darfur region of Sudan? No, silent indifference is almost as lethal as active criminality. If anything, the notion of *tikkun ha-olam* demands of us active involvement in ending such brutality once and for all and a passionate commitment beyond mere rhetoric and pious platitudes to do something about our world and its inhabitants before we succeed in incinerating ourselves altogether.

Judaism does demand of us that we challenge evil. The psalmist admonished us, "Flee from evil and do good!" (34:15). And the psalmist insisted, "Those who love the Lord hate evil" (97:10). When we see an injustice done, we are required to protest and not sit by with folded hands or avert our gaze. "It is a mitzvah to protest an evil," ruled the sages. "Jerusalem was destroyed because the sages did not protest injustices they witnessed with their own eyes," suggests the Talmud (*Git.* 56a). When scholars and saints witness evil in silence rather than protest, "they, too, are ensnared in the punishment of their generation" (*Shabb.* 54b–55a). Rabbi Israel Salanter declared: "A rabbi who has no one battling him is no rabbi. A rabbi who is constantly fighting with people is no *mensch.*" There are certain principles for which we must be prepared to do battle—not only rabbis but, indeed, all Jews and all of God's children.

The first chief rabbi of Eretz Yisrael, Rabbi Abraham Isaac Kook, wrote the following:

> The truly righteous do not complain about wickedness
> but add righteousness;
> They do not complain about heresy but add faith;
> They do not complain about ignorance but add wisdom.

This is our task, as I understand it in the light of everything Jewish tradition and teachings inform me: to actively seek to mend and heal and improve this world, and to fashion a better and more benevolent one than the world we have received from our predecessors.

Points to Ponder:
Can We Repair the World?

1. Why do you think *tikkun ha-olam* has become so popular in so many circles?

2. What are the roots of the notion of repairing or fixing the world?

3. Why is it significant that most references to *tikkun ha-olam* appear in the fourth and fifth chapters of *Gittin*?

4. The author states that the sages expanded the principle of *tikkun ha-olam* into economic, criminal, and civil laws. Can you give examples of that fact?

5. How did the *Aleinu* prayer radically reinterpret the notion of *tikkun ha-olam*?

6. How did the Zohar and the system of Kabbalah reinvent the notion of *tikkun ha-olam*? What implications are there in this new understanding of its meaning?

7. How did Rabbi Isaac Luria revolutionize our understanding of the concept and how did his view empower human beings as never before?

8. The Hasidim consider their *rebbe* or *tzaddik* as essential to the process of *tikkun*. What dangers are inherent in this philosophy?

9. Emil Fackenheim wrote that the Holocaust has caused a rupture in the world and only *tikkun* can repair it. What elements does he single out as essential for effective *tikkun*?

10. Contemporary *tikkun ha-olam* seems synonymous with social activism and the struggle for justice. How did this come about? Do you view this as a good or bad development?

11. The author finds the concept of *tikkun* both exciting and stimulating. Do you agree or disagree?

12. The author decries silent indifference and subversive inactivity in the face of injustice and oppression. What is your reaction to his insistence that Judaism demands of us that we challenge evil.

13. How do you interpret Rabbi Salanter's statement that a rabbi who has no one battling him is no rabbi, but a rabbi who is constantly fighting with people is no *mensch*?

14

How Can Jews Relate to Other Faiths?

THERE ARE approximately six billion people on this planet as of this writing. About one billion are Roman Catholics; over 800 million are Protestants or Greek and Eastern Orthodox. There are over one billion Muslims on earth. We can only guess at how many Buddhists, Hindus, Sikhs, and assorted other religionists inhabit our planet. In the United States alone, we number several hundred Protestant denominations. "Man is a religious being," wrote Paul Hutchinson. And George Bernard Shaw speculated that, "There is only one religion, though there are a hundred versions of it." Of all the varied religious groups, we Jews are among the smallest, numbering only 13 million or so worldwide. Evidently, we humans are all searching for something intangible: We are seeking a sense of transcendence; we are endeavoring to find answers to gnawing problems and issues of life and death. We struggle to discover the way one must live and conduct one's affairs and the proper means of relating to one another. We are endeavoring to find the right path to "salvation," whether that special place is Heaven, Nirvana, *olam ha-ba*, or however we choose to define that term. Each faith has developed its own approach to these challenges; each believes it has a right path to truth, if not the right path to truth. How each group relates to one another presents one of the greatest challenges of civilization today. Up until now, humanity has performed poorly in this area, to put the case mildly. We have conquered, slaughtered, destroyed, ruined, expelled, tortured, and murdered countless millions in the name of a Higher Power. I dare say that the wars of religion have filled our planet with as much blood as all the secular battles among nations, tribes, and peoples. That fact should make each and every one of us deeply saddened and ashamed. And the greater shame is that in this twenty-first century, the phenomenon has yet to disappear.

Have we, Jews, learned anything from all of this sorry record? And have we anything to teach others about relating to others in justice, harmony, and peace? In short, what is Judaism's attitude toward other faiths and religions? And, more vitally, what must its attitude be if we are to witness a modicum of religious peace on earth?

The Bible certainly adopted a very negative attitude toward the pagan peoples who surrounded the Hebrews. The Bible terms those pagans, *nokhri* (plural, *nokhrim*). The word, *goy* (plural, *goyim*), with which we are most familiar, referred in the Bible to all peoples, including the Hebrews. Only much later on, in rabbinic days, was the term, *goy*, used in reference to non-Jews. In keeping with its severely critical attitude toward pagan religions, biblical Judaism called for the elimination of those pagan peoples whose very presence posed a grave danger for Judaism, threatening to overwhelm our ancestors with pagan pollution including false gods and idolatry, depraved morality, temple prostitution, child sacrifice, and all other manner of sinful and perverse behavior (Exod 17:14–16; Deut 25:17–19, and parallels). Joshua is supposed to have crushed and dispossessed those peoples, although the book of Judges indicates that the process was not total. The Torah admonishes us to abhor the pagan idols and totems and to shun and destroy them utterly (Deut 7:25–26). But as late as the fifth century B.C.E., Ezra and Nehemiah were constrained to struggle with numerous Jews who were intermarried and whose spouses were seducing them into various pagan practices, including worship of fetishes and totems (Ezra 9–10; Neh 9:1–2, 10:31, 13:1–3). Evidently Ezra and Nehemiah forced the Jewish spouses to either divorce or convert the non-Jewish partners to preserve the integrity of the Jewish religion. But many centuries later, rabbinic laws record that descendants of those original nations were still to be found in Israel in the days of the Second Temple, an indication that the ethnic absorption was far from complete.

However, that is only part of the tale of Judaism's relationship to other faith groups. The Torah commands us on numerous occasions to love the *ger*, the stranger and foreigner, because we, too, once were strangers and foreigners in the Land of Egypt; we understand only too well the sense of estrangement and feeling of discrimination experienced by strangers in a foreign land (Exod 22:20 and many parallels). The Book of Ruth depicts in charmingly touching fashion how a young Moabite woman was accepted into the fold of Israel and, in fact, became an ancestor of King David. Nor should we overlook the fact that God entered into a covenant with all peoples, not just Jews. The Noahide laws and covenant are indications of the love God has for all peoples, including pagans. These laws include six negative commandments: no idolatry, no blasphemy, no murder, no sexual immorality, no stealing, and no eating a limb from a living animal.

The positive commandment is the establishment of courts of justice (Gen 9:1–17; *Sanh.* 56a).

The rabbinic attitude toward pagans was profoundly negative and critical. Idol worshipers were viewed by the sages of the Talmud and Midrash as killers, thugs, sexual perverts, people of loose morals, untrustworthy, and dishonest individuals. An entire Talmudic tractate, *Avodah Zarah*, is devoted to the subject of the relationship between Jews and non-Jews. It does not portray non-Jews in a sympathetic or positive light. Undoubtedly, the Jewish hatred for pagans deepened after the disastrous Roman Wars that left the Temple destroyed, Jerusalem in ruins, and much of the country devastated. There are a considerable number of negative statements about Rome or "Edom," a pseudonym for the Roman government, in rabbinic literature. We are not to do business with pagans three days prior to and on their festivals. Why not? The Talmud (*m. Abod. Zar.* 1:1 and *Gemara*) explains that we must not give them joy on their festivals or a reason to bring a thanksgiving offering to their idolatrous temples in gratitude for a successful business deal with the Jews.

But there is another side to the picture. Some rabbis were of the opinion that the pagan who studies Torah stands on a level with the High Priest (*Abod. Zar.* 3a). Torah may not be found among pagans but wisdom certainly is. We learn many things from pagans, including, in one specific case of a pagan named Dama, son of Netinah, the mitzvah of honoring a parent. A Jewish physician is permitted to heal pagan sick for a fee. We must support their poor, especially in the Sabbatical years when the land lies fallow, and visit their sick. We may not kill a pagan, except in war. And we should, indeed, greet them for the sake of peace (*mipnei darkhei shalom*) and in order to avoid enmity (*mipnei eivah*), and wish them a good harvest. In fact, Rabban Yohanan ben Zakkai would always greet pagans in the market place (*Ber.*17a). Some sages insisted that dishonest behavior towards gentiles is allowed. But Rabbi Akiva ruled that if there is the possibility of a desecration of God's name (*hillul ha-Shem*), then we may not trick, deceive, defraud, or profit from a gentile's mistakes but we must sanctify God's name (*kiddush ha-Shem*) via honest behavior (*B. Qam.* 113a–b).

Whether the commandment, "You shall love your neighbor as yourself" (Lev 19:18), includes non-Jews was hotly debated and the interpretation varied with the political circumstances. As Jews were increasingly marginalized by religious or state laws and decimated in wars, their understanding of this great commandment narrowed and became more parochial. Still, we detect an inescapable move to reevaluate our perception of the pagan world. Rav Nahman stated in the name of Rabbah bar Abuha that gentiles outside of Eretz Yisrael are not really idolaters; they merely follow the customs of their ancestors (*Hul.* 13b), and the medieval Tosafists expanded the rule to include gentiles living in Eretz Yisrael. Further, we are told that Rav Yehudah sent a gift to a pagan friend on the latter's holiday because he was confident that his friend did not worship idols. Likewise, Rav sent a gift to a pagan friend on a pagan festival because, he too, was certain that his friend did not worship idols (*Abod. Zar.* 64b). This last passage is quoted numerous times by medieval scholars in justifying their more liberal stance toward gentiles.

An even more profoundly meaningful debate centers on the matter of "salvation": obtaining a portion in the afterlife. Rabbi Eliezer argued that the gentile nations do not have a portion in the afterlife. But Rabbi Joshua disagreed, insisting that "there are *tzaddikim* (righteous) among the nations and they, indeed, have a portion in the afterlife" (*t. San.* 13:2, p. 434). This famous formulation, dating to the second century C.E., that the righteous people (*tzaddikim*) of the non-Jewish nations have a share in the afterlife became the normative Jewish view. So, for example, when the Roman Emperor Antoninus (his identity is uncertain) asked his friend, Rabbi Yehudah Ha-Nasi, the Prince, whether he might enter the world to come, Rabbi Yehudah replied, "Yes, indeed. Only when a non-Jew behaves like the wicked Esau is he denied a share in the afterlife; if the person is righteous, the portion awaits him" (*Abod. Zar.* 10b on Obad. 1:18). I challenge anyone to show me any other Western religion that arrived at such a conclusion then or now.

So much for Judaism's attitude towards the pagan world: What of Judaism's attitude toward other monotheistic religions, specifically, Christianity and Islam?

Surprisingly, the Talmud has virtually no references to Christianity. There are perhaps four authentic references to Jesus in the Talmud. Only one verse from the Gospels (Matt 5:17, "I come not to abolish the law but to fulfill it") is quoted (*Shabb.* 116a–b). We can understand that the Babylonian Talmud rarely mentions Christians or their new faith because there were so few in Babylonia, but it is puzzling that the Palestinian Talmud, whose sages did encounter early Christian communities, is almost silent on the subject. One possibility is that there were so few contacts that the rabbis ignored the matter entirely. Another possibility is that they were contemptuous of this new group of *minim* (heretics, sectarians) and were indifferent to them. It is also conceivable that with the conversion of Constantine to Christianity, they were fearful of punishment if their criticisms were too unguarded. A final possibility is that there were, indeed, references to the Nazarenes (*notzrim*), as they were called, but internal and external censorship deleted the relevant references from our editions. Obviously, since the Talmud was edited before the advent of Islam, there are no allusions to the new faith, although there are references to Islam in some of the later *Midrashim*.

As the situation of the Jews in Christian lands became more precarious, the medieval Jewish view of Christianity turned more hostile and demeaning. Forced conversions, expulsions, compulsory attendance at conversionist sermons, public disputations defending Judaism against the onslaught of the dominant faith, censorship and burning of Hebrew books such as the Talmud, all contributed to the increasing disdain the Jewish teachers and scholars felt for Christianity. This contempt was confined, for obvious reasons, to polemical writings that refuted the Christian claims concerning the messianic role of Jesus, and a few scurrilous books and tracts that expressed insulting views of Jesus and Christianity. Many of the early sages equated Christianity with paganism, partly because of its cult of the divinity of Jesus, partly as a reaction to the triune God, partly due to the presence of statues in churches and cathedrals. Jews shunned priests and monks, avoided contact with Christian holy objects, and refused to even enter a church. In the wake of the Crusades, Christian-Jewish relations deteriorated sharply and were further poisoned by the increasingly anti-Jewish legislation of popes and councils, especially after Lateran Council IV (1215), when, at the instigation of Pope Innocent III, the Jew badge was introduced, further segregating Jews from their Christian neighbors and marking them as ready targets for insults and even injury and death.

Sometimes, economic considerations overcame many of the qualms Jews felt about interacting with Christians. The ancient prohibitions against doing business with pagans on or just before their holidays created an unbearable burden for Jews, especially where they constituted a small minority. In Babylonia and Eretz Yisrael, the Jewish communities were sufficiently large to avoid dealing with pagans without damaging their economies. But in Europe where Jews formed a small or even tiny part of the greater Christian world, those old rabbinic caveats were no longer feasible. Jews were required to do business on Christmas and Easter in order to survive, and they needed to be present at the various fairs that attracted thousands of merchants, from far and wide. They engaged in the wine and cattle trade, businesses that inevitably compelled them to deal with Christians. But if Christians were considered by halakhah to be pagans, how could Jews possibly deal with them and stay afloat in a gentile world? A creative and revolutionary approach to the halakhah dealing with pagans was required, and it was forthcoming. This is one of the striking illustrations of how halakhah responded to economic necessities boldly and radically.

Rabbi Natronai Gaon of Babylonia (ninth century) is reported to have ruled that we may trade with Christians and Muslims, even on their festivals, to avoid creating enmity. Rabbenu Gershom of Mayence (tenth-eleventh centuries) also ruled that we may trade with Christians even on Christmas and Easter lest we ruin the Jewish merchants economically, "for it is better that they sin inadvertently rather than deliberately since their very livelihoods depend on trade." Moreover, he added, this is an urgent situation and it is proper for us to recall the words of Rabbi Yohanan, "Gentiles outside of Israel are not idolaters; they merely follow the custom of their ancestors" (*Hul.* 13b).

Still, the prevailing view was that Christians are idolaters; the economic alleviations did not reflect a change of thinking or bring a rapprochement on that issue. The great Rashi (1040–1105), who was a vintner by trade, followed the same course of action, based on Rabbenu Gershom's ruling. But gradually, a different approach was suggested by Rabbi Isaac Or Zarua and two of Rashi's distinguished grandsons: Rashbam and Rabbenu Tam. They gravitated toward the view that contemporary gentiles are not pagans; they no longer pour libations to the gods with the harvested wine, and they no longer sacrifice animals on pagan altars. Consequently, the twelfth-century sages allowed doing business on Christian holidays, permitted Christian workers to handle the grapes, grape juice, and casks of wine, sanctioned partnerships between Jews and non-Jews, and, according to some, even accepted Christian oaths because "although they swear by the name of Jesus, their intention is to swear in the name of the God of heaven and earth." *Sefer Hasidim* indicates that German Jewry in the thirteenth century was also admonished to deal fairly and honestly with non-Jews in business dealings, that we were never to cheat or deceive them, or curse them secretly. Maimonides, however, considered Christians to be idolaters, and he therefore specifically prohibited doing business with them on Sundays and Christian festivals. But his view was a minority one; the prevailing opinion of both Sephardic and Ashkenazic authorities, certainly by the twelfth century, was that we allow business dealings with Christians because they are not pagans. The later codes, including the *Shulhan Arukh*, do not view Christians as idolaters, require Jews to return their lost property, and insist that Jews are to deal with them honestly and fairly (*Shulhan Arukh, Yoreh Deah*, 148:4,12 and parallels).

The most revolutionary advances in relating to Christians came from the pen of the remarkable Provençal Rabbi, Menahem Meiri of Perpignon (d.1316). Meiri essentially created a new category of religious human beings: "*umot ha-gedurot be-darkhei ha-datot ve-nimusim*, people who are regulated by the laws and norms of religion." This category raised Christians and Muslims above the level of nations bound by the seven Noahide laws while not quite situating them at the level of the Jewish people who are obliged to observe 613 *mitzvot*. Meiri specifically placed Christians and Muslims in this new category, and he argued that whenever the Talmud refers to a *goy* or *nokhri*, it refers to pagans of those days, not to contemporary Christians or Muslims. Consequently, we are obliged to save a Christian or Muslim whose life is threatened; we are to deal fairly and honestly with them in business as we would a fellow-Jew; we are to return their lost property; and we ignore the Talmudic prohibitions against associating with non-Jews lest they rape our women and children or copulate with our animals, because that only applied in pagan times. In short, as Jacob Katz and Moshe Habertal have demonstrated, Meiri essentially removed all legal discrimination against non-Jews since today's Christians and Muslims are not pagans and may not be treated as such. Meiri's view remained in manuscript for many centuries and was, at first, only a minority opinion. But gradually, over the centuries, his remarkably fresh approach to interfaith relations has gained increasing numbers of adherents and served as a precedent for a new attitude toward the other faith groups.

So much for the legal standing of Christians and Muslims in Jewish law: What of the theological opinions of Jewish thinkers and philosophers toward Christianity and Islam? As I noted in a previous chapter, virtually all Jewish commentators and sages viewed Islam as a monotheistic religion. Despite their negative views of Muhammad and their battle against the Islamic teaching that Jews had falsified the Scriptures, Maimonides, Solomon ibn Adret (Rashba), Yehudah Halevi, Joseph Albo, all considered Islam a pure, monotheistic faith. Yehudah Halevi and Maimonides both viewed Islam and Christianity, as poor imitations of the original faith of Judaism, but both affirmed the monotheistic nature of Islam. Yehudah Halevi introduces something precious and new. At the same time that he insists there cannot be two competing truths in religions, he states that Judaism is like the seed of a tree; that all subsequent monotheistic religions drew their nourishment from the original: "They merely serve to introduce and pave the way for the expected messiah: he is the fruit; all will be his fruit, if they will acknowledge him, and will become one tree. Then they will revere the root they formerly despised . . . ." (*Kuzari* 4:23, p. 252).

Medieval Judaism's view of Christianity is much more complex. The sages had developed the notion of *shittuf* (association), that is, a person who prays to God and, in his mind, associates another deity with the concept of God, is an idolater. The question is: Since Christians associate Jesus with God, are they idolaters? Maimonides believed they were idolaters, although his views changed with the circumstances that precipitated his written opinions. He was terribly critical of Jesus and Christianity in his famous Letter to Yemen in which he sought to bolster the faith of Yemenite Jewry that was being seduced by a false messiah. However, in his law code he built on the concept that the two daughter religions of Judaism are designed to help spread the message of Judaism far and wide. In one of his most famous passages on the subject, in the uncensored version of his *Mishneh Torah* (*Melakhim*, 11:4) we find the following:

> The missions of Jesus and Muhammad have helped pave the way for the coming of the messiah by improving the nature of mankind through the universal worship of God that has brought them near to His service . . . The whole world has been saturated with the teachings of the messiah, the Torah, and the commandments. These doctrines have been spread to the furthest isles and among numerous heathen peoples who are now engaged in the various commandments of the Bible . . . But I believe that when the true king messiah rises among us and triumphs over all and is exalted and honored, then all religions will acknowledge his teachings and will return to the source of their faith and correct the errors of their prophets and ancestors.

Most importantly, Maimonides ruled in his *Mishneh Torah* (*Teshuvah*, 3:5; *Melakhim*, 8:10) that, "*Hasidei umot ha-olam*, the pious of the nations have a portion in the afterlife." He defined the "pious" as those people who adopt the seven commandments given to Noah. Maimonides' remarkable formulation is accepted by virtually all who followed him, including kabbalists and legal scholars, Hasidim and their opposing *Mitnagdim*. Moreover, Maimonides ruled that we may not force a non-Jew to convert to Judaism, although we may compel a pagan to accept the Noahide laws. Over time, the codifiers accepted the notion that whereas Jews who associate God with another deity are guilty of idolatry, this prohibition does not apply to non-Jews. In other words, even if a Christian thinks of Jesus when praying, we accept the view that he really is praying to the one true God of heaven and earth. The codified halakhah in the *Shulhan Arukh* (*Orah Hayim*, 156) states precisely this position.

As the modern period approached, how did Jews revise their attitudes towards non-Jews? Glimmers of a new approach to other faiths appeared at first in Italy where Jewry was generally more progressive and worldly than elsewhere. Rabbi Abraham Farissol of Ferrara (d.1528), a member of the circle of the eminent Christian Hebraist and kabbalist, Pico Della Mirandola, expressed, what I believe to be, a remarkably unique view of Jesus. He affirms that the messiah has come for the non-Jewish world in the person of Jesus of Nazareth because he purified their beliefs of the pollution of idolatry and eliminated idol worship in most of the then known world. But he had not come to save Israel since he failed to rebuild the Temple and usher in a new era of universal peace; therefore, he may not be called the Jewish messiah. Moreover, "because of him and his apostles and disciples, the peoples of the earth have been brought to a belief in the unity of the First Cause."

This extraordinary understanding of Jesus as, indeed, the messiah for the gentiles, appears again in the writings of the famous Venetian Rabbi Leone Yehudah Aryeh Modena (1571–1648). Modena wrote that Jesus never pretended to be God or a part of God, but was, rather, a "great prophet who was close to God and he never foresaw what resulted after his death." However, the prophets of Israel looked forward to the end of days when the messiah would bring salvation to Israel and then to the entire world. Jesus claimed he was sent to save Israel, but in fact, he nearly destroyed them: "Who can believe it to be God's will that He would send a messiah to cause destruction and annihilation of the body and soul of His chosen people while saving the rest of humanity?" Although Modena denounced the cult of Mary as smacking of idolatry, he did not consider praying to Jesus idolatry since Christians identify Jesus with God. His younger Venetian contemporary, Rabbi Simhah Luzzatto, maintained that we are all created in the image of God, that there is no distinction between Jew and non-Jew; consequently, it is a sin to injure or exploit a non-Jew because that constitutes *hillul ha-Shem*, a desecration of God's name. He interpreted the passages in the Bible regulating relations with our "brother" or "neighbor" to include non-Jews as well as Jews and he insisted that, "Jews believe gentiles and those of other faiths are part of the human family, provided they keep the natural moral laws and accept the concept of a Higher Power."

The renowned Talmudist and physician of Ferrara, Rabbi Isaac Lampronti (1679–1756), in his pioneering Talmudic encyclopedia, *Pahad*

Yitzhak, writes: "Whenever I use the term, '*goy*,' I refer to the pagans of ancient times. It is not my intention to refer to Christians because they are not idolaters and they believe in the unity of God. Moreover, they are not suspected of bloodshed, or of sodomy or of theft, but, indeed, are more strict than we are in punishing violators; all those who shed blood or commit bestiality or homosexuality are severely punished. They are severe in executing thieves, whereas we merely impose monetary fines on thieves." He adds, "Whenever the sages of old refer to *goyim*, they mean pagans of their time who worshiped stars and constellations; who did not believe in the Exodus from Egypt and in the creation of the universe out of nothing. But today's *goyim*, among whom we dwell and to whom we turn for protection, believe in the creation of the universe out of nothing, and in the Exodus from Egypt, as well as other basic principles of religion. When they pray, their intention is to the Maker of heaven and earth, as many of our decisors have written."

Rabbi Lampronti had in mind some of the great Polish annotators of the authoritative code of Jewish law, the *Shulhan Arukh*, and he actually quotes several of them in noting their revised view of the non-Jew. For example, Rabbi Moses Isserles of Krakow (1525?–1572), whose glosses on the *Shulhan Arukh* of Joseph Karo are accepted as binding by virtually all Ashkenazic Jews, wrote, "Israel, Esau [Christians], and Ishmael [Muslims] are all children of Abraham . . . the father of all believers . . . and they all received their beliefs equally from Abraham. Consequently, even though Esau and Ishmael err and add strange elements into their faiths and worship in a strange cult, nevertheless, they all acknowledge God as the ruler of the world. This is their nature because the custom of their father, Abraham, is part of their lives." Isserles allowed business partnerships with non-Jews and consuming their wine and bread because, "Today's non-Jews do not swear to pagan gods . . . but their intention in oaths is to the Maker of heaven and earth, and if they associate some other power [Jesus] with God, this is no violation . . . because gentiles are not prohibited from such association [*shittuf*]." Rabbi Moshe Rivkes (d.1671–72) in his authoritative commentary on the *Shulhan Arukh*, follows the same argument in distinguishing between the pagans of antiquity and today's Christians and Muslims who believe in the creation out of nothing, the Exodus from Egypt, "and the main principles of religion, and their whole aim and intent is to the Maker of heaven and earth."

As we enter the modern era, we must note the remarkable views of the distinguished German Rabbi Jacob Emden (1697–1776), whose views on Jesus and Christianity were revolutionary, to say the least. He wrote that Jesus and his apostles never intended to abolish the *mitzvot* (he cites Matt 5:17 ff. in this regard), but he hoped to "establish a new religion for the gentiles from that time onward." This new religion was actually not completely new but consisted of the seven commandments given to Noah and his descendants; only Jews are obligated to keep all 613. But Jesus knew this would be too difficult for the non-Jews, so he actually forbade circumcision for their males:

> The Nazarene brought a double blessing to the world. On the one hand, he strengthened the Torah of Moses majestically, . . . and on the other hand, he did much good for the gentiles . . . by doing away with idolatry and removing the images from their midst. He obligated them with the seven commandments so that they would not be as the beasts of the field. He also bestowed on them ethical ways, and in this respect he was much more stringent with them than the Torah of Moses . . . for they even said we must love one's enemies. How much more so us! In the name of heaven, we are your brothers! One God has created us all.

Emden extended this new appreciation of Christianity to Islam as well, since Muslims, too, recognize the Creator of the world and abide by the seven basic laws of Noah, believe in the difference between good and evil, and look forward to an afterlife. Emden's celebrated contemporary and literary friend, Moses Mendelssohn (1729–1786), shared these views, extending them further. He indicated that he acknowledged the innocence and moral goodness of Jesus on the conditions that he never meant to regard himself as equal to the Father, that he never proclaimed himself a divinity, that he never claimed the honor of worship, and that he did not intend to subvert the religion of his fathers. Mendelssohn wrote: "Since the Creator intended all humans for eternal bliss, an exclusive religion cannot be a true one. I venture to state this as a criterion for truth in religious matters. No revelation purporting to be alone capable of saving man can be the true revelation if it does not harmonize with the purpose of the All-Merciful Creator."

The nineteenth and twentieth centuries witnessed yet new appreciations of the other faiths by some of Judaism's most profound thinkers. One of the most interesting and unusual approaches was championed by an Italian rabbi, philosopher and kabbalist, Rabbi Elia Benamozegh of Livorno (1823–1900). Benamozegh urged a universal religion for non-Jews based on the seven Noahide laws, in what he called "a religion of Noahism." This is a "universal law that exists alongside Mosaism." Since Judaism does not require a non-Jew to convert and accept the mitzvah system of the Torah, all that is necessary is for non-Jews to accept the Noahide laws. At the same time, Benamozegh wrote:

> There is no Jew worthy of the name who does not rejoice in the great transformation wrought by Christianity and Islam in a world formerly defiled. We cannot listen to the noblest and most precious names in Judaism, the echoes of its holy books, the recollection of its great events, its hymns and prophecies, in the mouths of so many millions of former pagans of all races, joined together to worship the God of Israel in churches and mosques, without feeling imbued with a legitimate pride of gratitude and love towards the God who affected such great miracles.

While paying tribute to the teachings of Jesus that are marked by "simplicity, grandeur, and infinite tenderness," Benamozegh indicated that Jesus never set out to form a new religion. His mission failed in the sense that the world is not redeemed. But his second coming can be brought about with all the hoped-for blessings of universal salvation, if the two sister religions are reconciled and foster "Noahide universal religion." Benamozegh's unique proposal has met with virtually no success and has been relegated to the realm of curiosity.

Far more powerful in impact have been the teachings of the renowned German-Jewish philosopher, Franz Rosenzweig (1886–1929). Rosenzweig wrote in his *Star of Redemption* that, "Before God, Jews and Christians both labor at the same task. He [God] cannot dispense with either. The truth, the whole truth, thus belongs neither to them nor to us. Just for this we remain. Thus we both have but part of the truth. Only God has the whole truth." Consequently, Jews and Christians now wait and hope "only for the great reconciliation on the very last day." Many have deduced from Rosenzweig's words that he was propounding a theory of two covenants: one with Israel, the other with Christianity. In truth, he never quite says this. But we can infer from his remarks that he was, indeed, committed to the notion that no one faith group has a monopoly on truth; that we all have but a part of the whole truth, known to God alone; and that it follows that each is to be respected and honored for its own particular contribution to human salvation, the ultimate unfolding of which is God's secret will.

How have the various streams in Jewish religious life related to the other faiths? The answer is that each group carved out its own niche in interreligious work, some more intensively committed to it, some less; some embracing with fervor the need to work together, others rejecting any significant contact.

The Orthodox stream in Judaism has been loathe to involve itself in interreligious work. For many years, Orthodox rabbis were reluctant to meet with their Christian counterparts. Above all, they have been resistant to theological discussions. Much of this stems from deep-seeded prejudices, the result of centuries of suffering at the hand of the daughter religion, and the fear that such discussions are merely camouflage for proselytizing. I know of Orthodox rabbis who refuse even to enter a church, and for many years, the various Orthodox rabbinical groups invoked sanctions against their members who did so. Some, of course, have been involved in such outreach to other faith groups; but the vast majority has not and the Orthodox rabbinic bodies have consistently opposed such endeavors except in the realm of social justice.

The Reform movement has stood in the vanguard of interfaith efforts. From its very beginnings, Reform Judaism has insisted that Jews work together with all faith groups in the search for a better society and more peaceful world. Most Reform rabbis are involved in dialogues with Christian, and even Muslim, colleagues. The Hebrew Union College has included courses in Christianity in its curriculum. From time to time, the leaders of the movement have urged that Jews reclaim Jesus as one of their native sons. When Rabbi Stephen S. Wise delivered a talk on this subject in 1925, advocating the restoration of Jesus to the ranks of one of Israel's great teachers and prophets, he garnered national attention, and earned the vilification of many Jews. The Reform position is clear, however, that if we fail to talk and dialogue with one another, nothing will be accomplished in improving relations between faith groups.

The Conservative movement has also been involved in interfaith dialogue, but to a lesser degree than the Reform movement. Rabbi Louis Finkelstein, late head of the Jewish Theological Seminary, pioneered in outreach to non-Jewish theologians and scholars. The periodic meetings and conferences as well as the volumes that emerged from those gatherings were important contributions to interreligious work. Dr. Abraham Joshua Heschel was profoundly immersed in discussions and study with Catholic and Protestant scholars and teachers. In sum, the movement recognizes that "although we have but one God, God has more than one nation" with whom He has entered covenants. Conservative Judaism is committed to improved understanding of other faiths and joint efforts to fashion a better society and world.

Reconstructionism has not been overly enamored of interfaith work. Dr. Mordecai M. Kaplan was badly shaken by the Holocaust and remained wary of faiths claiming to possess "the truth," and he had little patience for "gestures of good will." In a position curiously close to that of Orthodoxy, he suggested that the best we can do is work together on common ethical ideals and strive for civic justice, elimination of poverty, fight disease, defend the oppressed, and foster mutual respect and affection. More recently, the Reconstructionists have engaged increasingly with other faith communities in both social justice and theological concerns.

The impact of the *Shoah* on interreligious affairs has been nothing less than traumatic. The fact that this greatest crime was committed on the soil of Christian Europe impelled both Catholic and Protestant denominations to reexamine their relationship to Judaism and the Jewish people. Protestant theologians such as Reinhold Niebuhr, James Parkes, Roy and Alice Eckardt, and others, posed powerfully searching questions: Had Christian teachings prepared the soil for the Holocaust? Did the churches aid or abet the Nazi crimes? Did church leaders do all they might have done to oppose the murderous regime of the Nazis? Did Christians do all in their power to protect and save Jewish victims of the Nazi fury? These were profoundly painful questions that prompted deep soul-searching among Protestants. But a more powerful catalyst was called for, and that catalyst was provided by Pope John XXIII, Vatican Council II, and its historic pronouncement on relations with other religions, *Nostra Aetate* ("In Our Time").

Pope John XXIII had served as nuncio in Turkey and Bulgaria during the Second World War. He knew what was happening to European Jewry and was deeply chagrined at the inactivity of his church. When he became pope, he was determined to turn a new page in Catholic-Jewish relations and uproot the "teaching of contempt" that had prepared the soil for the *Shoah*. The result was section four of *Nostra Aetate*, on relations with the Jews, a document that changed the religious world. Promulgated in October of 1965, the document was revolutionary because it states that Jews are still and forever in the covenant with God; that Christianity's roots are from Judaism, and that Jesus and his disciples were all Jews. Furthermore, it states clearly that the crucifixion cannot be ascribed to all Jews then or now so that Jews are not a deicide people; it urges understanding and respectful studies and dialogue between the faith groups; and it deplores anti-Semitism and mandates the removal of the teaching of contempt from textbooks, catechism, teaching, and sermons. Unquestionably, *Nostra Aetate* sparked a Copernican revolution that led to several important documents that fleshed out this sea change in relations between the two faiths.

The late Pope John Paul II dedicated much of his pontificate to build-ing on the foundation laid at Vatican Council II. Undoubtedly, his Polish background and intimate acquaintance with Jews and their tragic fate shaped his thinking and actions. He visited the Rome synagogue in 1986, denounced anti-Semitism as a sin against God and humanity, and referred to Judaism as the "elder brother" to Christianity. The Pope extended dip-lomatic recognition to the State of Israel, went on a remarkable pilgrim-age to Israel and the Western Wall, visited Auschwitz, where he begged forgiveness for the sins of Catholics during the *Shoah*, and called for the "purification of memory" in facing up to the tragedy of those times. He did more than any pope in history to set Catholic-Jewish relations aright.

In the wake of this historic change, Protestant and Eastern Orthodox churches began to revise their teachings about Jews and Judaism. A new spirit of amity has filled the air; meaningful dialogues and study pro-grams are flourishing between the Jewish community and the Protestant and Orthodox world. The most significant Protestant groups have issued documents expressing remorse for the *Shoah* and have begun urging a new understanding of the meaning of Judaism for Protestants.

How has the Jewish world reacted to this new spirit emanating from Christian quarters? For many, it is a matter of indifference. Having lived through 19 centuries of Christian anti-Judaism, and having endured the unspeakable *Shoah* in Christian Europe, many simply ignore the new out-reach as too little, too late. Most Orthodox Jews have either been indiffer-ent or rebuffed any friendly overtures from Christians. Much of this is due to the unfortunate 1964 article by Rabbi Joseph Soloveitchik, in which he insisted that we may not discuss theological matters with non-Jews because our universe of discourse is totally different. At best, we may only work to-gether in the secular realm, in social action and programs to achieve social justice. Rabbi Moshe Feinstein went even further: He expressed the view that dialogue is merely a thin cover for proselytism and can only lead to assimilation. He described Christianity as idolatry, and he therefore pro-hibited all Jews from contact with Christians because "only isolation can assure our survival." These views have prevailed in Orthodox Jewish circles until quite recently, when we are finally witnessing Orthodox discussions with Christians on theological issues. In fact, the Israeli chief rabbinate is officially engaged in such discussion with the Vatican's Commission for Religious Relations with Jews. On the other hand, the other streams in Jewry have accepted the outstretched hands of Christians and dialogues, joint study programs, and university departments are intensely involved in efforts to better understand one another and to build cordial relations.

A group of over 200 rabbis, theologians and educators from all streams of Judaism, signed a document called, *Dabru Emet* ("Speak Truth") in 2000. This document is an attempt to respond to the efforts of the Christian world to turn a new page in our relations. It indicates that we worship the same God, share part of Sacred Scriptures, adhere to a similar moral standard, and need to work together to improve our world. Since there is no one central religious body for American Jewry, the document has no official standing. Additionally, it was severely criticized by some for blurring crucial differences between the faiths. But despite its imperfections, it is an important first step in responding from the Jewish side to the over 40 years of outreach from the Christian world, and I trust, it will not be the last response. We have much material on Christianity and Islam in legal discussions and halakhic rulings, but no one, so far as I know, has tackled the problem of crafting a theology of the other faiths and our relationship to them.

The critical questions, then, are these: How shall Jews relate to other faiths? How shall we view other religions in the light of our theological convictions coupled with our bitter past experiences of over 19 centuries? Can we develop a theology of the other, or are we to go our separate ways, never speaking or touching or engaging one another in anything resembling true conversation?

First, I believe we must stress that God has drawn up many covenants with many different peoples on earth. The Bible indicates God entered into covenants with Adam and Eve, Noah, Abraham, Israel at Mount Sinai, Joshua, King David, as well as others. God's ability to enter covenants is never limited since God is unlimited and capable of infinite love. Sister Mary Boys poses this question, in her book, *Has God Only One Blessing?* And, of course, her answer is: "Certainly not! God has innumerable blessings and can shower them on whomever He chooses." Rabbi Irving Greenberg, in a similar vein, writes in his volume, *For The Sake of Heaven and Earth,* that God has enough love to extend to as many people as He sees fit. To insist that His love only extends to a few or only one nation is to limit His infinity. Professor Michael Wyschogrod, in his volume, *Abraham's Promise,* spurns the notion that other nations have no covenant with God, because to do so "ignores the promise to Abraham that through his election, the nations, too, will be blessed; it further ignores the covenant with Noah . . . ." To say that God has only sufficient love for one people, only adequate salvation to bestow on but one religion, only enough compassion to extend to but one nation or tribe is to limit the infinite God and place the Creator of the universe in a theological straightjacket and I believe that is a ludicrous and unacceptable position.

Second, I believe that we religious beings are all striving for the same goal, albeit by different routes. We want to "know" God by learning the ways of the Lord. We want to lead the proper, good, and righteous life so that we might achieve "salvation" no matter how one defines that amorphous term. For some it is *olam ha-ba*, an elusive notion, as we shall see in the chapter on the afterlife in Judaism. For yet others, it is Heaven or the Garden of Eden. For still others, it is Nirvana. No matter what we call it, it is the ultimate goal of the striving religious person. This is the way the great Hebrew poet of Spain, Solomon ibn Gabirol (1021–1053 or 1058) conceived of this striving:

> You are God and all creatures are Your servant and worshipers,
> Your glory can never be lacking among the congregation of those
> who serve You alone.
> For the intention of all of them is to reach out to You,
> Even if they stray from the highway of the King and lose the way.

Third, I am absolutely convinced that religions can no longer engage in religious imperialism; in exclusive claims to truth; in a campaign to bring "light and truth" to those immersed in darkness. We must understand that we do not possess the "keys to the kingdom" (Matt 16:19); that "there are many rooms in my Father's house" (John 14:2); that the "pious of all nations have a share in the afterlife." We cannot insist that "I'm in—you are out," because only God truly knows who is in and who is out. The cost of religious imperialism in human blood and anguish, suffering and oppression has been appalling. The bloody borders are not just confined to Islam or Christianity or Hinduism, but to all imperialistic faiths that have been delusional enough to believe that they have a monopoly on truth and it is their manifest destiny to bring that truth to benighted non-believers. The religious wars in history have soaked this planet in enough blood and gore to match any political wars we have endured over the centuries. I watched a documentary program on TV hosted by Barbara Walters on the subject of Heaven and Hell and was appalled by some of the things I heard. A Muslim suicide bomber stated bluntly to Walters, "Of course you Christians and Jews will go to and burn in Hell." And then I watched in dismay as an American Evangelical preacher said exactly the same thing about non-Christians. Such arrogance! The old notion, *extra ecclesiam nulla salus*, there is no salvation outside of the church, is, tragically, very much alive. It is impossible to enter any sort of trusting dialogue with persons who insist that my faith has been superseded or displaced by the other; that one group is in covenant with God while the other is outside; that one is assured "salvation" while the other is forever "lost" or "damned."

A recent scandal that highlighted this issue was the revelation that the Mormon Church has been busily baptizing posthumously millions of non-Mormons, including tens of thousands of Holocaust victims. In the face of bitter protests from the organized Jewish community, and especially from Holocaust survivors who are incensed at this chutzpah, Mormon leaders have adamantly refused to cease and desist from this outrageous practice (despite a 1995 written agreement) because they truly believe that all non-Mormons are barred from heaven unless they are baptized even after death! I believe that this attitude must be banished if ever we are going to enjoy the fruits of religious amity and respect and bring peace to our earth. We have got to learn the lesson Abraham taught us when he cajoled his nephew, Lot, to end their feud, "Let there not be strife between us . . . After all, we are kinsmen" (Gen 13:8).

Let me pose these elementary questions: Since we all, more or less, accept the concept of an omnipotent God who is capable of doing anything He wishes, why has He not led Jews to the truth of Christianity or Islam these past 20 centuries? Does it not seem plausible that we remain stubbornly attached to the faith of Israel despite all pressures, benign and no so benign, because it is God's will?

Fourth, we Jews must adopt the viewpoints of those rabbinic sages and scholars who included all non-Jews who, at the very least, abide by the seven laws of Noah, under the category of "neighbor" and "brother-sister." We must deal with them, as Menahem Meiri ruled, as we would with fellow-Jews, even as we would want them to deal fairly and justly with us. All remnants of legal discrimination against non-Jews in halakhah must be discarded in order to sanctify God's name (*kiddush ha-Shem*). We have sufficient precedents for such a policy, as I have tried to demonstrate. There is simply no room in Judaism for defamatory statements or discriminatory treatment of the other.

Fifth, Jews must realize that Christianity is a faith of over 1.8 billion people on our planet. Are they just to be written off as heretics? Likewise, the over 1 billion Muslims, our half-brothers whose monotheism is pure, even if our understanding of Sacred Scriptures differs: Are they not essential in the process of spreading the essence of Jewish faith "to the furthest isles," as Maimonides had written in the twelfth century? The role of Jesus is problematic, I readily concede. There are those among us who should like to regard Jesus as a great teacher and even a prophet of Israel, for he was, remained, and died a loyal son of Israel. The eminent twentieth-century French-Jewish philosopher, Emanuel Levinas, disagreed: He wrote in his volume, *Difficult Freedom*, "It is not enough to call Jesus Yechou and Rabbi to bring him closer to us. For us, we who are without hatred, there is no friendship. It remains far off. And on his lips, we no longer recognize our own verses." Irving Greenberg has espoused the unusual notion that Jesus was not a "false" messiah but "failed" messiah. His intention was pure and noble; he sought to bring about the Kingdom of Heaven. He failed in that respect but he did serve as the catalyst for hundreds of millions of pagans to accept the notion of one God and the basic doctrine of the Hebrew Scriptures and its ethical system. As Abraham Farrisol, Leone Modena and Jacob Emden suggested, he was indeed the messiah for the pagan world that accepted Christianity but could not submit to the yoke of *mitzvot* of Judaism. Judaism, as we note in our chapter on the messiah, did propose the notion of several messiahs, of forerunners to the true and final messiah, who would lay down their lives in the process of nudging humanity closer to the ultimate redemption. Perhaps we might view Jesus as one of those preliminary messiahs whose role was fulfilled via the ultimate conversion of the pagan world. Likewise we should honor Muhammad, who successfully weaned the Arab world away from idolatry. But the full messianic revelation has yet to come. As long as the wolf does not lie down with the lamb; as long as we cannot sit peaceably under our vine and fig tree; as long as humanity has not yet beaten swords into plowshares and learned not to wage war any longer, He has not yet come. Christians, therefore, look forward to the second coming (*Parousia*); we Jews await the first. In this sense, we are, indeed, "partners in waiting."

Finally, we must continue to talk, dialogue and study together. We must reach out to each other in the spirit of Isaiah (1:18), "Come, now, let us reason together." Abraham Joshua Heschel admonished us that "it is barbaric not to talk with one another," for "no religion is an island." And Michael Wyschogrod, breaking ranks with his revered teacher and mentor, Rabbi Soloveitchik, criticizes Orthodoxy for refusing to talk with the other, noting, "Where there is communication there is hope, but where there is no communication, the very basis of hope is absent." Albert Camus wrote: "What we must fight is fear and silence, and with them the spiritual isolation they involve. What we must defend is dialogue and the universal communication of men." I think we have learned that people who don't talk, shoot and it is the same with nations and religions. Dialogue, of course, must never be a camouflage for proselytism. Dialogue means conversation, not conversion, consultation, not confrontation. Sadly, there is currently no meaningful dialogue with our Muslim cousins. But we must not give up. Once, we Jews, living side by side with Muslims in Spain during its Golden Age, enjoyed cordial relations and enriching dialogues with our Muslim neighbors. That seems impossible in these days as *jihad* (holy war) has assumed such bloody and maniacal proportions and as liberal and forward-looking Islam seems to have been hijacked by fanatics and haters of non-Muslims. Do we really want to continue on the same, well-worn, bloody path of the past 19 centuries? Or do we not accept the need to tear down the walls of suspicion and hatred and erect in their place bridges of understanding and trust?

We have come a long way these past 40 years or so from the days when Christians and Jews scorned each other; when clergy of both faiths were contemptuous of each other and refused to traffic with one another; when a Catholic would avoid stepping into a synagogue and a Jew would cross the street rather than walk in front of a church; when Christians viewed Jews as a deicide people and Jews considered Christians idolaters; when mistrust, suspicion and even hatred marred the relationship between the two faiths. We who are committed to the religious way, are, after all, working towards the same goal. We are striving for the day when, "The Lord shall be one and His name one" (Zech 14:9). And we struggle for the fulfillment of the prophecy, "For then I will turn the people to a pure language, that all may call upon the name of the Lord, to serve Him with common purpose" (Zeph 3:9). In God's good time this dream will be realized. In the meantime, it is up to us to make us worthy of His promised blessings.

Points to Ponder:
How Can Jews Relate to Other Faiths?

1. The author writes that the wars of religion have filled our planet with much blood. Do you agree? And if so, does this not negate the positive value of religion?

2. The Jewish view of pagans was ambivalent. Why do you think that was so?

3. What are the implications of the Noahide laws for Jewish relations with other faith groups?

4. "The righteous of the nations have a portion in the afterlife." How can this teaching bring religious peace to our world?

5. How did political conditions affect Judaism's view of other faiths?

6. Why did many rabbis consider Christianity idolatrous? Why was Islam viewed as monotheistic?

7. The author notes that economic considerations forced a reevaluation of Christianity. What is your reaction?

8. What was so remarkable about the opinions of Yehudah Halevi and Maimonides of Jesus and Muhammad? Are their views helpful to us in formulating a theology of the other faiths?

9. What factors caused early modern rabbis to revise their views of Christians?

10. Why do you think Elia Benamozegh's program of a universal religion failed?

11. Franz Rosenzweig suggested that Judaism and Christianity—and, presumably, other faiths—possess only a part of the whole truth of God. Is this the right approach to interreligious peace?

12. How did Vatican Council II revolutionize Christian-Jewish relations?

13. How have the various streams in Jewish life responded to the new Christian outreach to us?

14. The author offers six suggestions for a Jewish understanding of the other faiths. How do you react to these suggestions?

15. The author insists that "religious imperialism" and "exclusive claims to truth" are at the heart of religious wars and oppression. Do you agree? And can we uproot these notions once and for all?

15

Messiah: Fact or Fancy?

A BIZARRE EVENT captured world attention in January of 1993. A frail, ill, paralyzed and stroke-afflicted old man was about to be crowned and acknowledged as the messiah. The man was the Lubavitcher Rebbe, Rabbi Menachem Mendel Schneerson. The site of this momentous event was the Lubavitcher headquarters at 777 on Eastern Parkway in Brooklyn. Silenced forever by a devastating stroke, the Rebbe could not convey his true feelings nor shall we ever decipher them. Did he approve of his enthusiastic followers' actions? Was he even aware of what was going on? Or was he truly mentally incompetent? The furor that resulted from this messianic pronouncement was palpable. Signs began to sprout like spring flowers with the Rebbe's picture and the slogan, "We want *mashiah* now!" The Jewish community was in turmoil; the non-Jewish community was either befuddled or snickered. Incredibly, the death of the Rebbe in 1994 did not put an end to this messianic fever. Signs appeared in America and Israel with the familiar face and a new legend, "Long live our master and teacher, the King Messiah, Rabbi Menachem Mendel Schneerson!" More sober Orthodox rabbis were deeply troubled by this messianic fever and some, such as Professor David Berger, demanded we put an end to this embarrassing folly at once. Berger convinced the Rabbinical Council of America, the mainstream Orthodox rabbinic group, to denounce this messianic madness, but not without a sharp battle. And still the craze endures. In a letter to *The New York Times* in 1994, Rabbi Shmuel Butman defended the messianic movement and wrote, "Lubavitcher Hasidim believe the time we have to endure without the Rebbe's physical presence will be very short and very soon the Rebbe will lead us to the great and final redemption." The massive placards proclaiming his messianic role that line roads and adorn buildings both in America and in Israel attest to the vitality of this cult.

Why? What is this matter of the messiah? Is this concept an intrinsic part of Judaism? Is it a miracle or is it a form of madness? Joseph Klausner wrote in his pioneering study, *The Messianic Idea in Israel*, that the three gifts Jews left the world are monotheism, refined morality, and prophets of truth and righteousness. To this group, we must add a fourth, he suggested, namely, the belief in the messiah. It is a powerful notion and noble ideal; it is a source of courage and hope. The roots of Christianity lie in the soil of the Jewish idea of the messiah, and to a lesser degree, the roots of Islam. It is a complex concept and often confusing. It comprises many strands and themes, much bipolarity and tensions. Do Jews believe in a personal messiah or a messianic age? Do we believe that the messiah will usher in a catastrophic era for humanity or a utopian society? Is the messiah to be a real human being or a supernatural person? Can our actions hasten the coming of the messiah or is the time of salvation pre-set by God? These are just a few issues engendered by the messianic concept.

The seedbed of the messianic concept in Judaism is the Bible. The ancient Hebrews believed that political and military defeats and natural calamities were all attributable to moral and ritual sins. Only repentance and righteousness could right the scales and achieve atonement and reconciliation with God for the people. But there were times in Israel's history when salvation and political security seemed a distant and unattainable dream, material well-being a distant goal, and freedom an impossible ideal. The slavery period in Egypt was a moment of the deepest despair. Similarly, the era of the Judges was marked by a mood of chaotic hopelessness. But the blackest mood of all was experienced in the time of the Babylonian Exile when it appeared that all was lost, that hope was dead, that Israel, in Ezekiel's matchless words, was but a fossil, a people of dry bones. Similar moods of depression gripped the people in Maccabean times and in the era of the Roman Wars, as well as in the days of medieval calamities, expulsions, and persecutions. In such calamitous days when hope flagged, the people yearned for a strong savior who would smite their enemies and redeem them. This savior was destined to be anointed by God (*mashiah*) even as the High Priests, prophets, and kings were anointed with olive oil as a symbol of their Divine mission or sacred purpose. The term, "messiah," is from the Greek version of the Hebrew, *mashiah*—"anointed one." In the Bible, the Lord Himself is the redeemer; the messianic agents merely carry out His will, whether it was Moses or Joshua, Gideon or Saul, David or Hezekiah—even the Persian King Cyrus the Great, who invited the Hebrew exiles to return to their homeland and rebuild their Temple. In other words, in the Bible, the messiahs are not supernatural beings but leaders who are human agents carrying out the will of God who, alone, is the redeemer and savior.

Israel's prophets developed the notion of the messianic era to the richest and fullest expression. They looked forward to *aharit ha-yamim*, "the end of days, the future time," when a savior would deliver Israel from her enemies, free the nation from oppression and bondage, restore political independence and stability to Jewish life, and return the exiles to the homeland. But they also preached a utopian vision of cosmic proportions: They anticipated a golden age in the future when humanity as a whole would evolve into a higher state of development; when spiritual bliss will reign; when humankind will be restored to the utopia of the Garden of Eden and the golden age of harmonious nature will be realized; and when nature will be radically altered. In short, their vision was both national and universal: it embraced both Israel and the world.

The prophets of Israel invested these messianic ideas with richness and variations that would provide a rich lode for later sages and philosophers to mine. They expounded on two basic themes: a belief in a strong, charismatic leader who would serve as God's emissary in leading Israel to national rejuvenation and glory; and a belief in a new age or end of time or human history when God's words would be implanted in the human heart, nature would be altered, violence disappear, and universal peace and justice would reign supreme. Isaiah, Micah, Jeremiah, Hosea, and other prophets expanded on these themes broadly and deeply. They developed the philosophy of the end of time, "eschatology," from the Greek word, *eschaton*, meaning, "end."

Amos, the earliest of the literary prophets, was obsessed with visions of doom and gloom that will precede the messianic era. He depicted the "Day of the Lord" as a dreadful day of reckoning for Israel. Hosea added a new element or two as he viewed punishment as a means to moral reform. He also anticipated a righteous leader who would succeed in ending anarchy and political corruption of the monarchy of the Northern Kingdom of Israel. He went further by predicting a change in nature for good and blessing and an era of world peace and universal disarmament—the first author ever to espouse this dream.

No one was richer or more poetic in his messianic themes than Isaiah. He looked forward to a strong, charismatic leader (apparently, King Hezekiah) who would exemplify the highest political, spiritual, ethical, and physical qualities. The Davidic dynasty served as a paradigm of great leadership because David was beloved as the ideal king who had founded the dynasty of kings and unified the people. He was also known as "the sweet singer of Israel"—the author of the cherished Psalms. Hence, the commonly held view was that the messiah would emerge from the descendants or house of King David (*beit David*). He will be filled with "a spirit of wisdom and insight, a spirit of counsel and valor, a spirit of devotion and reverence for the Lord: he shall not judge by what his eyes behold, nor decide by what his ears perceive. Thus he shall judge the poor with equity and decide justice for the lowly of the land" (11:1 ff.). Isaiah's greatest prophecy (2:1 ff.) of the end of history envisions an end to wars and human and natural evil, an end to suffering and death, and a radical transformation of nature, with peace and brotherhood triumphant:

> The wolf shall dwell with the lamb, the leopard lie down with the kid; the calf, the beast of prey and the fatling together, with a little boy to herd them . . . In all of My sacred mount nothing evil or vile shall be done; for the land shall be filled with the knowledge of the Lord as waters cover the sea. . . . For Torah shall come forth from Zion, the word of the Lord from Jerusalem. . . . And they shall beat their swords into plowshares and their spears into pruning hooks: Nation shall not take up sword against nation; they shall never again learn war.

Each of the prophets added a special ingredient of his own to the messianic mix. Micah predicted that God would forgive all our sins and cast them into the sea. Habakkuk disagreed with the others who maintained that repentance (*teshuvah*) and righteous deeds will hasten the coming of the messiah. He stated that humans must await the final reckoning for, in His own good time (*ketz*), God will send forth salvation (2:3 f. and 14). Jeremiah looked forward to the time when God will make "a new covenant with the House of Israel and the House of Judah" that will differ from all previous covenants that they broke, causing God to punish them. This new covenant will be radically different: "But such is the covenant I will make with the house of Israel after these days . . . I will put my teaching into their inmost being and inscribe it upon their hearts. Then I will be their God and they shall be My people. No longer will they need to teach one another and say to one another, 'Heed the Lord'; for all of them from the least of them to the greatest shall heed Me" (31:30 ff.). Ezekiel prophesied that God would redeem the people from exile not for its sake but for "the sanctification of God's name in the eyes of the gentiles." His extraordinary vision of the valley of the dry bones is a prediction of the restoration of the shattered and exiled Israelites who had dried up from loss of hope, and he introduced a new motif by describing a catastrophic war of Gog, king of Magog, against Jerusalem as a prelude to the defeat of the pagan armies and the new era (36:20 ff. 37:1–14; 38–39).

Deutero-Isaiah is saturated with messianic visions and messages about the future time. He depicted Israel as the "suffering servant of the Lord" who would redeem humanity through its travails. He looked forward to the conversion of pagans to the service of the Lord and envisioned Jerusalem as a world capital to which the nations would come to pray (40–48; 53:1ff.; 56:6–9; 59:21; 60–66). The last of the prophets, Haggai, Zechariah, and Malachi also developed special views of messianic redemption. Both Haggai and Zechariah believed Zerubabel, the Persian-appointed leader of the reconstituted nation of Judea, to be the promised Davidic leader who would restore greatness to Israel and usher in a new era of material, spiritual, and political prosperity. But Zerubabel never quite lived up to expectations. Malachi injected the notion that the Prophet Elijah would play a role in the final redemption as the harbinger of messianic salvation (3:22–24). This explains why, until this day, Elijah is viewed as the herald of the messiah and is invited to our Passover Seder as well as to the *brit milah* (circumcision) of every Jewish male baby. In Daniel, the angel Michael occupies that role and also is the agent of God who will resurrect the dead. But future generations preferred Elijah rather than Michael, and so it is even today. At any rate, the last of the prophets introduced the notion of a supernatural messiah-redeemer or apostolic prophet who would combine prophecy, messianism, and political and military prowess into one.

Post-biblical literature added some new elements to the messianic concept. For example, the sect of the Dead Sea Scrolls believed in two messiahs: one messiah will contend with Israel's enemies and die in battle; the other messiah will bring about the ultimate redemption. This motif eventually entered rabbinic and mystical literature dealing with the messiah in the Middle Ages. The first messiah, who will die in battle, is described as the son of Joseph, whereas the ultimate messiah, a descendant of King David, will usher in the messianic era.

Rabbinic literature deftly weaves a great tapestry from these strands. The bipolarity that we noticed in the Bible is evident in the Talmud and Midrash. Some sages believed in a personal messiah; others prayed for a messianic era. Some viewed the process as a supernatural one; others believed in a natural process. Some stressed the catastrophic element of messianism while others emphasized the restorative and utopian aspects. Some sages strove to calculate the date of the arrival of the messiah, while others sharply condemned such speculation. Some viewed messianic salvation in a nationalistic and particularistic setting; others adopted a universalistic and cosmic stance. Some believed the messiah would abolish the halakhah whereas others cautioned that not a single law would be changed. Some rabbis believed that no matter what we humans do, God has set the time of redemption. But others stressed the human role in hastening the final coming. These deeply ambivalent trends continued throughout the Middle Ages and, indeed, are still evident in our time. Additionally, there are all sorts of disagreements as to the messiah's true name, his birth, his stature, and character. Simply put, there is no shortage of messianic speculation.

One profound and long-abiding debate centers on the question of what would quicken the coming of the messiah (*biat ha-mashiah*) and the ultimate redemption (*geulah*). Two great *tannaim* of the second century adopted different views. Rabbi Eliezer ben Hyrcanus took an activist position, arguing that *teshuvah* would hasten the coming of the messiah. Rabbi Joshua ben Hananiah espoused a passive stance, insisting that no human action could shorten the time that must elapse before the final salvation, but in its own time (*ketz*), redemption will come and not before (*Sanh.* 97b and parallels). Followers of Rabbi Eliezer suggested that the performance of specific *mizvot* would precipitate the coming. Public prayer, fasting, study of Torah, and deeds of loving-kindness would certainly hasten the event. Some suggested that if Israel would observe a single *Shabbat* properly, the messiah would come. Others opined that if all Israel would repent for just one day, immediately the son of David would appear. One sage went so far as to urge that if we would just quote a saying in the name of its author, redemption would follow (*Abot* 6:6). But disciples of Rabbi Joshua were equally insistent that "the messiah will only come after the elapsed time has passed" no matter what we do or don't do. Some later teachers combined the two views and taught that, "Humanity will be redeemed through repentance and the observance of the *mitzvot*, God's compassion, the merit of the ancestors, extreme suffering, and the elapsing of the appointed time" (*y. Ta'an.* 1:1, 63d and parallels). The activist position of Rabbi Eliezer would, curiously, spawn the false messianic movements and agitations and eventually give birth to the Zionist movement, while the others of the more passive type (such as the Satmar Hasidim) belong in Rabbi Joshua's camp.

Yet another split developed around the issue of whether sins or virtue would hasten redemption. One school of thought insisted that only when Israel is fully purified of sin will the messiah come. The other school argued that only when Israel sinks to the depths of depravity and sinfulness will the messiah reveal himself. And yet another view held that, "When we all despair of redemption, then will he come."

An issue that was to plague Jews for centuries revolved around the date of the messianic redemption. Some sages in the Talmud and Midrash tried valiantly to calculate the set time, while others condemned sharply "those who seek to calculate the time of his coming." This strange enterprise would occupy the attention of some of the greatest of Judaism's sages throughout the ages into modern days. Not only mystics and kabbalists engaged in calculation of the date, but even the great rationalist, Maimonides, sought the date of redemption, noting that his family had a tradition that prophecy—a necessary prelude to the messiah—would be restored in the year 1210.

The sages disputed whether there would be radical changes in nature with the arrival of the messiah. Some suggested that the sick would be healed and the blind restored to vision; that sin would disappear and humanity return to a pristine state with a mythical banquet of epic proportions for the righteous. But Mar Samuel and his school of thought espoused the opposite view that taught: "There is no difference between this world and the next except that tyranny and political oppression will disappear" (*Ber.* 34b).

The sages preached both the particularistic and universal notion of the messiah. Some stressed that he would bring the dispersed Israelites home to Jerusalem, rebuild the Temple, and restore our independence. Others emphasized the universal aspect: He will usher in an era of justice and peace for all humanity with Jerusalem serving as a spiritual center as pagans recognize His sovereignty. The crowning achievement will be the resurrection of the dead (*tehiat ha-metim*), followed by the last judgment and the new age, the age or world to come (*olam ha-ba*).

Some sages insisted that the messiah will abolish the Torah and the *mitzvot* and issue a new set of laws. "In the days of the messiah, the pig will be kosher," runs one adage. Others insisted equally passionately that no new Torah or regulations will be issued. Of course, the notion of the abolition of the laws by the messiah was pregnant with dangerous ramifications, and Paul expanded on this teaching and created a new faith stripped of *mitzvot*. Later mystics and pseudo-messiahs (notably Shabbatai Zevi and Jacob Frank) preached these heretical views and shook traditional Judaism profoundly.

Perhaps the most significant dispute concerned the question of *personal messiah* versus *messianic era*. The school that held to a belief in a personal messiah expanded the earlier notion of two messiahs—an idea we have already encountered. The first one, son of Joseph, will die in battle and prepare the way for the messiah, son of David who will bring salvation. This strange notion gave birth to a string of false messiahs from Bar Koziba (Bar Kokhba, who had been endorsed by Rabbi Akiva, no less) down to Shabbatai Zevi and Jacob Frank and cost our people dearly. Painfully aware of the dangers implicit in personal messianism, especially after the Bar Koziba fiasco, Rabbi Hillel II, a descendant of the great Hillel, who lived in the fourth century C.E., insisted that, "There would be no messiah for Israel, since they had already enjoyed him in the days of King Hezekiah" (eighth century B.C.E.; *Sanh.* 99a). Rabbi Helbo, Rabbi Yohanan and Rabbi Samuel bar Nahmani stressed that God alone, not an angel or messenger, not Elijah or the messiah, will redeem Israel. This school of thought clearly felt the need to curb personal messianic speculation that had already caused such damage to Israel (*Midr. Pss.* 31, p. 237; 107, p. 462).

The messianic picture is certainly confusing and multifaceted. But, as I have stressed often throughout this book, this is quite typical of rabbinic speculative thought. To summarize briefly the confusing and complex rabbinic views on the subject: The time of the messiah or messianic age (*yemot ha-mashiah*) will be of limited duration; it will be accompanied by signs and wonders and most notably by the resurrection of the dead (*tehiat ha-metim*); it will effectuate the restoration of Israel and ingathering of its exiles; and it will culminate with the inauguration of *olam ha-ba*. In short, the arrival of the messiah is a *prelude* to the age to come.

It is instructive to note how the sages who edited the liturgy handled the concept of the messiah. The liturgy is remarkably free of personal messianism, although the concept of the messiah or messianic age is sprinkled throughout the prayers. Strikingly, the Passover *Haggadah* eliminated Moses entirely, except for one brief biblical reference. "How can that be?" I am invariably asked at my Seder. I see this as a deliberate attempt to play down the human role in the process of redemption and avoid the cult of the personality that might result if Moses were highlighted in the story. This paragraph from the *Haggadah* is especially telling:

> "And the eternal brought us out of the land of Egypt" (Deut 26:8). Not by an angel, not by a seraph, not by a messenger, but the Holy One, blessed be He, in His own glory and by Himself, as it is said, "And I will pass through the land of Egypt on that night, and I will smite all the first born in the land of Egypt" (Exod 12:12) . . . . I and not a messenger . . . I am He and none other.

The *Amidah* contains but one clear reference to a personal messiah and several references to messianic times. The usual rabbinic term, *mashi-*

ah ben David, messiah the son of David, is missing and in fact is found only once or twice in all the standard liturgy. Instead, the more ambiguous term, *goel*, redeemer, is used. In all of the blessings of the *Amidah*, it is God who is our savior, healer and redeemer. He will sound the shofar of freedom; He will gather our exiles from the four corners of the earth; He will destroy Israel's enemies; He will return to Jerusalem and rebuild the city, restore the dynasty of David, and rebuild the Temple. Both the *Kaddish* and *Aleinu* prayers look forward to the day when God will establish His Kingship and all human beings will acknowledge Him. A short prayer derived from the Talmud that is chanted in the Sabbath and festival morning service sums up the rabbinic view succinctly: "There is none like You, Lord, in this world, nor is there any king beside You in the life of the age to come. There is no redeemer besides You in the days of the messiah, and there is nothing to compare to You as our savior in the era of the resurrection of the dead."

Why did the sages who edited our liturgy play down the element of personal messianism and supernatural redemption by a superhuman messiah? Why did they displace the messiah, son of David, and substitute God instead in so many prayers? It cannot be an accident. Undoubtedly, they were appalled at the cult of Jesus and the spread of Pauline Christianity, as well as the tragically bloody fiasco of the Bar Koziba rebellion. Consequently, they realized the folly of unbridled messianic agitation that could only result in suffering and disappointment for the people and even breed a cult of worshiping a human.

Medieval Jewish thought reflects all the hues and variations of the classical teachings. Messianic speculation waxed and waned depending on the degree of Israel's suffering. A good rule of thumb in this regard is: the greater the oppression, the greater the messianic agitation.

Saadia Gaon, for example, borrowed heavily from the more wild and speculative messianic works and looked to a supernatural messiah who would perform miracles and wonders for Israel. He wrote that the messiah would come whether or not we repent, and that the messiah son of Joseph would first clear the way and die in battle with Israel's enemies. Saadia even tried to calculate the date, based on verses in Daniel.

Maimonides, on the other hand, was a rationalist who did not stress the personality of the messiah. He wrote (*Introduction* to *Commentary* on *m. Sanh.* 10, pp. 110–136 and parallels):

> The Jews . . . must . . . believe that the messiah will issue forth from the House of David . . . and he shall far excel all rulers in history by his reign, which will be glorious in justice and peace. Neither

impatience nor deceptive calculation of the time of the advent of the messiah should shatter this belief. Still . . . he must be regarded as a mortal being like any other and only a restorer of the Davidic dynasty. He will die and leave a son as his successor, who will, in turn, die and leave the throne to his heir. Nor will there be any material change in the order of things in the whole system of nature and human life; accordingly, Isaiah's picture of the living together of lamb and wolf cannot be taken literally but are metaphors.

Maimonides suggested that the messianic kingdom would bring Israel its political independence without subjugating the pagan nations. The people of Israel will enjoy an era of affluence and peace and devote themselves to the study of Torah, "leading all mankind to the knowledge of God and help them share in the eternal bliss of the age to come." In his famous letter to the Jewish community of Yemen that was roiled by a false messiah in its midst (1171), he adopted a much more personal concept of the messiah, whom he envisioned to be an eminent prophet greater than all the prophets who followed Moses, who would perform signs and miracles and never negate the teachings of Moses. He added, as I've noted before, that he possessed an old family tradition that the return of prophecy, the forerunner of the messiah, would occur in 1210. Let us remember that Maimonides died in 1204. Did he fancy *himself* the messiah? Abraham Joshua Heschel suspected so and wrote a fascinating essay on this subject. It seems that even the rationalist Maimonides had his mystical side. Let us also recall that he included the belief in the coming of the messiah in his Thirteen Principles of Faith: "I believe with perfect faith in the coming of the messiah. And although he may tarry, still I do believe."

Nahmanides, Moses ben Nahman, was a kabbalist and mystic who surely accepted the belief in a personal messiah but was very circumspect about teaching and preaching about it or revealing the date of redemption. He viewed the messiah as a king of flesh and blood who will reign over the entire world and bring the knowledge of God to the human heart, as well as universal peace. He rejected the crasser notions of those who predicted the fabulous pleasures of food and drink awaiting us, insisting that we look forward to saving our souls from Hell and approaching God in the Holy Land where His *Shekhinah* abounds. The messiah will also "abolish the evil urge and help us attain the profound truth."

Yehudah Halevi, curiously, barely mentioned the messiah in his writings. Joseph Albo rejected Maimonides' view that the messianic belief is a fundamental tenet (*ikkar*) of Judaism, the denial of which makes one a heretic. Albo conceded that it is an important article of faith but not a dogma or essential belief, and he accepted the view we mentioned earlier of Rabbi Hillel II, that Israel enjoyed messianic bliss in the days of King Hezekiah.

The Kabbalah followed the pattern of rabbinic Judaism in all of its richness. These elements include: future disasters, natural calamities, the redemption and in-gathering of Israel's exiles, miracles in nature, and the explication of the secrets of Torah. Lurianic Kabbalah took a new turn, in the view of Gershom Scholem, perhaps in response to the tragedy of the expulsions from Spain and Portugal. Personal messianism was played down; instead, the entire people of Israel was identified with the messiah and charged to uncover the sparks of divinity and remove the shell of sin through the process of *tikkun*, amendment, restoration, or repair. But in truth, personal messianic hopes did not totally disappear from the Lurianic version and there were those who believed that Rabbi Isaac Luria himself was the messiah!

The Hasidic movement, certainly in its later stages, restored personal messianism, even to the point of extolling the *tzaddik* or rebbe to such adulation, that the *tzaddik* is viewed at least as a harbinger or forerunner of the messiah, if not the messiah himself. Therein lay the roots of the Lubavitcher's conviction that its late leader, Rabbi Menachem Mendel Schneerson, is, indeed, the messiah.

Modern Jewish religious movements have assessed and reinterpreted the messianic idea. Mainstream Orthodoxy seems to accept it in its classical exposition, retaining all the traditional liturgical passages on the subject, although I think many modern Orthodox rabbis and thinkers espouse the notion of a messianic age rather than a personal messiah. Religious Zionists write and speak of the State of Israel as, "The beginning of the era of redemption"—a position that has spawned the Greater Israel movement that has battled so tenaciously to retain the extended borders of the State, rejecting the policy of "land for peace." Rabbi Abraham Isaac Kook articulated a rather unique position: He suggested that the evolution of humanity to a higher life form represents messianism.

On the other hand, the Reform movement in Judaism that succumbed to the heady optimism and notion of social progress typical of the nineteenth century stripped the personal messiah from the prayer book but accepted the idea of "Israel's great messianic hope for the establishment of the kingdom of truth, justice, and peace among all men." The liturgical reference to a *goel*, redeemer, was changed to read *geulah*, redemption. The 1976 "Centenary Perspective" declared, "We have learned again that the survival of the Jewish people is of highest priority, and that in carrying out our Jewish responsibilities we help move humanity toward its messianic fulfillment." The latest word of the Reform movement is found in its "Ten Principles of Reform Judaism" (1999), where we read: "Partners with God in *tikkun olam*, repairing the world, we are called to help bring nearer the messianic age."

Conservative Judaism has followed a similar, non-personalized messianic route, retaining the traditional wording of the prayers mentioning the messiah but translating the prayers to mean, "messianic age." In its *Statement of Principles of Conservative Judaism* (1988), the movement affirms a "gradualist" or "evolutionary" approach to the issue stating that "we do not know when the messiah will come, or whether he will be a charismatic figure or is a symbol of redemption of humankind from the evil of the world." The *Statement* adds that every individual must live his or her life "as if he or she, individually, has the responsibility to bring about the messianic age."

Rabbi Mordecai M. Kaplan rejected the notion of a personal messiah as supernaturalism and insisted that we preserve a belief in human progress towards redemption of humanity. He taught his Reconstructionist movement a philosophy of human history as the evolutionary process of human progress to a higher stage of human development, "a higher type of man."

Unquestionably, the messianic ideal, while not a dogma, is one of the greatest teachings of Judaism. It has imbued us with hope in hopeless times. It has sustained our spirits when despair engulfed us. It has prodded us to better society and heal the world when madness and bestiality have raged. It has exposed for us shafts of light when all seemed dark and bleak. But I am convinced that personal messianic beliefs are both foolish and dangerous. We have paid a heavy price for this naive notion that a sort of "superman" can lead us to redemption. We have fallen for the nostrums of a variety of charlatans and deluded dreamers and downright scoundrels who have filled us with false hope and led us astray. Do we really believe in a superhuman who will come riding on a white ass and battle Israel's enemies in a supernatural fashion? Do we truly seek a fusion of nationalism and religious messianism, knowing that such combinations invariably prove lethal? Our sages muted the theme of personal messianism and were wise to do so. They never gave up the ideal of a messianic era, even while seeking to rein in the potentially tragic tendencies toward personal messiahs. We have witnessed false messiahs in our times who, in the Communist version, promised "pie in the sky, bye and bye," and slaughtered millions in the process. We have experienced the secular movements of fascism and

Nazism and their "charismatic leaders" who brought untold suffering to nations.

I believe that the modern Jew wants and needs a belief in messianic fulfillment because the modern Jew—indeed, all humans—needs to look beyond the bleak present, to tomorrow's new sunrise, to an era of justice and prosperity, of happiness and harmony, of prosperity and peace. As partners with God in this great process of *tikkun ha-olam*, mending the world and improving society, we humans hasten that messianic fulfillment and justify our faith that, "Weeping may linger for the night, but at dawn there are shouts of joy" (Ps 30:6).

But when will that time be? Perhaps this little Hasidic tale gives us a clue. One day, a student rushed breathlessly into the *shtiebel*. He made his way to the side of the rebbe and excitingly told him: "Rebbe, I've just heard great news. The messiah is at the gate of our town! The messiah has come at long last!" The rebbe hastily put on his coat and fur hat, adjourned the class, gathered the disciples and rushed off with the student, bursting with eagerness to finally greet the messiah. As they passed a courtyard, the rebbe observed a teamster mercilessly beating his horse. The rebbe restrained his disciples, sighed, and urged them, "Let's go back home. He has not come yet. Not yet."

When there will be no more brutality or cruelty toward humans and animals, when peace and harmony will reign, then we shall know: The era of the messiah is upon us.

Points to Ponder:
Messiah: Fact or Fancy?

1. How do you react to the messianic cult that has sprouted around the late Lubavitcher Rebbe?

2. Biblical Judaism preached the twin doctrine of national and cosmic redemption. How is this so? And what relevance does this have for us today?

3. Why did Judaism insist that the messiah will spring from the house of David?

4. Explain how each of the prophets added a special, individual ingredient into the messianic concept.

5. What is the difference between the activist and passivist positions regarding the messiah? How have these two divergent views affected Jewish life, thought, and action over the ages?

6. Why did so many seek to calculate the date of the messianic redemption? Why is this so perilous?

7. Why do you think Mar Samuel insisted that the only difference between this world and the next is that political tyranny and oppression will disappear?

8. Why do you think Moses is eliminated from the Passover *Haggadah*? The Reconstructionists have restored him to the *Haggadah*. Do you favor their restoration of Moses?

9. How do you feel about the concept of resurrection of the dead?

10. Why is belief in a personal messiah perilous?

11. What does the Hasidic tale of the rebbe, the alleged messiah, and the teamster say to you?

12. Do you accept the idea of a messiah? Do you believe in a personal messiah or messianic age?

16

Is There an Afterlife?

IN VIRTUALLY every civilization on earth humans developed the notion of an afterlife. The Egyptians, the Canaanites, the Mesopotamian peoples, the American Indians—all formulated concepts of what is to happen to a person after death. Alan F. Segal's richly documented, *Life After Death*, contains over 750 pages describing beliefs in the afterlife among a variety of peoples on different continents. All kinds of books and poems and philosophical treatises have been devoted to the subject, none more celebrated, perhaps, than Dante's *The Divine Comedy*.

Why the preoccupation with life after death? For two main reasons, I believe. First, we find it terribly difficult to accept that death is the end of it all, and that after we expire nothing remains—we simply crumble in the grave to dust and ashes. Consequently, we fear death. As a well-known comedian put it, "I'm not afraid of dying! I just don't want to be there when it happens."

Second, the problem of evil gnaws at us, allowing us no respite. Why do righteous people suffer on this planet while so many wicked ones seem to prosper? Is there no justice? No reckoning? No final moral settling of accounts?

Consequently, Judaism constructed its unique version of what the prophets dubbed, "*aharit ha-yamim*, the end of days," and what the sages termed, "*atid la-vo*, the coming future." In the sage's construction, the coming future time includes several key elements: *yemot ha-mashiah*, the days of the messiah, followed by *tehiat ha-metim*, the resurrection of the dead, followed by *din ve-heshbon*, judgment before God at which time *sekhar*, reward, and *onesh*, punishment, will be meted out. This includes *Gan Eden*, heavenly reward for the virtuous, and *Gehinnom*, Gehenna or Hell and punishment for the wicked. Thus, humanity will enter *olam ha-ba*, the age (or world) to come. The subject is terribly complex and often confusing in the rabbinic construction that evolved over several centuries as it was amplified in the Talmud and Midrash and it is truly difficult to discern emphatic trends and dominant themes. But the earlier biblical layer is far simpler to fathom.

Unquestionably, the Bible knew of belief in the afterlife. How could it not? After all, we were in contact with various civilizations that constructed elaborate theories of life after death. The Canaanites, the Assyrians, the Babylonians all believed in an afterlife. The Egyptians made it a cornerstone of their belief system, as we know from their Book of the Dead and their remarkable tombs and elaborate burial patterns. In fact, the Egyptians were a very other-worldly culture that laid enormous stress on the next life. My visit to the exhibit of King Tut's opulent tomb artifacts several years ago (and this represented but a small fraction of the over 5,000 artifacts among his treasures), reinforced my impression that the ancient Egyptians believed you *can* take it with you! But the Bible rejected most of these beliefs and practices. Why? Yehezkel Kaufmann opined that pagan beliefs were so inextricably bound up with pagan worship that we utterly shunned the idea of an afterlife. Perhaps so: but the fact is, the Bible clearly rejects the notion of life after death.

That the Bible rejects the concept of reward and punishment after death is clearly indicated in numerous passages in virtually every book of the Bible. Reward for keeping God's commandments and punishment for rejecting His *mitzvot* are in the here-and-now, on earth, in this world. The virtuous are granted length of days, the blessings of fertile crops and herds, rain and wind (Deut 7:12 ff.; 11:13 ff.; 22:6–7; 28:1–14). Conversely, sins against God lead to dire punishment against individuals, nations, crops, and herds, the ultimate punishment being exile from our land (Lev 26:14–45; Deut 28:15–68). We are commanded to live by the *mitzvot* and strive for long life, prosperity, personal happiness, and communal welfare, enjoying life to the fullest since both humans and beasts end up in the same place, viz., the grave (Lev 18:5; Ezek 20:11; Deut 30:19; Qoh 3:18 ff., 9:3–6; Jer 21:8; Ps 30:3–4: Prov 3:2; Job 7:8–21). In short, virtue leads to blessings while sin results in curses.

Significantly, the Bible explicitly rejects a belief in the afterlife. This is clear from a plain reading of a host of texts. Job queries rhetorically, "There is hope for a tree; if it is cut down, it will renew itself . . . If a person dies can he live again?" (14:7ff.). Qohelet states several times his view that human and beast, righteous and sinful, end up alike in the grave (3:18 & 22; 12:7). The psalmist stresses on any number of occasions that there is nothing beyond this existence. "What is to be gained from my death, from my descent into the Pit? Can dust praise You? Can it declare Your faithfulness?" (Ps 30:7–10). "The dead cannot praise God, nor can those who descend into the grave" (Ps 115:17). And Isaiah depicts the critically ill King Hezekiah as pleading, "For it is not *Sheol* that praises You, nor the land of Death that extols You; nor do they who descend into the Pit hope for your grace. The living, only the living can give thanks to you as I do this day" (Isa 38:18–19).

In sum, the Bible stresses this life over the next and rejects the notion of reward and punishment in the next life. "Behold, the righteous shall be rewarded on earth, how much more so shall the wicked and the sinner be punished" (Prov 11:31). The fact that the sages devoted the better part of chapter ten of the Talmudic treatise, *Sanhedrin*, to detecting biblical "proofs" of this belief underscores this point all the more graphically.

Then, late in the biblical era, perhaps in the second century B.C.E., we glimpse a perceptible shift. The pious editor of Qohelet adds the notion of spiritual immortality to the book whose author had steadfastly denied an afterlife. He adds the gloss, "And the dust returns to the ground as it was, *and the spirit returns to God who bestowed it*" (12:7). Isaiah, in chapters 25:8 and 26:19 (chapters that seem to postdate the great Prophet), injects the notion of the resurrection of the body. Daniel, apparently the last book of the Hebrew Bible, states, "Many of those who sleep in the dust of the earth will awake, some to eternal life, others to reproaches, to everlasting abhorrence" (12:2). Was it Greek influence that injected the belief in immortality of the soul? Was it Persian religion that introduced the concept of physical immortality into Judaism? Most scholars believe this to be the case. At any rate, both ideas took root in Judaism and are developed more fully in the books of the Apocrypha that were composed just after the conclusion of the biblical period and prior to the rabbinic era. In 2 Maccabees 7:9 and 12:43 and in the Wisdom of Solomon 3:1–4, bodily resurrection begins to assume full formulation, setting the stage for the elaborate exposition in the rabbinic literature of the Mishnah, Talmud, and various *Midrashim*.

Rabbinic theology created a huge complex of beliefs and practices that reflected this new view of the afterlife, contrasting *olam ha-zeh*, this life (or world) with *olam ha-ba*, the next or coming life (or world). The first-century historian, Josephus, as well as the New Testament and later rabbinic sources, inform us that this item was one of the major issues roiling the relations between various Jewish groups or sects in the first century C.E. The Sadducees denied a belief in resurrection, although they apparently affirmed a belief in the immortality of the soul, which probably came from Plato and other Greek thinkers. The Pharisees, on the other hand, affirmed the concept of resurrection of the dead, which was a borrowing, it seems, from the Persians. The dispute between these two groups was marked by acrimony and even violence. Gradually, the Pharisees conflated the two points of view, so that belief in the resurrection of the dead followed by immortality of the soul became a cardinal dogma of Judaism.

The rabbinic concept of the afterlife consists of several elements. First, the rabbis referred to that future time as *atid la-vo*, the future to come. The first step in the unfolding of the future is to be the coming of, or the days of the messiah, *biat ha-mashiah, yemot ha-mashiah*. The next step is to be resurrection of the dead, *tehiat ha-metim*, which the sages crystallized into one of the few genuine dogmas of Judaism. Following that, *olam ha-ba*, the new age (or world) will be ushered in. The souls of all beings will be judged by God, *din ve-heshbon*. The righteous will be sent to *Gan Eden* or Paradise, Heaven; the wicked will be dispatched to *Gehinnom* or Hell. The whole notion of the afterlife is so complex and multifaceted and the opinions so innumerable and diverse, so complex and controversial that it is almost impossible to extract a clear picture of what *olam ha-ba* will be like. Louis Finkelstein was of the opinion that the sages deliberately left the concept vague. After all, nobody living has ever seen what the next life is really like. Well, not quite: The Talmud records (*Ketub.* 77b) that Rabbi Joshua ben Levi stole the Angel of Death's knife, jumped across the fence and entered *Gan Eden*. His son, Rabbi Joseph, saw in a vision the next world in which everything will be topsy-turvy: those important here will be of no importance there; the insignificant here will be significant there (*Pesah. 50a*). But these are merely charming legends. In truth, in the words of Shakespeare, "Death is the undiscover'd country from whose bourn no traveller returns."

The sages emphatically articulated their belief that there is, indeed, an afterlife even if their speculation as to the details of what it will be like differed radically. "All Israel has a portion in the world to come," they taught (*Abot* 1:1; *m. Sanh.* 10:1). In a rare statement of dogmatic belief, they ruled that, "Whoever denies that resurrection is from the Torah, who maintains that the Torah is not from Heaven, and the Epicureans lose their portion in the age to come" (*m. Sanh.* 10:1). The righteous on earth store up capital for the next life and those who perform *mitzvot* will find that the principle accrues to the future life. Even sinners who repent have a share in the next life, as do the righteous men and women of all nations.

But rabbinic speculation on the next life displays a certain chaotic indeterminacy. Some argue that this world is merely a corridor to the next and that this life is merely a prelude to the next. Others insist that it is better to enjoy the legitimate pleasures of this life than the entire next one. Some argue that the reward of virtue is virtue itself; the doing of the mitzvah is its own reward. Others maintain that reward and punishment await a human being in the next world when there will be a proper moral reckoning. Rabbi Yaakov presents us with a paradoxical view of this life as contrasted with the next: "Better one hour of repentance and good deeds in this life than all of the next life. But better one hour of spiritual calm in the next life than all of this life" (*Abot* 2:2, 16; 3:1; 4:2, 16, 17; 5:20).

The descriptions of what Heaven and Hell must be like are notable for their confusing chaos. Some sages believed in judgment of the souls of the departed for a period of twelve months as God examines their earthly record. The righteous are to be sent to Heaven (*Gan Eden, Pardes*), to await the final judgment triggered by the coming of the messiah. God then sends the virtuous to eternal bliss in Heaven while the wicked are dispatched to Hell. The School of Shammai maintained that the righteous will be rewarded with eternal life while the wicked will go to Hell forever. The average folk are scourged for a time in a sort of purgatory and then ascend to Heaven. The School of Hillel, including Rabbi Akiva, disagreed, insisting that the righteous go at once to Heaven while the sinners are judged for twelve months and then their souls are destroyed (*m. Ed.* 2:10; *Shabb.* 152b; *Midr. Ps.* 31, p. 120a).

When it comes to descriptions of Heaven and Hell, free reign prevailed and the fancy of the sages seemed to know no bound. Generally speaking, there was a split between those who argued for a fantastic conception and others who insisted on a more spiritual concept in describing the pleasures and pains of the next life. Many maintained wild and fanciful ideas of what Heaven will be like. The virtuous will be treated to all kinds of sensuous pleasures, excluding sexual ones. They will feast on the flesh of a remarkable bull, the mythical fish, Leviathan, and drink a rare wine saved up from the days of Creation. Muslims may look forward to 72 virgins in Paradise; Jews prefer to anticipate 72 slices of gefilte fish. Moreover, Heaven contains seven layers depending on the level of one's virtues, with the highest rung reserved for the martyrs who gave their lives for the faith. Hell will also contain seven levels, with the worst sinners consigned the lowest depths where their punishment will not be mitigated and where they will burn with a fire unlike any other known to humans. The following text from the Midrash (*Exod. Rab.* 15:21) summarizes the literalist view of the afterlife:

> Ten things will the Holy One, blessed be He, renew in the next life. He will illuminate the world; He will cause running water to issue from Jerusalem; He will cause trees to bear fruits every

month and people to eat them and be healed; He will rebuild all the ruined cities so that no waste place will remain on earth; He will rebuild Jerusalem with sapphires; peace will reign throughout nature; He will assemble all the beasts, birds and reptiles and make a covenant between them and Israel; weeping and wailing will cease in the world; and there will be no more sighing, groaning or anguish—but all will be happy.

Conversely, some very eminent rabbis maintained far less literal and much more spiritual notions of the afterlife. They insisted that Heaven and Hell are merely metaphors; that reward and punishment are not to be interpreted in crude and tangible ways. Mar Samuel, for example, speculated that, "There is no difference between this world and the days of the messiah except that tyranny and political oppression will disappear" (*Ber.* 34b). Rav suggested that, "In the next life there will be neither eating nor drinking nor sexual relations, no business affairs, no envy or hatred and no competition, but the righteous will sit around the banquet table with garlands on their heads and they will enjoy the splendor of God's *Shekhinah* (sacred presence: *Ber.* 17a). Resh Lakish stated clearly, "There is no Hell in the next life but the Holy One, blessed be He, will remove the sun from its sheath. The righteous will be healed by its rays while the wicked will be judged by it" (*Ned.* 8b).

The crystallization and final version of rabbinic thinking on this momentous subject is found in the liturgy of the synagogue. The prayer book codifies much of the sages' views on the afterlife. The belief in resurrection, one of the few authentic rabbinic dogmas, appears in several key places in the prayers, notably in the *Amidah* which is recited three times daily and four times on Sabbaths and festivals. There we read: "Your might, O Lord, is boundless. You give life to the dead; great is Your saving power . . . Faithful are You in giving life to the dead. Praised are you, Lord, who revives the dead." This is a creedal statement and we are told in the Talmud that it became one of the red flags to identify heretics such as the Sadducees who denied a belief in physical resurrection. Anyone who omitted this phrase from the prayer service was barred from leading the prayers (*m. Ber.* 9:5).

The prayer book codifies other statements of belief in an afterlife. The burial *Kaddish* speaks of the resurrection and renewal of life in the next life. The *Aleinu* prayer looks forward to the day when God will repair and improve the world under His mighty kingship. The *Yizkor* memorial prayer and the *El Maleh Rahamim* in the Ashkenazic festival service, as well the *Hashkabah* memorial prayer in the Sephardic service, speak of life eternal in *Gan Eden*. Interestingly, as Louis Jacobs points out, there is no mention of Hell in the standard prayers. This passage in the Sabbath morning service succinctly summarizes the official rabbinic position: "You are our King incomparable in this world, inimitable in the world to come, peerless Redeemer in the days of the messiah, singular in resurrecting the dead."

Saadiah Gaon (882–942) took a very literal view of the afterlife, describing in concrete terms the eternal punishment of the wicked while accepting the literal views of the eternal reward of the righteous as an incentive to lead the good life here on earth (*Emunot Ve-Deot*, Treatises 7–9, pp. 264–356). Maimonides, on the other hand, seemed to have been deeply ambivalent about the meaning of the next life. In his *Mishneh Torah* law code (*Teshuvah*, 3:6; 8:1, 5) he mentions those wicked ones who go to Hell but takes that to mean *karet*, extirpation or annihilation. He also advocates this position in his *Commentary* to the Mishnah (*Sanh.* 10:1) and in his Thirteen Principles of Faith. In his "Essay on Resurrection," he seeks to calm the spirits of critics who accused him of slighting the belief in physical or bodily resurrection. He indicates his belief in bodily resurrection at the time of the messiah, but insists that this will last for but a moment. He cites the view of Rav, that I have described previously, that in the future life there will be neither eating nor drinking nor copulation nor any of the other bodily functions, but humanity will enjoy a purely spiritual existence. Maimonides then quotes another source in the Talmud that states that God has not created anything in vain; that all of His creations have a purpose. Since there will be no need for bodily functions in the next life, what need is there for a body? Hence, the resurrection will last for but a moment after which the body will be totally annihilated, leaving the soul to enjoy eternal spiritual bliss. Nahmanides (1194–1270) stated his firm belief in bodily resurrection in the time of the messiah but diluted the view of eternity of the body by maintaining that the righteous will live eternally in a refined, spiritual body while the wicked will be condemned to eternal suffering in Hell. Joseph Albo describes elaborately the fires of Hell that will torture the souls of the wicked who will be pulled in two conflicting directions, one towards desire, and the other towards fulfillment.

The Zohar graphically depicts the eternal punishment in Hell awaiting the unrepentant sinners. There are seven levels in Hell to which sinners will be sent depending on the severity of their sins. Various demons will torture the sinners accordingly. The notion of *gilgul ha-nefesh* (transmigration of the souls, reincarnation, metempsychosis), which probably originated in Hindu philosophy, was borrowed by the Zohar and became a dominant theme in kabbalistic thought, then entering Hasidic theology. This doctrine states that the soul of a human undergoes a process of migration from body to body over the ages until it is finally united with the Source of All Souls.

Rabbi Moses Haim Luzzatto (1700–1746 or 47) assimilated much of the doctrine of the Zohar, stating that this world is merely preparatory to the next. The goal of a human being is nearness to God. But interestingly, he suggests that the holy person is accounted to have beheld the presence of God even though he is still in this world. Likewise, not all Hasidic masters subscribed to the totally literal view of the afterlife. For example, Rabbi Shneor Zalman of Liady described *olam ha-ba* as the ability of the soul to enjoy the radiance of the *Shekhinah*, that is, the full comprehension of the Divine. Rabbi Elimelekh of Lizhansk wrote that the *tzaddik* (righteous person) who keeps the *mitzvot* achieves pure communion (*devekut*) with the Divine and need not wait for the afterlife since he enjoys those delights in this world.

The challenge of modernity, and specifically, the Enlightenment in Europe, dealt a severe blow to religion in general and to the supernatural beliefs including revelation, messiah and afterlife in particular. Spinoza in Holland, Voltaire and his colleagues in France, Hume and his friends in England, assailed some of the basic beliefs of the Jewish and Christian faiths. The idea of resurrection and an afterlife seemed preposterous to the new generation of the enlightened West. The Reform movement was keenly aware of these challenges and responded accordingly. The Pittsburgh Platform (1885) clearly rejected the traditional views as this paragraph indicates: "We reassert the doctrine of Judaism, that the soul of men is immortal, grounding this belief on the Divine nature of the human spirit, which forever finds bliss in righteousness and misery in wickedness. We reject as ideas not rooted in Judaism the belief both in bodily resurrection and in Gehenna and Eden (hell and paradise), as abodes for everlasting punishment or reward." The liturgy of the movement reflects this theological shift. The *Union Prayer Book* (1894) deleted the classical blessing, "Who resurrects the dead," and references to resurrection and afterlife and substituted the English phrase, "Who has planted immortal life in us." The *Gates of Prayer* (1975), that contains eight different Sabbath services, offers the phrase, *mehayei ha-kol*, in lieu of *mehayei ha-metim*, and translates in several different ways, "whose gift is life," "Source of life," or "Creator of life." The "Ten Principles of Reform Judaism" (1999) seem to combine the Reform movement's passion for social action together with a messianic thrust. It states: "Partners with God in *tiqqun olam*, repairing the world, we are called to bring nearer the messianic age. We seek dialogue and joint action with the people of other faiths in the hope that together we can bring peace, freedom and justice to our world."

The Conservative movement approaches the problem somewhat differently. Always reluctant to drop the traditional liturgy, the Conservative prayer books in use since 1945 retained the traditional blessing of God who resurrects the dead, as well as other passages alluding to the afterlife and messiah, but translated the key blessing, "who calls the dead to life everlasting." The *Sim Shalom* prayer book (1985) translates the phrase differently: "Master of life and death" and "faithful are You in giving life to the dead"

The Reconstructionist movement of Rabbi Mordecai M. Kaplan applied its usual cold logic and rationalism to the question of the afterlife. Dr. Kaplan wrote unequivocally: "Men and women brought up in the atmosphere of modern science no longer accept the notion that the dead will one day come to life. To equate that doctrine with the belief in the immortality of the soul is to read into the text a meaning which the words do not express." But Kaplan did affirm his belief in the immortality of the human soul. The 1945 edition of the *Reconstructionist Prayer Book* inserted a substitute Hebrew text for the traditional blessing about resurrection which reads, "Who in love rememberest Thy creatures unto life." But the 1994 *Kol Haneshamah* prayer book that replaced the original seems to flirt with the restoration of the notion. Its version of the blessing reads, 'Who gives and restores life."

As we have already noted in our discussion of prayer, the Orthodox movement is officially unruffled by these various challenges to classical concepts. After all, if God can create life out of nothing, why can He not recreate life from the dead? Consequently, the liturgy of the Orthodox group remains unchanged and unrevised. The blessings and all the classical concepts about messiah, resurrection, and *olam ha-ba* appear in the prayer books without emendations or amendments. The English translations may fudge the issue a bit, but that is the only concession Orthodoxy makes to modernity in this regard.

It is rather intriguing to note the various theologians from different camps who have been wending their way back to a more traditional acceptance of resurrection, messiah and a life after death. Will Herberg, already in the 1950s, began to find his way back from Marxism to classical beliefs in the personal messiah and the life to come. Reform theologians such as Steven Schwarzschild and Eugene Borowitz abandoned the classical Reform position and returned to a belief in resurrection and immortality. In the Conservative ranks, Hershel Matt and Neil Gillman have argued vigorously for a restoration of the traditional beliefs and liturgical statements—including resurrection of the body. But the late Conservative theologian, Louis Jacobs, rejected the idea of resurrection while affirming a belief in spiritual immortality. I believe that the matter is not yet closed for any of the various groups.

Where does all of this leave us modern Jews? I cannot imagine that most modern Jews can accept with any enthusiasm or passion the crass notions of what Heaven and Hell will be like. The very earthy and sensuous descriptions of the rewards of Heaven and the punishments of Hell simply defy our imagination and fly counter to our logical beliefs and scientific understanding of the universe. Nor can most of us accept the concept of physical resurrection of the dead. Even Maimonides had his own problems with that idea, as we have noted. The sages stated, "Righteous people even in death are described as living" (*Tanh. Berakhah* 7, 2:28b–29a). That is, their influence is a living legacy; it is as if they had not really died. Additionally, they taught that whoever raises up a righteous child it is as if that parent never died (Rashi on Gen 18:19). Immortality is therefore achieved by righteous living on earth and by training children who walk in the ways of the Lord and are just and honorable, kind and compassionate to fellow beings. Through the genes we transmit to the next generation; through the influence we exert on our children or students, we pass on a legacy. And that, I believe, is our measure of immortality. "When we quote the teachings of a deceased scholar by name," taught the sages, "his lips quiver with joy in his grave" (*Sanh.* 90b). This, too, is a form of immortality, I think.

Additionally, despite our doubts and skepticism, there is within the human being a spirit, an indefinable element beyond mere flesh and bone. We call it the "soul"—the *neshamah* or *nefesh*. The Bible describes the human soul as "the lamp of the Lord" (Prov 20:27). And the kabbalists speak of the Divine *nitzotz*, spark, within each of us, that yearns and strives to return to its source, the *Ein Sof*, the Infinite One. We all, deep down, aspire to return to the Source of all life; we believe that there is something within a being that outlasts the body and the crumbling of flesh and blood in the grave. That elusive, indefinable something is—the soul, the breath of the Divine. And it yearns to return to its Creator in immortal embrace. In the words of Lord Byron:

> My mind may lose its force, my blood its fire
> And my frame perish in conquering pain;

But there is that within me which shall tire
Torture and Time, and breathe when I expire.

Does this imply that Judaism is an other-worldly religion as some have charged? I think not: We believe in living the good and moral life in the here-and-now. We urge humans to enjoy all legitimate pleasures on earth and in this fleeting life. Rabbi Hiya observed that some people might think that the Sabbath was given to Israel for ill or in order to force them to suffer through privation. But that is not the purpose of the Sabbath, he stressed. "God gave Israel the Sabbath for their benefit. How so? You must sanctify the Sabbath with good food and drink, with clean garments and physical pleasures. If you do this, I will reward you accordingly" (*Deut. Rab.* 3:1). Rabbi Eliezer observed that on a festival, a person ought to indulge all day in eating and drinking or else sit and study Torah. Rabbi Joshua disagreed and insisted that one should divide the day in two: half for eating and drinking, half for study in the academy (*Pesah.* 68b). Asceticism was not the norm for Jews. True, there were ascetics from time to time in Jewish life. The destruction of the Second Temple caused a wave of asceticism to flood the guilt-ridden Jewish community of Eretz Yisrael. Some refused meat and wine arguing that it would be sinful for Jews to indulge in such luxuries when they could no longer bring such sacrificial offerings to the Temple. Others abstained from marriage or curbed the festivities of marital celebrations as a sign of mourning for the lost Temple. But soon, saner minds prevailed and Jewish life returned to its more wholesome and natural patterns. Still, Maimonides took a dim view of sexual intercourse even in marriage (no doubt a reflection of his revulsion with the lascivious harem life he witnessed as physician to the vizier), limiting it to procreation and the satisfaction of female needs. Similarly, many of the kabbalists of the Lurianic school limited sexual relations with their wives to Friday evenings when the act of coitus assumed cosmic import by uniting God with the *Shekhinah*. But this was hardly the Jewish norm that maintained the importance of enjoying the legitimate pleasure of daily life. As the eminent Rav put it, "When a person is called to judgment in the next life, he or she will be held accountable for not having enjoyed all the legitimate pleasures on earth" (*y. Qidd.* 4:12, 66d).

At the same time, we believe there is a reckoning so that sooner or later the moral person reaps a reward while the evil person harvests punishment. Is Judaism, therefore, a this- worldly or other-worldly faith? Rabbi Louis Jacobs was quite right, I think, in stating: it is both. We live life to the fullest here and now; we hope instinctively that there is more to just this present existence. The Laws of Conservation of Energy and Matter are suggestively intriguing. Those Laws posit that during an ordinary chemical change, there is no detectable increase in the quantity of matter and energy. Energy cannot be created or destroyed but can change its form. Additionally, the total quantity of matter and energy available in the universe is a fixed amount and never more or less. Might that suggest that immortality is not merely a pious hope? That the laws of the universe are so constructed as to guarantee that, in some form or other, we humans do survive death?

A final thought. Even the sages who did firmly and fervently accept the concept of resurrection and an afterlife expressed their humility in the face of the great mystery of death and its consequences. They were candid enough to admit: "We simply don't know everything." They taught (*Sanh.* 99a; *Ber.* 34b): "All the prophets prophesied about the days of the messiah. But as to the next age, 'No eye has seen it except You, God' (Isa 64:3) and no one can fathom 'the goodness You have stored up for those who revere You'" (Ps 31:20). We shall just have to wait and see what God has in store for us all. Until then, we might be comforted by the final words of the beloved hymn, *Adon Olam*, with which most Ashkenazic synagogues close their morning Sabbath and festival prayers:

> I place my spirit in His care, when I wake and as when I sleep.
> God is with me, I shall not fear, body and spirit in His keep.

Points to Ponder:
Is There an Afterlife?

1. Why do you think virtually all civilizations developed a belief in the afterlife?

2. Why do you think the Bible rejected a belief in an afterlife? What historical-theological developments prompted the sages to incorporate the belief in an afterlife in our theology?

3. What impact did Persian and Greek cultures exert on Judaism in regard to the afterlife?

4. Louis Finkelstein opined that the sages deliberately left the concept of an afterlife vague. Why do you think this is so?

5. Why do you think many Jews are ignorant of Judaism's teachings that there is an afterlife?

6. Do you personally believe in life after death? Do you believe in Heaven and Hell?

7. Why do you think Maimonides seems to equivocate in his view of resurrection?

8. How has Jewish liturgy reflected our belief in the afterlife? How do the modern Jewish movements deal with this theme in the liturgy?

9. Does not emphasis on the afterlife or *olam ha-ba* make Judaism into an other-worldly faith?

10. Asceticism has never been the norm in Judaism. Can you prove or disprove this assertion?

11. Louis Jacobs argues that Judaism is both this-worldly and other-worldly. Explain how it can be both simultaneously.

12. Deniers of the afterlife and skeptics have derided it as an anodyne for the credulous and seekers of comfort from the perils and evils of this life. How do you react to this charge?

13. The sages admitted that, concerning the age to come, no one has seen it and no one can fathom its blessings. How do you interpret this?

Afterword

I HAVE DEVOTED this book to an analysis and exposition of the basic tenets of the Jewish faith in the fervent hope that the reader and student will be encouraged to reflect on his or her own theological beliefs and delve deeper into the mine of Jewish ideas, whose surface I have merely scratched. If my readers do so, I will be amply rewarded. We have a plethora of books on "how to live as a Jew" and "how to observe the various rituals and festivals"—all of which is very good and useful. Judaism is, preeminently, a legal religion comprised of numerous laws and regulations, of halakhah and *mitzvot* so that it is quite important for us to instruct our laity in the proper observance of our faith.

I remind my readers that Judaism, while stressing proper action, is a religion of great *ideas and principles*. And whereas we have certainly affected much of the Western world's notions of law and justice, our greatest impact on Western civilization has been in the realm of *ideas*. We conquered paganism and shaped Christianity and Islam into monotheistic faiths. We implanted in them the concept of human dignity. We instilled in them the notion of social justice and righteousness. And we infused them with a belief in messianic redemption. I dare say these are no insignificant legacies.

Clearly, ideas are significant components in any religion and civilization. With ideas we capture the minds and hearts of millions. With ideas we energize humans—for good or for ill. With ideas we may build great cultures—or destroy them. With ideas we are capable of inspiring souls and encouraging spirits. To downplay the importance of ideas and concepts, beliefs and notions in Judaism does not, in my view, serve any positive purpose. Quite the contrary: We need both halakhah and aggadah; if we accept one and reject the other, we skew the balance of Judaism and disturb the vital blend of our faith. And we certainly run the risk of alienating the vast reservoir of intelligent and secularly educated Jews who comprise the bulk of modern Jewry, not just in America but in other lands as well.

In 1702, Queen Anne of England awarded a peerage to the Duke of Marlborough in recognition of his great military prowess and heroism. When he took his place in the House of Lords, he was spurned and scorned by the blueblood Lords who disdained his humble background. One Lord sneeringly questioned him: "And whose descendant are you, sir?" Marlborough replied: "I, sir, am no descendant; I am an ancestor." Indeed, his most illustrious descendant was—Winston Churchill. I readily concur that it is very inspiring and uplifting to reflect that we are descendants of Abraham, Isaac and Jacob, Sarah, Rebecca, Rachel, and Leah. It is prideful to note that our ancestors number Hillel and Rabbi Akiva, Maimonides and the Gaon of Vilna. But it is infinitely more important that our children and theirs after will live as proud and practicing Jews for whom the principles of our religious forebears will not just remain a dead letter or a musty bundle of nostalgia, but will be a perennial inspiration and a living and vibrant faith by which to live and die. That has been both my goal and my incentive in writing this book.

Glossary

Aggadah. Literally, "the telling." Narrative portions of rabbinic literature containing theology, law, folklore, legends, etc.

Amidah. The standing devotion prayer; the most important prayer apart from the **Shema**. It is recited three times daily and four times on the Sabbath and festivals.

Am Yisrael. The Jewish people.

Aliyah. Literally, "going up." 1. Going up to the Torah for an honor. 2. Going up to settle in the land of Israel.

Amora (plural: *amoraim*). The sages who created the **Gemara**.

Ashkenazim. Originally, Jews of German origin, but extended to include Polish, Austro-Hungarian, Russian, and other European Jews.

Beit Din. A Jewish religious court, usually consisting of three judges.

Berakhah (plural, *berakhot*). A blessing; a prayer praising God for the gift of food, drink, health, joyous occasions, etc.

Bimah. The raised platform used for prayer and Torah readings in the synagogue.

Brit. A covenant. Jews believe that at Sinai, God entered into a covenant with the Jewish people.

Eretz Yisrael. The land of Israel as the Bible envisioned it, not to be confused with *Medinat Yisrael*, the modern State of Israel.

Galut (or, *Golah*). The Jewish Diaspora or exile from the Land of Israel.

Gan Eden. The Garden of Eden, Paradise.

Gehinnom. Gehenna, Hell.

Gemara. Literally, "teaching, conclusion." The discussions and debates based on the **Mishnah** and its legal rulings.

Genizah. A repository for old and worn-out books, usually found in synagogues. The famous Genizah in Old Cairo, discovered by Solomon Schechter at the end of the nineteenth century, yielded tens of thousands of manuscripts.

Get. A Jewish religious writ of divorce.

Goy (plural: *goyim*). 1. Nation (including Israel); 2. Non-Jewish people.

Haggadah. 1. Hebrew for, **Aggadah**; 2. The book that recounts the Passover story and is read at the Seder.

Halakhah. Jewish law dealing with civil, criminal, domestic, and ritual matters.

Hazzan. The cantor who leads the prayer service in the synagogue.

Hillul Ha-Shem. Literally, "the desecration of God's name." An action that brings shame upon Judaism, **Torah**, and the God of Israel.

Ikkar. A basic principle of Judaism.

Kabbalah. Jewish mystical lore and teachings.

Kaddish (root: *kadosh*, "holy"). 1. A prayer praising God's glory and greatness that signals the end of a section of the prayers or the culmination of a study session. 2. A prayer recited by mourners as they recall deceased loved ones.

Kashrut (root, *kasher* or *kosher*, literally, "fit, proper"). The Jewish dietary laws including: humane slaughtering of animals; consumption of animals that chew their cuds and have split hooves; of fish that have both fins and scales; of domestic, rather than scavenger birds; and separation of meat and milk foods and dishes.

Kavvanah. Intention, direction, inner concentration and devotion in prayer and in performing **mitzvot**.

Kiddush Ha-Shem. Literally, "the sanctification of God's name." In the performance of a **mitzvah**, a Jew sanctifies God's name in the eyes of contemporaries. The ultimate *Kiddush Ha-Shem* is martyrdom.

Mahzor. The prayer book used on Jewish festivals.

Mashiah. Literally, "the anointed one." The messiah.

Mezuzah. A small container mounted on the doorpost of homes and rooms containing passages from the **Torah** including the **Shema**.

Midrash (plural: *midrashim*). Expositions and interpretations of the Bible. The various collections deal with both law and theology and were edited around the time of the Mishnah and Talmud and into the early middle ages.

Minhag (plural: *minhagim*). Custom.

Mishnah. The first codification of the Oral Torah, edited by Rabbi Judah Ha-Nasi (the Prince) around 200 C.E. and divided into six sections and 63 tractates.

Mishneh Torah. Maimonides' codification of the entire body of Jewish law completed in the year 1176, consisting of fourteen volumes and subdivided into subjects.

Mitzvah (plural, *mitzvot*). 1. A divine commandment. Traditionally, the sages tallied 613 *mitzvot* in Judaism, many of which are no longer relevant. 2. A good and righteous deed.

Nusah. 1. The liturgy. 2. The melodic modes and patterns of the prayers. The main prayer patterns are Ashkenazic, Sephardic, Middle Eastern, and Italian.

Noahide Laws. The seven commandments allegedly given by God to Noah after the Flood. They include: No murdering, no stealing, no sexual immorality, no idolatry, no blaspheming God's name, no consuming the flesh of a living animal, and the positive commandment to establish courts of justice in communities. They are viewed as the basics laws of civilized society and are roughly the equivalent of natural law.

Olam Ha-Ba. The age or world to come; the afterlife.

Pikuah Nefesh. Saving a human life. This **mitzvah** is so important that it transcends all others.

Piyyut. A sacred poem, generally inserted in the prayer book.

Qoheleth (or Kohelet). The Hebrew name for Ecclesiastes.

Sefer Hasidim. A compendium of medieval German piety, ethics and morals edited by Rabbi Judah He-Hasid (the pious) around 1200.

Sefirot. Literally, "numbers." The ten emanations of God's attributes according to the kabbalistic theological system.

Sephardim. Jews from the Iberian Peninsula who fled from or were expelled from Spain and Portugal.

Shabbat. The Jewish Sabbath.

Shema. The most important Jewish prayer, proclaiming God's unity. It is found in Deuteronomy 6:4 ff. and is recited several times daily and at the moment of death.

Shekhinah. The Divine Presence; the indwelling spirit of God.

Shoah. The Hebrew word for the Holocaust that decimated European Jewry.

Shul. The Yiddish word for synagogue.

Shtiebel. A small prayer room used by the Hasidim.

Shulhan Arukh. The Code of Jewish Law edited by Rabbi Joseph Karo in 1564. Together with the glosses of Rabbi Moses Isserles, it has become the standard code of religious practice for Orthodox Jews and other observant Jews.

Seder. The ritual meal on Passover evening that includes tales about the Exodus from Egypt, Torah study, songs, and discussion.

Siddur. The Jewish prayer book used daily and on the Sabbath.

Sitra Ahra. Literally, "the other side." The Aramaic term for the evil or Satanic forces in this world, used primarily by the kabbalists.

Sukkah. The frail, rustic hut in which Jews dwell during the Sukkot Fall harvest festival.

Takkanah. An ordinance or legislation of the rabbis.

Tallit. A prayer shawl.

Talmud. The vast corpus of the rabbis' oral discussions of the Bible, encompassing debates and discussions of law and lore from 200 B.C.E. to 600 C.E. The Talmud consists of two layers: the Mishnah and *Gemara*, and is divided into six divisions and sixty-three tractates in over 5,800 pages, incorporating the teachings and opinions of several thousand sages. There are two versions of the Talmud: the Palestinian (popularly called the Jerusalem Talmud, or *Yerushalmi*) edited in Eretz Yisrael around 400 C.E., and the Babylonian (popularly called the *Bavli*), edited between 500–600 C.E., the latter being the more complete and authoritative.

Tanakh. An acronym for the three divisions of the Hebrew Bible: **Torah** (five Books of Moses), *Neviim* (prophets), *Ketuvim* (writings).

Tanna (plural: *tannaim*). The sages who developed the **Mishnah**.

Tefillah. The most common Hebrew word for prayer.

Tefillin. The phylacteries worn at daily morning prayers consisting of two small black boxes containing biblical passages, wrapped by leather straps around the head and arm.

Teshuvah. Literally, "returning, turning." Repentance.

Tikkun Ha-Olam. Mending or repairing the world; improving society. The term is often a modern synonym for social justice. In **Kabbalah**, *tikkun* assumes mystical, cosmic proportions.

Torah. Literally, "teaching, instruction." 1. The Five Books of Moses. 2. The Bible. 3. The entire corpus of Jewish learning.

Tzaddik. A righteous person. In Hasidic circles, the rebbe or rabbi is viewed as a *tzaddik*.

Tzedakah. 1. Righteousness. 2. Charity.

Tzimtzum. Literally, "contraction, recoiling." A kabbalistic term indicating that God contracted into Himself and withdrew from the universe after the creation.

Yetzer Tov. The good instinct or urge in a human being.

Yetzer Ha-Ra. The evil or destructive instinct or urge in a human being.

Yizkor. The memorial service for the dead in Ashkenazic synagogues, held four times yearly.

Yom Tov. A Jewish festival including Rosh Hashanah, Yom Kippur, Sukkot, Passover, and Shavuot.

Zohar. The classic text of the Kabbalah ascribed to Rabbi Shimeon ben Yohai (second century C.E.) but actually edited by Rabbi Moses de Leon of Spain in the thirteenth century.

References for Modern Quotations

P. 9: Albert Einstein essay in *Science, Philosophy and Religion: A Symposium* (New York: Conference on Science, Philosophy and Religion in Their Relation to the Democratic Way of Life, 1941).

P. 10: Leo Tolstoy, *My Confession, My Religion: The Gospel in Brief* (New York: Crowell, 1927).

P. 15: Solomon Schechter, "Jewish Dogmas," *Jewish Quarterly Review* 1 (1889) 115–27. Reprinted in *Studies in Judaism* (Philadelphia: Jewish Publication Society of America, 1945) 1:147–81.

P. 15: Abraham Joshua Heschel, *God in Search of Man: A Philosophy of Judaism* (New York: Farrar, Straus & Cudahy, 1955).

P. 20: Martin Buber, *I and Thou*, translated by Walter Kaufmann (New York: Scribner, 1970).

P. 20: Emanuel Levinas, *Nine Talmudic Readings*, translated by Annette Aronowicz (Bloomington: Indiana University Press, 1990) 30.

P. 34: Bertrand Russell, "A Free Man's Worship," in *Selected Papers of Bertrand Russell* (New York: Modern Library, n.d.) 6. Original pub. 1903.

P. 46: Heschel, *God in Search of Man*, 274.

P. 46: Mordecai M. Kaplan, *Judaism as a Civilization* (New York: Macmillan, 1934) 414, 510.

P. 46: Ibid., *The Greater Judaism in the Making* (New York: The Reconstructionist Press, 1960) 506–11

P. 53: William Faulkner, Acceptance speech for Nobel Prize for Literature, December 10, 1950. <http://www.rjgeib.com/thoughts/faulkner/faulkner.html>

P. 54: Sigmund Freud, Letter to Oskar Pfister, October 9, 1918. See *Letters of Sigmund Freud*, selected and edited by Ernst L. Freud, translated by James Stern (New York: Basic Books, 1960).

P. 54: Aharon Appelfeld, *Masa el Ha-Horef* (English title, *A Journey into Winter*, Jerusalem: Keter, 2000) 62.

P. 58: Reinhold Niebuhr, *Moral Man and Immoral Society* (New York: Scribner, 1932). Reprinted, Library of Theological Ethics (Louisville: Westminster John Knox, 2001).

P. 62. Immanuel Kant, "Idea for a Universal History from a Cosmopolitan Point of View," in *Philosophical Writings*, edited by Ernst Behler, The German Library (New York: Continuum, 1986).

P. 62: Mark Twain, *Pudd'n'head Wilson: A Tale* (London: Chatto & Windus, 1894).

P. 63: William Butler Yeats, "The Second Coming," in *Michael Robartes and the Dancer* (Churchtown: Cuala, 1920; reprinted, Shannon: Irish University Press, 1970).

P. 65: William James, *Memories and Studies* (New York: Longman Green & Co., 1911) 299–306.

P. 66: David J. Gross. Address at the Nobel Foundation banquet, December 10, 2004. <http://nobelprize.org/nobel_prizes/physics/laureates/2004/gross-speech-e.html>

P. 76: Heschel, *God in Search of Man,* 423–26.

P. 76: Mordecai M. Kaplan, *Judaism as a Civilization,* 43.

P. 77: Eugene Borowitz, *Renewing the Covenant* (Philadelphia: Jewish Publication Society, 1991).

P. 78: Markus Barth, *Israel and the Church: Contribution to a Dialogue Vital for Peace* (Richmond: John Knox, 1969; reprinted, Eugene, Ore: Wipf & Stock, 2005).

P. 83: Menachem Fisch, *Rational Rabbis* (Bloomington & Indianapolis: Indiana University Press, 1997) 78–96.

P. 88: W. Gunther Plaut, "Religious Discipline and Liberal Judaism," CCAR *Yearbook* 85 (1975) 163–73.

P. 88: Arnold J. Wolf, "Repairing *Tikkun Olam,*" *Judaism* 50, 4 (Fall 2001) 479–82.

P. 88: As quoted in Benjamin Cardozo, *The Nature of the Judicial Process* (New Haven: Yale University Press, 1921).

P. 109: William James, *Varieties of Religious Experience* (New York: The Modern Library, n.d.) 454.

P. 109: Heschel, *Man's Quest for God: Studies in Prayer and Symbolism* (New York: Scribner, 1954) 78.

P. 116: Albert Einstein, letter to Max Born, 12 December 1926, quoted in Ronald W. Clark, *Einstein: The Life and Times* (New York: World, 1971).

P. 120: Rabbi Eric Yoffie, sermon at the 65th Biennial Convention of the Union for Reform Judaism, December 15–19, 1999. <http://www.urj.us/orlando/speakers/ysermon.shtml>

P. 124: Yoffie, Biennial sermon.

P. 152: Jonathan Swift, "Thoughts on Various Subjects."

P. 162: Isaiah Berlin, *The Proper Study of Mankind* (New York: Farrar, Straus & Geroux, 1998) 9.

P. 179: Heschel, *God in Search of Man,* 70, 375.

P. 180: Kaplan, *The Meaning of God in Modern Jewish Religion* (New York: The Jewish Reconstructionist Foundation, 1947) 63, 72–76, 80.

P. 180: Ibid., *The Future of the American Jew* (New York: Macmillan, 1948) 236–42.

P. 180: Richard L. Rubenstein, *After Auschwitz: Radical Theology and Contemporary Judaism* (Indianapolis: Bobbs-Merrill, 1966) 223–25.

P. 188: Isaiah Tishby, *Mishnat Ha-Zohar,* 3 vols. (Jerusalem: Mossad Bialik, 1961) 2:261, 3:955.

P. 191: Martin Buber, *Israel and the World: Essays in a Time of Crisis* (New York: Schocken, 1948) 185–87.

P. 191: Heschel, *God in Search of Man,* 379–80.

P. 191: Eugene Borowitz, *Renewing the Covenant,* 50–51.

P. 191: Ibid., *Studies in the Meaning of Judaism,* 331.

P. 191: Arthur Green, *These Are the Words: A Vocabulary of Jewish Spiritual Life* (Woodstock, VT: Jewish Lights, 1999).

P. 192: Irving Greenberg, *For the Sake of Heaven and Earth: The New Encounter between Judaism and Christianity* (Philadelphia: Jewish Publication Society, 2004).

P. 192: Jonathan Sachs, *Tradition in an Untraditional Age* (London: Valentine, Mitchell, 1990).

P. 192: Ibid., from a speech to the West Coast Convention of the Union of Orthodox Jewish Congregations (December 1997).

P. 192: Ibid., *To Heal a Fractured World: The Ethics of Responsibility* (New York: Schocken, 2005).

P. 193: Arnold J. Wolf, "Repairing *Tikkun Olam*," *Judaism* 50 (2001) 479–82.

P. 195: Abraham Isaac Kook, *'Arpilei Tohar* (Jerusalem: Ha-Makhon al Shem ha-Rav Z.Y.H. Kook, 1983) 39.

P. 197: George Bernard Shaw, "Preface," in *Plays Pleasant and Unpleasant*, vol. 2 (Chicago: Stone, 1898).

P. 208: Franz Rosenzweig, *The Star of Redemption,* translated by William W. Hallo (New York: Holt, Rinehart and Winston, 1971) 415–16.

P. 212: Mary Boys, *Has God Only One Blessing?: Judaism as a Source of Christian Self-Understanding* (New York: Paulist, 2000).

P. 212: Irving Greenberg, *For the Sake of Heaven and Earth.*

P. 212: Michael Wyschogrod, *Abraham's Promise: Judaism and Jewish-Christian Relations,* edited by R. Kendall Soulen, Radical Traditions (Grand Rapids: Eerdmans, 2004).

P. 215: Ibid.

P. 215: Emanuel Levinas, *Difficult Freedom: Essays on Judaism,* translated by Sean Hand (Baltimore: The John Hopkins University Press, 1999) 105.

P. 215: Albert Camus, "Neither Victim nor Executioner," translated by Dwight MacDonald. <http://www.ppu.org.uk/e_publications/camus8.html>

P. 220: Joseph Klausner, *The Messianic Idea in Israel from Its Beginning to the Completion of the Mishnah,* translated by W. F. Stinespring (New York: Macmillan, 1955).

P. 230: *Emet ve-Emunah: Statement of Principles of Conservative Judaism* (New York: The Jewish Theological Seminary, 1988).

P. 233: Alan F. Segal, *Life after Death: A History of the Afterlife in the Religions of the West* (New York: Doubleday, 2004).

P. 236: William Shakespeare, *Hamlet*, Act 3, Scene 1.

P. 241: Mordecai M. Kaplan, Introduction to *The Siddur for the Sabbath* (New York: The Jewish Reconstructionist Foundation, 1945) xxvii; *Questions Jews Ask* (New York: The Jewish Reconstructionist Foundation, 1956) 220.

P. 243: Lord Byron, *Childe Harold's Pilgrimage,* Canto the Fourth, CXXXVII. <http://www.online-literature.com/byron/childe-harolds-pilgrimage/4/>

Index

B

C

D